The Heart
is the Teacher

by LEONARD COVELLO
with
GUIDO D'AGOSTINO

A great and dedicated teacher's success at one of the most challenging educational assignments of our times forms the basis of this inspiring educational autobiography. It is the story of Leonard Covello, who, starting life as an Italian immigrant in the 1890s, became a beloved teacher and later principal in the teeming, poverty-ridden melting pot of New York's East Harlem. *The Heart Is the Teacher* takes an unusual and optimistic view of the "blackboard jungle" of modern big-city education. For Leonard Covello proved, through half a century of teaching and encouraging boys, that even seemingly incorrigible delinquents can be turned into useful and productive citizens, given affection, attention and guidance.

The boys who came under Dr. Covello's influence were frequently wild and rebellious, mostly from impoverished homes, many without any comprehension of English. In touching and exciting anecdotes, Dr. Covello tells how he handled the "bad boys" he refused to believe were bad. His work took him from the classroom into

(continued on back flap)

(continued from front flap)

the homes of his students, into the alleys and streets which were their playgrounds. He taught evening language classes at the YMCA; he organized "store front" schools to carry education to adults as well as the children. The best schools, Dr. Covello believes, are those that are deeply rooted in their communities and that give their pupils a sense of place and responsibility in the neighborhood and the world at large.

Through dramatic episodes drawn from his own experience, Leonard Covello re-creates the struggles, the triumphs, the heartbreaks of an extraordinary teaching career. His colorful and inspiring story will give the reader new faith in the creative powers of the human heart.

About the authors:

Leonard Covello is qualified as few other educators are to understand the problems of American immigrants. When he was nine years old, his family moved from Italy to the Italian section of East Harlem. Despite poverty, he managed to finish high school and won a Pulitzer scholarship to Columbia University. Now retired from teaching, he is presently Educational Consultant for the Migration Division of Puerto Rico's Department of Labor.

Guido D'Agostino is author of four novels, including *Apples on the Olive Tree,* and is a successful writer of short stories and magazine articles. Born in Greenwich Village, N.Y., of Sicilian parents, Mr. D'Agostino attended the city's public schools and Columbia University.

The
Heart is
the
Teacher

LEONARD COVELLO

with

GUIDO D'AGOSTINO

The
Heart is
the
Teacher

McGraw-Hill Book Company, Inc.

NEW YORK   TORONTO   LONDON

THE HEART IS THE TEACHER

To those who believe

that the struggle for a better world

will be won or lost in our schools

Acknowledgment

No formal acknowledgment can adequately express my gratitude to my boys at De Witt Clinton High School, who opened my mind and heart to the role that a teacher can and should play in our American life; and to the many students, teachers, parents, and civic-minded men and women who helped in a pioneer effort to create a Community School in East Harlem.

I would also like to commend the High School Division of the New York City Board of Education, which gives to the principals of high schools great latitude in developing special educational programs to meet the needs of the communities in which their schools are located.

AUTHOR'S NOTE

For obvious reasons, in dealing with case histories
of boys who were at one time or another in trouble
I have used fictitious names and composite cases.

1/ Forty-five years of my life I spent as a
teacher in the New York City public schools. Twenty-two of
these years I was principal of the Benjamin Franklin High
School located in the East Harlem district of Manhattan
Island.

In this long lifetime of teaching, I have learned much about
the ways of immigrant peoples and their American-born children. I was an immigrant boy myself. I know what the American school can do to maintain family unity. I also know how
the school can function as the integrating force in our democracy and in the molding of young citizens.

After half a century as teacher and principal, I retired—with
the greatest regret. But I went right back to work with migrants. As educational consultant in New York City to the Migration Division of the Department of Labor of the Commonwealth of Puerto Rico, I am trying to give the latest of our
migrants—the Puerto Ricans—what I tried to give to the
Italians and the Negroes, to the Irish and Germans, to the rest
of the nationalities and races that make up that human mixture
known as East Harlem: my time, my affection, and above all,
my understanding. For only he who has suffered, directly or
indirectly, the degrading insults of *wop* or *nigger* or *spick* or

mick or *kike*—or whatever else the unwanted or newcomer to
this land is called—can readily understand.

I have known all of these things. I have known the hunger
for food and the much greater hunger for knowledge. I have
known fighting and stealing and the life of the back alleys and
the city pavements, and also the life of the spirit at the mission
house and the helping hand of some truly magnificent men
and women. I have known all of these things, and if I had it to
do over again, it is hard to say what change, if any, I would
make.

From the window of my office at the Benjamin Franklin
High School, I can see the East River Drive and the surging
traffic of high-powered motor cars. It is Wednesday—the last
Wednesday in August. For me it is the last Wednesday in
school. It is the end of my life as a teacher in a public school.
It seems impossible. I cannot quite convince myself that it is
or could be the end. I had walked into a New York City classroom forty-five years ago. Life, for me, at that period,
stretched interminably into the future. I always felt that my
life in a school would go on and on until my last day.

I know that in September the now-empty classrooms and
silent halls will once again feel the pulse of life as the boys—my
boys—pour into every nook and corner of the building and
take it over as they have done for so many, many Septembers
—and I will not be there. It will seem strange not to stand
again on the front steps and watch them as they converge
upon the school, greet them as they come up the steps—children of the great metropolis: Negroes, whose parents migrated
from the deep south; Italians, whose parents had forsaken the
poverty-ridden villages of southern Italy; Puerto Ricans, from
that stricken island in the Caribbean; Irish, Jews, Germans,
Finns, and Swedes, migrants from every corner of the world,
from near and distant places; people on the move, uprooted
people, disinherited, seeking a new and better way of life,

fleeing from lands where oppression and exploitation had been their daily lot, in search of the land that would give them the status and dignity of free men.

Once more the exuberance of my boys will fill the corridors. Their energy and vitality will fairly burst the seams of this great building as they pour in. I see them, the fair-haired and the dark, in the colorful array of their clothing and the pigmentation of their skin. How difficult it is to leave them!

I get up from my desk. Beyond is the East River, catching a brilliant reflection of sunlight. In this dazzling blur and in the pain within me, I see another land and another sun and the first of all those leave-takings which are part of life and, at the same time, a bit of death.

"Narduccio," my mother is saying, "come away from the window. Your father is gone now. We must wait. We must be patient until he calls for us and we can go to him in America."

All around is the dead pastel of an Italian landscape in the year 1891. And the solid masonry of walls that have withstood the centuries, as if the town had emerged from the mountain itself. The winding cobbled streets of the mountain town converge upon the *piazza* below. And the hot, humid wind from the south tortures the mind and can spell ruin for the peasant and his meager patch of land just outside the walls of Avigliano.

The town of Avigliano faced west, and it was westward that my father had gone, one more among the thousands upon thousands of southern Italians traveling to America in search of bread for his family. I was the oldest of three children, and already the idea of family and the sense of responsibility was taking hold of me.

"Why did he leave us? He said he was coming back."

My mother drew me away from the window. "These are the things men feel they must do. It is destiny. We cannot question it. It is God's will. We can only hope that in the end it will work out best for all of us."

I was still too young for her to explain the fever that had gripped my father—to explain that he had to go to America with the others. As a boy, my father had tried the shoemaker shop. Then the family sent him off to Naples to learn upholstering. Diligence and industry at this time of his life did not seem really important. He had a good voice, liked to sing, and liked to go to the *cantina*, or wine shop, where his companions would gather around as he told them, in his inimitable way, stories, anecdotes, and incidents of people and events in Avigliano. This did not help him financially in a town like ours, where work must be continuous and everything was scarce, even the water we drank.

"You must watch for the butterfly," my mother said, trying to comfort me. "When a butterfly enters the window, then we will have news of your father, and it will be news that he is sending for us."

I remember how I caught butterflies and turned them loose in the house. My mother smiled and tried to pretend and play the game with me, but it was an empty smile which fooled no one. My father had troubles of his own in America. He sent what money he could, but he did not write very often. It was difficult for him to set words to paper, as it was with all our people in those days.

When someone returned from America to Avigliano it was a big event. "An *Americano* is here," people would say, and gather in the *piazza*, or square of the town, for a personal interview with this extraordinary Aviglianese who had ventured across so many thousand miles of ocean to a wonderful new world and come back again. Usually the *Americano* had a huge gold chain spread across his vest, at the end of which reposed some masterpiece of the watchmaker's art—tremendous in size. He spoke slowly and deliberately, as though his native Aviglianese dialect were now an effort for him, and

his conversation was spiced with such phrases as *Nuova Yorka!*
La jobba! Lu bosso! Alò—gooda-by. And we hung on his
words.

Once I wormed my way through the crowd and tugged at
the sleeve of such an adventurer. "Have you seen my father?
In America? Compare Pietro? Pietro Coviello?"

Amid general amusement the man ruffled my hair and said,
"Compare Pietro? Of course. Everyone in Nuova Yorka
knows Mista Coviello. He is the bigga bossa on a bigga jobba.
Tell your mother he will send the money very quick now for
l'umbarco," by which he meant the passage money.

I ran all the way home and breathlessly told my mother the
wonderful news, embellishing it as I went along. My mother
tried not to listen. She clasped her hands in her lap and closed
her eyes. I rattled on about the money that was coming with
the next mail. Finally, when she could stand it no longer, she
grasped my shoulder and gently pushed me away. I was hurt.
The words choked back in my throat. I hurried off to hide my
tears. At that time I had no way of knowing that the man had
never seen my father, that he had never been anywhere near
where my father lived or worked.

These were hard times for us. My mother, my two younger
brothers, Raffaele and Michele, and I occupied one room in
the house of my father's brother, Zio Canio. But we also spent
a great deal of time in the home of my mother's brother, who
was a priest—Giuseppe Genovese. Zio Prete, or Uncle Priest,
we called him. As the oldest males in the two families, Zio
Canio and Zio Prete shared responsibility for our upbringing.
It was their duty. However, all major decisions had to receive
the blessing of my paternal grandmother, Nonna Clementina
—matriarch by right and personality. As the first-born, I kept
close to my own mother—the place reserved for the oldest son
in a southern Italian family.

During the day I went to school, and after school I worked
in my Uncle Canio's shoemaker shop. Then if there were a

few moments to spare I played. But play, in the town where I was born, was not a part of life, as it is here in America. Life was difficult and exacting. From the moment of birth you had to learn to assume your responsibility in the life of the family. Everyone had to contribute to the work of the *paese*, or town. Every hand was necessary. You had a purpose in living and that was to work and be of service. Play was a thing that happened sometimes in the process of being alive. There were no such things as organized play activities or toys, except an occasional rag doll for a girl child, and this was merely preparation for the more serious task of raising a family.

I was born and grew up among the men who had fought in the wars of Italian unification. My uncles, cousins, and other relatives related stories about Mazzini and Garibaldi and particularly about the brigands who infested the region of Lucania—stories told around the fireplace with just the light from the burning logs. Children listened to their elders. We rarely ventured even a question and never offered a comment, for that was the way to absorb knowledge and wisdom. Duty was stressed. *"E il tuo dovere!"* "It is your duty!" It was your duty to prepare yourself for a useful life.

There were many of us apprenticed in the shoemaker shop of Zio Canio. We never received money, except a few pennies on festival days. It would have been morally wrong to accept money to learn how to work. And from the discipline of the work there was no escape. On sunny days we would work outside the shop, learning how to soften the leather by working it in water, how to use the awl, fasten a pig's bristle at the end of the thread, and gradually how to shape the leather and form the shoe.

I had a dog named Leone. He was a shaggy mongrel with ribs showing through his hide, but I loved him as only a child can love a dog. One day he decided to take off on some dog business and was gone for some time. The thought that something had happened to him preyed on my mind. I could not concentrate on anything else. Instead of going to the shoe-maker shop this particular afternoon, as was my custom, I set off to search for my dog.

Avigliano was a town of some seven or eight thousand peo-ple. Yet, curious as it may seem, we never wandered far from the *piazza* or the immediate vicinity of our house, so that most people from the other end of the town were almost strangers to us. If we boys did go off, it was usually in little groups, to ward off the danger of other gangs of the town, and our dogs were part of our defense as well as our companions. This was the pattern of southern Italian living. First came the immediate family. Then the Coviello clan with its innumerable relatives. Then our loyalty extended in ever-diminishing waves from our street to our neighborhood, until it encompassed the whole town; so that anyone who came from outside the town itself was called a *forestiere*, or foreigner. And if someone from Avigliano married a girl from even a neighboring town he was looked upon with disapproval, as if the girls of his own *paese* were not good enough for him.

It was an oppressive, fitful kind of day—a day when the old men who hung around the *piazza* sucking their pipes would glance anxiously up at the sky and shake their heads—a day when tempers were short and even the town crier, announcing the local items of news, sang out in a different voice. From *Il Castello*, the section where my family lived, I made my way through the labyrinth of cobbled streets, under archways and through shaded alleys, to the lower section of the town known as *Bassa Terra*, urged on by the quarreling of dogs in the distance.

"Leone!" I kept shouting.

The search for my dog became an adventure. Never except in the company of elders had I wandered this far from home. From the substantial, several-storied houses of the artisans around and above the central *piazza*, I entered the section where the *contadini,* or peasants, lived. Here the buildings were all of one level, mostly one room with a dirt floor, where humans and livestock shared the same roof. Fascinated, I peered through the open doorways—at the old women, cooking and fanning the twigs of a fire, their ancient faces creased by the weather and age and the smoke of a million fires; at the strings of onions, garlic, and peppers hanging from the rafters; at the ragged children who stared suspiciously at me without approaching.

How far I wandered I no longer remember. The sky was getting darker. There was now the occasional rumble of thunder, but I paid no attention to the approaching storm. I wanted Leone.

Down the next street I caught a glimpse of a reddish-brown dog vanishing around the corner of a building, followed by another mongrel in swift pursuit. I started to run, shouting my dog's name. I ran until my legs gave out and I fell against a building trying to catch my breath. The dogs had by now gone through the main gate of the town and were heading toward the fields beyond, with their patches of yellowing wheat and thirsty green vineyards.

Suddenly a hand with the grip of an iron claw fastened on my shoulder, and I was struggling in the grasp of an unshaven *contadino.* "The nephew of Mastro Canio, the shoemaker! What are you doing in this part of Avigliano? What have you done? Why are you running when you should be at your uncle's bench, working like any honest Christian?"

"I am looking for my dog."

"What dog?"

Straightway he started marching me back up through the town to the *piazza.* "Are you a dog yourself to go chasing after dogs? Is it the life of a dog that you are preparing for? I suppose you have nothing better to do in this life?"

When we reached the *piazza* the storm was close upon us. My uncle, short, sturdy, with an impressive black beard down to his chest, was there waiting, along with my mother and her brother Zio Prete with his eternal Malacca cane. Whether they were there to watch the storm or were waiting for my return I have no idea. All I know is that this meddling *contadino* thrust me at my uncle. He removed his hat and bowed to my mother.

"You must excuse me. At *Bassa Terra* I found him, running after dogs, like a dog, as if he had four legs and a tail."

My uncle reached to cuff me. "*Stupido!*"

My mother exclaimed, "Do you want to frighten me to death?"

The Malacca cane stung me across the legs. "When he should be doing his lessons or communing with God!"

I retreated into the shop. The other apprentices looked at me with amazement, as if to say, "It serves you right for venturing so far out into the world." My older cousin grabbed me by the ear, stuck a broom in my hand and ordered me to clean up the shop and pick the nails out of the sweepings.

Outside the shop I could hear the *contadino* saying, "It was my duty."

"What is this life coming to when children go and come as they please?" Uncle Canio intoned. "You did right, Peppe. It was your duty as a good neighbor to bring him back."

My uncle came into the shop for a bottle of wine and a glass. He threatened me with a gesture. "We'll square accounts later. You were looking for Leone? Tonight Leone will eat your supper!"

"Cursed be America," my mother said. "Men are lured away. Women have to do their own work and enforce discipline besides. How can children grow up in this fashion?"

At that moment a much more calamitous event diverted their attention from me. There was a searing flash of light and the splintering, crackling sound of a powerful electric spark followed by rolling of thunder. A wind swept across the *piazza* and whirled the dust around in the shop where I was sweeping.

Then it came. First like the sound of distant machine-gun fire. Then closer and closer until an avalanche of hailstones was upon us. I went to the door of the shoemaker shop. There was not a soul in sight. You could hardly see across the *piazza*. Hailstones as big as marbles were dancing everywhere, bouncing into the air.

"*Maria Vergine Santissima!*" I heard my mother say.

My uncle, Zio Prete, pressed his palms together over the handle of his cane and closed his eyes. Uncle Canio held his head erect and bit his lip. The *contadino* stood appalled, a glass of wine in his hand, staring at the hailstorm. Slowly the glass tilted in his fingers and the wine spilled to the ground.

In my mind I could see the slopes of our mountain town. Where I had last seen the dogs among the patches of wheat and green verdure, it was as if everything had been cut with a scythe. In a very few moments the wheat which would have provided bread for the winter was gone.

"*Lo studente deve soffrire,*" Zio Prete would say, tapping the floor with his cane.

In Avigliano it was not only the student who suffered. There was suffering enough in the mere business of living. If it was not the hailstorm which destroyed the crops, it was the torrents of water which carried the land away in the spring and the lack of water in summer which caked the ground. But summer or winter, water was always precious. The age-old, empty promises of governments and politicians to build dams and create reservoirs were never realized. It was the daily task of the women to go to the few fountains of the town and bring back the water in barrels and jars, which they balanced on their heads. Whenever possible, rainwater was caught in tubs and used for washing.

Poets have sung of the sunny skies of Italy and of laughter and music and love. There were these things too. But poets seldom climbed the mountains of southern Italy, where from December to March there was snow and ice and bitter cold, and where fuel was scarce and clothing expensive and children did not play because to play was "to wear out shoes, undermine health, and waste time."

"The student must suffer to learn!"

A student from our town who was studying medicine in Naples had to give up school because family resources gave out. Loss of prestige and personal frustration were more than he could bear. He went out to the *camposanto*, or cemetery, on the outskirts of the town. Next morning they found him lying in the family plot with a bullet through his head. No one condemned this act. It was a matter of family honor.

To make ends meet, my mother rented a little cubbyhole on the *piazza*, where she sold small quantities of olive oil and bread and other staples. Sometimes she would make enough money for our own food, but more often we ate *acqua sale*, which was nothing more than hard bread soaked in boiling water with a little olive oil and salt added for flavor.

We never had breakfast at home. Some of the older men would take a small cup of black coffee and go to the shop. When I left for school, I took with me a piece of bread which my mother cut from an enormous Italian bread loaf—the portion depending on how much was available for the week— and an onion or a tomato when in season. Often we would share our food with some poorer classmate whose family was temporarily without bread.

In the winter a semblance of warmth filtered to us from the fireplace and from the charcoal fire in a brazier set on the platform at the teacher's feet. At stated times we would form a line, warm our hands, and then go back to our benches and continue our writing lesson. One of the requirements for school attendance was that each pupil bring daily to class one or two pieces of wood for the fire—and wood was scarce and hard to get.

School was from nine to eleven and from two to four in the afternoon. Sessions were short and attendance irregular.

Our class was in an enormous square room near the *piazza* of the town, rented for the purpose. Light came only from several windows in the front. On dark or rainy days we neither read nor wrote. We recited individually or in small groups—mostly from memory. Our teacher, Salvatore Mecca, or Don Salvatore as we addressed him, was young, strong, vigorous, with a military bearing, short-cropped mustache and a Prussian haircut in the style of Umberto I, King of Italy.

As he entered the room we sprang up to attention from behind our crude benches.

"*Buon giorno, ragazzi!* Good morning, boys!"

"*Buon giorno*, Don Salvatore!"

That was the signal for us to sit down again.

There were no girls in our school. Girls did not belong in the world of boys.

We had a book—one book which our parents bought when we began school and which we used through several grades before passing it on to a younger brother. Even at that early age pupils often dropped out of school and never came back again. No one thought much about it, not even Maestro Mecca, who would blow his nose and comment, "Better thus. He is better suited for a hoe than a pen."

We learned the alphabet and spelling by singing it in unison:

b—a, ba; b—e, be; b—i, bi; b—o, bo; b—u, bu; ba—be—bi—
bo—bu; ba—be—bi—bo—bu;

while the teacher strode around the room, the black ruler behind his back, apparently absorbed in his own thoughts.

Our one school book contained all the elements of instruction, from arithmetic and geography to Roman and Italian history. There was one small blackboard, where the teacher would demonstrate penmanship and write down important dates and events. We learned mostly by rote, in limited areas, but thoroughly. It was our memory that was trained.

If we violated a school rule, physical punishment was meted

out effectively, and that was only the beginning. The news of
any infraction reached home quickly. There was no escape.
We not only suffered cracks over the head for badly memorized lessons but also punishment on the knuckles from a
square black ruler even for the way we held our pens. According to Don Salvatore, there was only one way in the world to
hold a pen—his way. However, Salvatore Mecca was not a hard
man. He was a teacher, teaching in the way that was expected
of him, and to have taught differently would not have been
understood or accepted either by the family or by the town.

As my uncle, Zio Prete, used to say, sitting in his enormous
armchair, hearing my lesson and tapping his cane affectionately
against my legs, "What comes easy is soon forgotten. What
causes effort and torment is remembered all the days of one's
life."

Once we thought of a way to ease the raps on the head
and the blows of the black ruler across the hand. One of my
friends who worked with us in the shoemaker shop had an
idea. We called him Mingo. The idea was to bathe one's hands
and rub one's head with Holy Water.

Whether or not we expected punishment that day, I no
longer recall. However, the temptation to try this protective
ritual was too strong for either of us to resist, even at the risk
of facing a thrashing to test the result. When we saw the
sacristan crossing the *piazza* for his afternoon glass of wine at
the *cantina*, we sneaked over to the church, which was situated
in a small square of its own where the parishioners could gather
after mass to exchange greetings and the gossip of the town.

How quiet and ghostly a church can be on a late afternoon,
with just the faintest breath of air touching the flames of the
votive candles! We were both trembling with a fear that was
far more painful than any physical punishment which might
result from this adventure; and yet, above all, there was a
breathlessness and kind of excitement in doing the forbidden

which urged us on almost against our will. Many, many years
later I was to recognize in adolescent boys this agitation of the
senses which is almost intoxication. It helped me to understand
that very often what is mistaken for a delinquent act is, instead,
a part of the very normal process of growing up.

Over the hexagonal flagstone flooring we stole our way past
the Stations of the Cross to the baptismal font—a heavy, stone
basin set upon a pedestal near the main altar. We did not dare
look up into the faces of the saints, who seemed to know our
sacrilegious purpose. The feeling of guilt was growing so
strong that our one desire now was to get out of the church as
quickly as possible. In a wild gesture we sloshed Holy Water
over our hands and arms and heads and rushed from the
church, down the stone steps, across the square in the direction
of the *piazza*, and on further, stopping only when our legs gave
out behind the protective wall of an abandoned courtyard. At
any moment we expected the heavens to open and some terrible thunderbolt to come hurtling down upon us.

Nothing happened.

Mingo pinched his arm to study the effects of the Holy
Water. There didn't seem to be much sensation. He smiled.
"It works!" he said. "It works!"

I clenched my fist and looked at it.

"Try it against the wall," he suggested. "Hard."

I drew my fist back for an instant and then let it drop to
my side. "You try," I said. "My uncle, the priest, would be
very angry if I doubted the power of Holy Water."

As I look back upon my boyhood in Italy, I see many images
and people, submerged and half forgotten, yet woven inex-
tricably into the pattern of what was to be my life. I remember
the huge, square room of my Uncle Canio's house where we
used to spend the time after supper and before going to bed,
memorizing our lessons or listening to the stories of our elders
—legends and terrifying ghost stories and particularly tales of

the battles they had fought in the mountains of Lucania in that period when no man ventured outside the walls of the town without a musket on his shoulder.

We huddled about the fireplace for warmth in winter, but the solid masonry of the walls oozed dampness, so that it was never really possible to be comfortable. Closest by the fire, sitting straight in her chair, was Nonna Clementina, my paternal grandmother. Her gray hair, parted in the middle, was combed tight over her head and knotted. Her face was wrinkled and her hands bony and gnarled, and to us children she seemed as ageless as the mountains themselves and her position in the household just as secure. Even my Uncle Canio, stern-faced, bearded, and respected in the community, consulted her on all occasions and was swayed by her opinion. In our home she was the focal point around which all life revolved, even though now her vision was failing and it was difficult for her to get about. She knew all the herbs and remedies for every ailment. She could set a broken bone and apply the splints. I rarely saw a doctor in our home. And when there was a problem, she found the answer in the wisdom of her years and everyone listened to her.

Nonna Clementina had a way of placing her hand upon my forehead that was like a benediction. When I was bad or had been punished by my mother or one of my uncles, I would run to her for comfort, and she always ended by giving me a piece of bread and a sip of wine. But best of all was when she would walk slowly into her room, open a special drawer with a key which hung always at her waist, and offer me a spoonful of ground coffee mixed with sugar.

"*Te, figlio mio!*" she would say as I opened my mouth. "Here, my son!"

This was over sixty years ago, and yet I have only to close my eyes and the taste of burnt coffee and sugar is there in my mouth, better than the taste of any candy I have ever known.

My mother was never very demonstrative with us children. This was characteristic of all our people once a child was beyond infancy. Her deep affection manifested itself in complete devotion to taking care of her family. She was of medium stature, dark-complexioned, with black hair combed straight back, and she never wore jewelry or ornaments of any kind except her marriage ring. She spoke in a low voice, and never became excited. No matter what happened, it was always as God had willed.

Neither my grandmother nor my mother could read or write, even though schooling was highly respected in our family and my mother's brother was a priest and my grandmother's father had been a lawyer. Schooling played no part in the lives of women. A man studied for the purpose of bettering himself—to become a notary, a druggist, a doctor, a lawyer, or an engineer. What was the purpose of schooling in the life of a woman? Would it help her bear a child? Raise a family?

One of my earliest recollections is of the letters I used to write for my mother to my father in America. I sat at the heavy dining-room table under the light of a kerosene lamp, with a steel-point pen and an inkwell and a piece of ruled paper in front of me. My mother stood at my side while I slowly and painfully inscribed the introduction which was as unchangeable as the days of the week and which had to withstand the critical inspection of my uncle the priest.

My dear Husband:
    I am writing these few lines to let you know that we
    are all well and that we hope you are well too . . . .

The end of the pen would touch my lips and I would look questioningly at my mother until she went on.

Nonna Clementina sends her *saluti!* And Zio Prete. And Uncle Canio. And Raffaele. And Michele. And Mastro Peppe. And your old friend Gerardo Antonio."

"Anything else?"

"That we are anxiously waiting to hear from him."

"About *l'umbarco?*"

"No. Mention nothing about money. Just as I said it."

The letters were sealed with great care and went off with the weekly coach to Potenza, capital of the province, some twelve kilometers distant. And then the long, interminable wait for a message from my father in America. But neither the butterflies in the house nor the prayers and candles in church seemed to make any difference. All we knew was that our father was living with the family of Vito Accurso—his boyhood companion—in New York, and that work was seasonal and life difficult. In fact, Uncle Canio often shook his head and said, "It is all very confusing. Everything is supposed to be so marvelous in America and money so plentiful, yet it takes so long to put together the money for the passage." These were the mysteries which the people who remained behind could never understand.

When *l'umbarco,* or passage money, did arrive, it was received with mixed feelings—gladness because the painful period of waiting was over, and sadness because it meant going far away to a strange world of no return. And sadness, too, because Nonna Clementina at about this time had taken to bed, and it was obvious that the countless days and nights of her years on this earth had run out and that she was ready to die.

A week or so before we left Avigliano, she asked for me. I entered her room, which had an ageless smell of lavender and mildew and the olive oil with which she used to rub her hands. She was lying propped against the pillow, her small wrinkled face almost lost beneath the nightcap she wore. I leaned close to her and her fingers traced the outline of my face, as though to assure herself of what her ancient eyes could no longer distinguish. Her voice was weak, almost a whisper, but in her wisdom she had a final gift for me.

"Narduccio!" she said. "Narduccio *mio!* The gold you will find in America will not be in the streets, as they say. It will be in the dreams you will realize—in the golden dreams of the future."

2/ In the autumn of 1896, we arrived in America.

As a boy of nine, the arduous trip in an old freighter did not matter very much to me or to my younger brothers. A child adapts to everything. It was the older people who suffered, those uprooted human beings who faced the shores of an unknown land with quaking hearts.

My mother had never been further from Avigliano than the chapel just a few kilometers outside the town, where we went on the feast days of *La Madonna del Carmine*. Suddenly she was forced to make a long and painful trip from Avigliano to Naples, through interminable mountain tunnels where choking black smoke and soot poured into the railroad carriages. Then twenty days across four thousand miles of ocean to New York.

When the sea threatened to engulf us, she did not scream and carry on like the rest, but held us close with fear and torment locked in her breast—voiceless, inarticulate. And when finally we saw the towering buildings and rode the screeching elevated train and saw the long, unending streets of a metropolis that could easily swallow a thousand Aviglianese towns, she accepted it all with the mute resignation of *"La volontà di Dio,"* while her heart longed for familiar scenes and the faces of loved ones and the security of a life she had forever left behind.

We spent two days at Ellis Island before my father was

aware of our arrival. Two days and two nights we waited at
this dreary place which for the immigrant was the entrance to
America. Two days and two nights we waited, eating the food
that was given us, sleeping on hard benches, while my mother
hardly closed her eyes for fear of losing us in the confusion.
Once during a physical examination men and boys were
separated for a short time from the women. My mother was
frantic as the guard led me and my two younger brothers away.
When we ran back to her, she clutched us convulsively. Still
in her eyes there was the disbelieving look of a mother who
never expected to see her children again.

But her nightmare finally came to an end. We were on a
small ferry boat crossing the lower bay of New York, going
away from Ellis Island. My mother was standing at the railing
with my father, and both of them happy—my father taller,
more imposing than I remembered him, but still with his heavy
mustache and short-cropped hair in the style of Umberto I.
He held my younger brother by the hand and every once in a
while glanced at me affectionately. The sunlight shone upon
the water and upon the skyline of the city directly in front of
us. I was standing with my brother Raffaele and a girl several
years older than I who had accompanied my father to Ellis
Island. She was dressed differently from the women of Avigliano, and her voice was pleasant and warm, and she could switch
from our Italian dialect to English as she chose.

"You will like America," she chattered in Italian. "There are
so many things to see. So many things to do. You will make
many new friends. You will go to school. You will learn and
maybe become somebody very important. Would you like
that?"

My brother nodded vigorously. I was older. I only smiled.
The girl now addressed herself to me. "Wouldn't you like
that?"

I shrugged.

"Yes or no?" she teased.

"*Sì.*"

"Oh, but no! You must say it in English. Y—E—S, yes. Say it after me. Yes."

"Y—ess."

"Good! Bravo!" the girl laughed. "It is your first word in English and you will never forget it."

"Why?" I asked.

"Because I told you, foolish one! Because I told you, you will never forget the word and you will never forget me."

It was true. Mary Accurso was her name. It might have been possible for me to forget how I learned to say "yes" in English. But Mary Accurso—never.

Our first home in America was a tenement flat near the East River at 112th Street on the site of what is now Jefferson Park. The sunlight and fresh air of our mountain home in Lucania were replaced by four walls and people over and under and on all sides of us, until it seemed that humanity from all corners of the world had congregated in this section of New York City known as East Harlem.

The cobbled streets. The endless, monotonous rows of tenement buildings that shut out the sky. The traffic of wagons and carts and carriages and the clopping of horses' hoofs which struck sparks in the night. The smell of the river at ebb tide. The moaning of fog horns. The clanging of bells and the screeching of sirens as a fire broke out somewhere in the neighborhood. Dank hallways. Long flights of wooden stairs and the toilet in the hall. And the water, which to my mother was one of the great wonders of America—water with just the twist of a handle, and only a few paces from the kitchen. It took her a long time to get used to this luxury. Water and a few other conveniences were the compensations the New World had to offer.

"With the Aviglianese you are always safe," my father

would say. "They are your countrymen, *paesani*. They will always stand by you."

The idea of family and clan was carried from Avigliano in southern Italy to East Harlem. From the River to First Avenue, 112th Street was the Aviglianese Colony in New York City and closest to us were the Accurso and Salvatore families. My father had lived with the Accursos during the six years he was trying to save enough for a little place to live and the money for *l'umbarco*. In fact, it was Carmela, wife of his friend Vito Accurso and mother of the girl who met us at the boat, who saved his money for him, until the needed amount had accumulated. It was Carmela Accurso who made ready the tenement flat and arranged the welcoming party with relatives and friends to greet us upon our arrival. During this celebration my mother sat dazed, unable to realize that at last the torment of the trip was over and that here was America. It was Mrs. Accurso who put her arm comfortingly about my mother's shoulder and led her away from the party and into the hall and showed her the water faucet. "Courage! You will get used to it here. See! Isn't it wonderful how the water comes out?"

Through her tears my mother managed a smile.

In all of her years in America, my mother never saw the inside of a school. My father went only once, and that was when he took me and my two younger brothers to *La Soupa Scuola* (the "Soup School"), as it was called among the immigrants of my generation. We headed along Second Avenue in the direction of 115th Street, my father walking in front, holding the hands of my two brothers, while I followed along with a boy of my own age, Vito Salvatore, whose family had arrived from Avigliano seven years before.

My long European trousers had been replaced by the short knickers of the time, and I wore black ribbed stockings and new American shoes. To all outward appearances I was an American, except that I did not speak a word of English.

Vito kept chanting what sounded like gibberish to me, all the while casting sidelong glances in my direction as though nursing some delightful secret.

"Mrs. Cutter cut the butter ten times in the gutter!"

"What the devil are you singing—an American song?" I asked in the dialect of our people.

"You'll meet the devil all right." And again, in English, "Mrs. Cutter cut the butter ten times in the gutter! Only this devil wears skirts and carries a stick this long. Wham, and she lets you have it across the back! This, my dear Narduccio, is your new head teacher."

Was it possible? A woman teacher! "In Avigliano we were taught by men," I bragged to my friend. "There was Maestro Mecca. Strong? When he cracked your hand with his ruler it went numb for a week. And you are trying to scare me with your woman teacher. . . ."

I spoke with pride. Already "yesterday" was taking on a new meaning. I was lonely. I missed the mountains. I missed my friends at the shoemaker shop and my uncles and the life I had always known. In the face of a strange and uncertain future, Avigliano now loomed in a new and nostalgic light. Even unpleasant remembrances had a fascination of their own. Who had felt the blows of Don Salvatore Mecca could stand anything.

The Soup School was a three-story wooden building hemmed in by two five-story tenements at 116th Street and Second Avenue. When Vito pointed it out I experienced a shock. It appeared huge and impressive. I was ashamed to let him know that in Avigliano our school consisted of only one room, poorly lighted and poorly heated, with benches that hadn't been changed in fifty years. However, at this moment something really wonderful happened to take my thoughts from the poverty of our life in Avigliano.

Before entering the school, my father led us into a little store close at hand. There was a counter covered by glass and in it all manner and kinds of sweets such as we had never seen before. "*Candì!*" my father told us, grinning. "This is what is called *candì* in America."

"C-a-n-d-y!" know-it-all Vito repeated in my ear.

We were even allowed to select the kind we wanted. I remember how I selected some little round cream-filled chocolates which tasted like nothing I had ever eaten before. It was unheard-of to eat sweets on a school day, even though this was a special occasion. Anyway, the only candy I knew was *confetti*, the sugar-coated almond confection which we had only on feast days or from the pocket of my uncle the priest on some very special occasion, and for which we kissed his hand in return. But today my father was especially happy. He ate a piece of candy too. The picture of us there on the street outside the Soup School eating candy and having a good time will never fade.

The Soup School got its name from the fact that at noon-time a bowl of soup was served to us with some white, soft bread that made better spitballs than eating in comparison with the substantial and solid homemade bread to which I was accustomed. The school itself was organized and maintained by the Female Guardian Society of America. Later on I found out that this Society was sponsored by wealthy people concerned about the immigrants and their children. How much this organization accomplished among immigrants in New York City would be difficult to estimate. But this I do know, that among the immigrants of my generation and even later *La Soupa Scuola* is still vivid in our boyhood memories.

Why we went to the Soup School instead of the regular elementary public school I have not the faintest idea, except that possibly the first Aviglianese to arrive in New York sent his child there and everyone else followed suit—and also possibly because in those days a bowl of soup was a bowl of soup.

Once at the Soup School I remember the teacher gave each child a bag of oatmeal to take home. This food was supposed to make you big and strong. You ate it for breakfast. My father examined the stuff, tested it with his fingers. To him it was the kind of bran that was fed to pigs in Avigliano.

"What kind of a school is this?" he shouted. "They give us the food of animals to eat and send it home to us with our children! What are we coming to next?"

By the standards I had come to know and understand in Avigliano, the Soup School was not an unpleasant experience. I had been reared in a strict code of behavior, and this same strictness was the outstanding characteristic of the first of my American schools. Nor can I say, as I had indicated to Vito, that a blow from Mrs. Cutter ever had the lustiness of my old teacher, Don Salvatore Mecca. But what punishment lacked in power, it gained by the exacting personality of our principal.

Middle-aged, stockily built, gray hair parted in the middle, Mrs. Cutter lived up to everything my cousin Vito had said about her and much more. Attached to an immaculate white waist by a black ribbon, her pince-nez fell from her nose and dangled in moments of anger. She moved about the corridors and classrooms of the Soup School ever alert and ready to strike at any infringement of school regulations.

I was sitting in class trying to memorize and pronounce words written on the blackboard—words which had absolutely no meaning to me. It seldom seemed to occur to our teachers that explanations were necessary.

"B-U-T-T-E-R—butter—butter," I sing-songed with the rest of the class, learning as always by rote, learning things which often I didn't understand but which had a way of sticking in my mind.

Softly the door opened and Mrs. Cutter entered the classroom. For a large and heavy-set woman she moved quickly, without making any noise. We were not supposed to notice or even pretend we had seen her as she slowly made her way between the desks and straight-backed benches. "B-U-T-T-E-R," I intoned. She was behind me now. I could feel her

presence hovering over me. I did not dare take my eyes from
the blackboard. I had done nothing and could conceive of no
possible reason for an attack, but with Mrs. Cutter this held
no significance. She carried a short bamboo switch. On her
finger she wore a heavy gold wedding ring. For an instant I
thought she was going to pass me by and then suddenly her
clenched fist with the ring came down on my head.

I had been trained to show no emotion in the face of punishment, but this was too much. However, before I had time to
react to the indignity of this assault, an amazing thing happened. Realizing that she had hurt me unjustly, Mrs. Cutter's
whole manner changed. A look of concern came into her eyes.
She took hold of my arm, uttering conciliatory words which
I did not understand. Later Vito explained to me that she was
saying, "I'm sorry. I didn't mean it. Sit down now and be a
good boy!"

Every day before receiving our bowl of soup we recited
the Lord's Prayer. I had no inkling of what the words meant.
I knew only that I was expected to bow my head. I looked
around to see what was going on. Swift and simple, the teacher's blackboard pointer brought the idea home to me. I never
batted an eyelash after that.

I learned arithmetic and penmanship and spelling—every
misspelled word written ten times or more, traced painfully
and carefully in my blankbook. I do not know how many
times I wrote "I must not talk." In this same way I learned how
to read in English, learned geography and grammar, the states
of the Union and all the capital cities—and memory gems—
choice bits of poetry and sayings. Most learning was done in
unison. You recited to the teacher standing at attention.
Chorus work. Repetition. Repetition until the things you
learned beat in your brain even at night when you were fall-
ing asleep.

I think of the modern child with his complexes and his need for "self-expression"! He will never know the forceful and vitalizing influence of a Soup School or a Mrs. Cutter.

I vividly remember the assembly periods. A long narrow room with large windows at either end, long rows of hard benches without backs, and the high platform at one end with a piano, a large table, several chairs, and the American flag. There were no pictures of any kind on the walls.

Silence! Silence! Silence! This was the characteristic feature of our existence at the Soup School. You never made an unnecessary noise or said an unnecessary word. Outside in the hall we lined up by size, girls in one line and boys in another, without uttering a sound. Eyes front and at attention. Lord help you if you broke the rule of silence. I can still see a distant relative of mine, a girl named Miluzza, who could never stop talking, standing in a corner behind Mrs. Cutter throughout an entire assembly with a spring-type clothespin fastened to her lower lip as punishment. Uncowed, defiant— Miluzza with that clothespin dangling from her lip. . . .

The piano struck up a march and from the hall we paraded into assembly—eyes straight ahead in military style. Mrs. Cutter was there on the platform, dominating the scene, her eyes penetrating every corner of the assembly hall. It was always the same. We stood at attention as the Bible was read and at attention as the flag was waved back and forth, and we sang the same song. I didn't know what the words meant but I sang it loudly with all the rest, in my own way, "Tree Cheers for de Red Whatzam Blu!"

But best of all was another song that we used to sing at these assemblies. It was a particular favorite of Mrs. Cutter's, and we sang it with great gusto, "Honest boys who never tread the streets." This was in the days when we not only trod the streets but practically lived in them.

3/T hree or four years after we had established
ourselves in our first home in America, word got around that
the city was going to tear down several blocks of tenements to
make way for a park. The park took a long time in coming.
Demolition was slow and many families stayed on until the
wrecking crews were almost at their doors.

The buildings had been condemned and turned over to the
city, and together with Vito and my other companions, I
played in a neighborhood of rubble and debris and abandoned
buildings. We stole lead from the primitive plumbing to sell
to the junk man. We stole bricks and chipped off the old mor-
tar and sold them again. And in order to do this, we had to
scour around the area for old baby-carriage wheels to make
carts in which to carry off the stuff that we stole.

My father worked as general handyman in a German tavern
or café on 22d Street. Downstairs there were bowling alleys,
and during the winter he was kept pretty busy setting up
pins along with his other work, but in summer business slack-
ened and he was often without work for weeks at a time.
When he did work he made seven or eight dollars a week and
extra tips. But work or no work, money in our house was

scarce. My mother kept saying, "What are we going to do?" and my father would always answer, "What can I do? If there is no work there is no work. You'll have to do the best you can."

It was a curious fatalistic attitude among our people in America that while they deplored their economic situation they seldom tried hard to do anything about it. Generations of hardship were behind them. Life was such. *"La volontà di Dio!"* For them the pattern could never change, though it might, perhaps, for their children.

Our kitchen table was covered by an oilcloth with a picture of Christopher Columbus first setting foot on American soil. It was the familiar scene of Columbus grasping the flag of Spain, surrounded by his men, with Indians crowding around. More than once my father glared at this oilcloth and poured a malediction on Columbus and his great discovery.

One day I came home from the Soup School with a report card for my father to sign. It was during one of these particularly bleak periods. I remember that my friend Vito Salvatore happened to be there, and Mary Accurso had stopped in for a moment to see my mother. With a weary expression my father glanced over the marks on the report card and was about to sign it. However, he paused with the pen in his hand.

"What is this?" he said. "Leonard Covello! What happened to the *i* in Coviello?"

My mother paused in her mending. Vito and I just looked at each other.

"Well?" my father insisted.

"Maybe the teacher just forgot to put it in," Mary suggested. "It can happen." She was going to high school now and spoke with an air of authority, and people always listened to her. This time, however, my father didn't even hear her.

"From Leonardo to Leonard I can follow," he said, "a per-

fectly natural process. In America anything can happen and
does happen. But you don't change a family name. A name is a
name. What happened to the *i?*"

"Mrs. Cutter took it out," I explained. "Every time she pro-
nounced Coviello it came out Covello. So she took out the *i.*
That way it's easier for everybody."

My father thumped Columbus on the head with his
fist. "And what has this Mrs. Cutter got to do with my
name?"

"What difference does it make?" I said. "It's more Ameri-
can.The *i* doesn't help anything." It was one of the very few
times that I dared oppose my father. But even at that age I
was beginning to feel that anything that made a name less foreign was an improvement.

Vito came to my rescue. "My name is Victor—Vic. That's
what everybody calls me now."

"Vica. Sticka. Nicka. You crazy in the head!" my father
yelled at him.

For a moment my father sat there, bitter rebellion building
in him. Then with a shrug of resignation, he signed the report
card and shoved it over to me. My mother now suddenly entered the argument. "How is it possible to do this to a name?
Why did you sign the card? Narduccio, you will have to tell
your teacher that a name cannot be changed just like that . . . ."

"Mamma, you don't understand."

"What is there to understand? A person's life and his honor
is in his name. He never changes it. A name is not a shirt or a
piece of underwear."

My father got up from the table, lighted the twisted stump
of a Toscano cigar and moved out of the argument. "Honor!"
he muttered to himself.

"You must explain this to your teacher," my mother insisted. "It was a mistake. She will know. She will not let it
happen again. You will see."

"It was no mistake. On purpose. The *i* is out and Mrs. Cutter made it Covello. You just don't understand!"

"Will you stop saying that!" my mother insisted. "I don't understand. I don't understand. What is there to understand? Now that you have become Americanized you understand everything and I understand nothing."

With her in this mood I dared make no answer. Mary went over and put her hand on my mother's shoulder. I beckoned to Vito and together we walked out of the flat and downstairs into the street.

"She just doesn't understand," I kept saying.

"I'm gonna take the *e* off the end of my name and make it just Salvator," Vito said. "After all, we're not in Italy now."

Vito and I were standing dejectedly under the gas light on the corner, watching the lamplighter moving from post to post along the cobblestone street and then disappearing around the corner on First Avenue. Somehow or other the joy of childhood had seeped out of our lives. We were only boys, but a sadness that we could not explain pressed down upon us. Mary came and joined us. She had a book under her arm. She stood there for a moment, while her dark eyes surveyed us questioningly.

"But they don't understand!" I insisted.

Mary smiled. "Maybe some day, you will realize that *you* are the one who does not understand."

At what I nostalgically and possessively call *my* school—the Benjamin Franklin High School in East Harlem—there is a gold-medal award given at each graduation to the student who has been of greatest service to his school and his community. This is called the Anna C. Ruddy Memorial Award, and it commemorates a woman who, though not very well known to the outside world, was a tremendous influence in East Harlem during a lifetime devoted to the cause of the recently arrived immigrant and his children.

Miss Ruddy was the daughter of a Canadian pioneer from Ulster County, the Protestant stronghold in North Ireland. She came to East Harlem from Canada about 1890 to do missionary work among the Italians—a job for which she prepared herself by learning how to speak and read our language. She had no money. At first she had very little help of any kind, only an overwhelming desire to bring some measure of hope into the dinginess of the immigrant's very crowded tenement life.

Miss Ruddy preached the teachings of Christ. That she was Protestant did not make any difference to us. In general, our fathers looked upon religion through half-closed eyes while the women, with endless household chores and children to look after, found little time for regular church worship. The younger people were left pretty much to make decisions for themselves.

On Sunday afternoons when my father got together with his cronies for a game of cards and the wine flowed across the Christopher Columbus tablecloth, there were often arguments about religion. But no matter which way a religious argument turned, it always ended by someone mentioning the name of Miss Ruddy. Then a change took place. A quiet settled in the room as the card game got under way once more.

"A woman in a million," my father would say. "Protestant! Catholic! Egyptian! In the end, what difference does it make? Religion is a matter of the spirit and heart. I take my hat off to Signorina Ruddy."

His old friend Vito Accurso once said, "I am a freethinker, you all know that. I believe what I believe—that's the right God gave me when I came into this world. Some people are born idiots. Most people are born to a life which doesn't matter very much one way or the other. But every once in a while someone turns up that makes you stop and marvel. There you have La Signorina Ruddy. Special. Beautiful in her American way. She could have anything. Yet she spends her time here among us, taking care of our children and our sick, helping wherever she can. So God, if there is one, gave her the mind to call herself Protestant. For this, am I to deny my children the benefits of her teaching? Good is good and bad is bad, no matter how you name or color it . . . ."

Many years of my life were spent under the influence of Miss Ruddy and the Home Garden, as her little mission was called. Yet, to catalog or classify it exactly is as difficult as it is to describe the unusual character of the woman who was its head. There was Sunday School and Bible reading—Miss Ruddy standing there, tall and imposing, her auburn hair swirling over her head and catching the sunlight which came through the windows of the small brownstone building which she had converted into a haven for the Italian children and young people of the neighborhood. She wore immaculately laundered blouses which buttoned close about her throat and a gold cross suspended by a fine gold chain—her only adornment. She read the Bible with the book settled loosely in the palm of her left hand, talking in a low, softly modulated voice, reading mostly from memory and only occasionally glancing down to reassure herself.

What meaning could Biblical verses and quotations have for the children of the slums of East Harlem? Who would listen to language that was like the ripple of water when in our ears rang the madness of the elevated trains and the raucous bellowing of Casey the cop above the cries of the fish mongers and fruit and vegetable peddlers as he chased us down the street?

"For what shall it profit a man if he shall gain the whole world and lose his own soul?"

"What do these words mean? You, Leonard Covello. Tell me what you think. Stand up. Don't be frightened."

"I'm not sure, Miss Ruddy. It's like somebody had a lot of money and at the same time he's no good."

"Exactly. If you hurt someone in the process of making money, what good is the money? You not only have done wrong but you have sinned against Jesus Christ and you have hurt yourself."

Away from the Home Garden we fought the Second Avenue gang with rocks and tin cans and used garbage-can covers for shields. We scavenged the dumps and the river front for anything we could sell to make a penny. We had a hideout under the tenement rubble where we played cops and robbers and took the fruit and sweet potatoes stolen from the pushcarts to cook in our "mickey cans." But at the same time we spent Sunday afternoon and several nights a week at the Home Garden with Miss Ruddy, where we formed another club called the Boys' Club. We read books, put on plays, sang songs. There was nothing strange about this duality, although it may seem so to people who have never been poor or lived in crowded big-city slums. For the Home Garden had much to offer tough little "street Arabs" like us.

In the unfolding of our lives, Miss Ruddy and the Home Garden filled a need we could find nowhere else. It was Miss Ruddy who gave me an idea of how important the influence of a teacher can be in the life of a growing boy. Of all of us who went to the Home Garden, not one, to my knowledge, ever became a criminal or ended "bad" in the usual sense of the word.

"Mother of the Italians," Miss Ruddy was called, because so many of our people ran to her with their troubles. When sickness or disaster fell she was always there to give help or comfort. Once, when someone asked her about her work among the Italians, she said, "They are like frightened bewildered children in a strange land. Where are they to turn for help if not to me or others like me?"

4/ In Avigliano there were times when there was
no food in the house. Then we bolted the door and rattled
kitchen utensils and dishes to give the impression to our close
neighbors that the noonday meal was going on as usual. After
the *siesta* everyone went about his customary tasks and the
outside world never knew exactly how it was with us. The
intimate things of family life remained sealed within the family,
and we created for ourselves a reserve both as individuals and
as a group.

In America it was not much different. Our people had the
worst possible jobs—jobs that paid little and were very uncertain. A stonemason worked ten hours a day for a dollar
and a quarter—if there was work. When there was snow or
rain or ice there was no work at all. During slack periods men
just hung around the house or played *boccie* down in the vacant lot or played cards in the kitchen or in the café. They did
not talk about their troubles, but their games did not have
the usual gusto. The children especially could sense their feeling of helplessness in this land which offered little more than
strangeness and hardship.

My mother lived in constant fear from the uncertainty of
life. As the eldest child, I had been close to her in Avigliano.
I was still closer to her here in America. There were now

four boys in our family and my mother was expecting another child. I had to earn money somehow while I was going to school.

Miss Ruddy came to our assistance. One day after a Boys' Club meeting she called me into her office. She looked me over for a moment and then smiled. "How old are you, Leonard?"

"Twelve, ma'am."

"Would you like to work? If you had a job, that is? Are you strong enough?"

I could hardly control my excitement. "I'm as strong as any boy in the Home Garden. Is there a job for me?"

Miss Ruddy nodded. "Here, take this note to Mr. Griffin and let me know what he says."

I found out later that Mr. Griffin was one of the members of the Lexington Avenue Baptist Church that we attended with Miss Ruddy. Mr. Griffin owned a large bakery shop on 112th Street and Fifth Avenue. I hurried over to see him. He was seated in a large armchair in his office behind the shop. He was a well-built man, with gray, curly hair, a heavy mustache and a very friendly manner. He read Miss Ruddy's note and looked up at me.

"You're not much for size or weight," he said. "It's hard work, running around delivering orders early in the morning. And it's an all-year-around job—six days a week, except the Sabbath. People want their bread when they wake up. Five o'clock we begin. If you're willing, it's a dollar seventy-five a week with a cup of coffee and a roll thrown in to perk you up before you start working. You begin Monday."

"I'll be here, sir," I said.

He laughed and grabbed a loaf of bread and thrust it under my arm. "Here, fatten yourself up a little. I'll see you on Monday."

I literally leapt from his office in my excitement. I ran home to tell my mother and father that I had found a job and was ready to do my share in supporting the family. My mother put her hand on my shoulder. My father said, "Good. You are becoming a man now. You have grown up." I was only twelve, but I could feel that he was proud of me. And I was proud of myself because I had reached the age where I could do more than scrub floors and wash windows and look after my baby brothers. I could earn money and stand on my own two feet and help keep the family together, as I had been taught practically from the time I was born was my responsibility.

At four-thirty every morning I walked rapidly over to Fifth Avenue and 112th Street to the bakery shop. There the day's orders were waiting for me to put into bags for delivery. After a hurried cup of coffee and milk and a couple of rolls, I started out pulling a little wagon that I had constructed out of an old packing crate and baby carriage wheels.

Servicing the private houses was not so bad where there were only a few steps to climb. However, the apartment houses were quite different. The cellars were dark and I had to grope along, banging into walls, stepping on cats, hearing rats scurry out of my way, and always keeping a wary eye for janitors' dogs. Sometimes, in the beginning I carried a lantern, but this was awkward with the bags of bread, so I had to learn to make my way through the darkness in and out of serpentine alleys to the dumbwaiters where the coarse rope cut my hands as I whistled to faceless customers who lived somewhere high up in the air like inhabitants of another planet.

It was rush, rush, rush, back and forth from the bakery until all the orders were delivered. Then I had to run home and get ready for school. For this work I received one dollar and seventy-five cents a week. It was not very much but it helped a great deal in days when meat was twelve cents a pound and milk six cents a quart. Thus when I was twelve, work became an inseparable part of life.

Very early the essential difference between working hard

in Italy and working hard in America became apparent to us who were young. In Italy it was work and work hard with no hope of any future. A few years of schooling and then work for the rest of one's life—no prospect of ever going beyond the fifth grade or ever becoming other than what one started out to be, in my own particular case, probably a shoe-maker. But here in America we began to understand—faintly at first, without full comprehension—that there was a chance that another world existed beyond the tenements in which we lived and that it was just possible to reach out into that world and one day become part of it. The possibility of going to high school, maybe even college, opened the vista of an-other life to us.

This was the beginning of my work years—jobs after school and during summer vacation to help the family and in order to be able to continue in school. Next I worked for several sum-mers in a baking-powder factory downtown on Barclay Street, passing the bakery delivery job to my younger brother Ralph. The hours at the factory were from seven-thirty in the morning until six at night and from eight until three on Saturdays. The wages were three dollars, out of which came sixty cents a week for carfare and sixty cents a week for lunch. This left me with only one dollar and twenty cents to take home to my mother. But every penny counted and helped to keep us going.

Mrs. Cutter and the Soup School were behind me now, in time if not in memory. I was going to Public School 83 on 110th Street between Second and Third Avenues. What an impres-sive school that was to me! Five stories high. Hundreds of boys. Halls. Regular classrooms. And a teacher by the name of Miss Sayles who gave me twenty-five cents a week to run up to her home, a brownstone building at 116th Street and Lexington Avenue, to bring back her lunch.

Once a week the huge rolling doors which formed the class-rooms were rolled back and we marched into assembly. As at the Soup School, everything was done in silence, in unison, and at attention. From a side door Mr. Casey, the principal, would emerge—bearded, impressive, wearing a black skull cap, stiff white collar and black tie, and a long, loose black coat with white laundered cuffs which stuck out from his coat sleeves. There was the usual flag salute and the Bible reading. Mr. Casey swallowed his words and I could never understand what he was saying, except one favorite expression, "Make a joyful noise unto the Lord!" This completely baffled me because everywhere, in the classrooms, in the halls, on the stairs, strict silence was the rule.

At one assembly I remember reciting a poem. I had recited it in class and then spent hours at home in front of a mirror saying it over and over, just as if I were standing in front of my uncle, Zio Prete, and he were sitting in his huge armchair with his cane at his side, listening impassively, critically. Waiting with my classmates to march into assembly, I was overwhelmed with fear. Mr. Casey finished the Bible passage, blew his nose into a large white handkerchief, folded it carefully away into a hidden corner of his coattail and announced, "This morning Leonard Covello of Class 4B will recite a poem for us. Leonard Covello."

A paralysis gripped me. I was unable to move.

Mr. Casey coughed. "Leonard Covello!"

My teacher tapped me on the shoulder. I managed to walk stiffly to the front of the assembly and face about. In a voice which I could not recognize as my own, I began: "I shall now recite a poem by Eugene Field."

> Winken, Blinken, and Nod one night
> Sailed off in a wooden shoe—
> Sailed into a sea of misty light,
> Into a sea of dew. . . .

I finished the poem and walked back to my seat, bewildered, but with a wonderful feeling of exhilaration. I had overcome

a fear that had haunted me for weeks—fear of facing my more
"American" classmates, fear of mispronouncing some of the
difficult words, fear of my accent or of forgetting my lines. To
my amazement, what had seemed so difficult was easy, much
easier than I had ever dreamed—an experience which has repeated itself often during the course of my life.

The teaching at Public School 83 was thorough for those
who could learn and who wanted to learn. Even in those days
there was the truant officer, but he could hardly cope with the
unwilling learner for whom school was no more than a prison
or with the parent who considered too much schooling unnecessary. Two boys whose father had an ice and coal business
were taken out of school at the age of twelve to help at home. It
didn't bother them. In fact, they were happy about it.

The constant drilling and the pressure of memorizing, the
homework, and detention after school raised havoc with many
students. For me, this type of discipline seemed merely the
continuation of my training in Italy. I wanted to go to school.
School meant books and reading and an escape from the world
of drudgery which dulled the mind and wore out the body
and brought meager returns. I had seen it often with my father
and his friends when they came home at night tired and dis-
pirited.

"Nardo," my father repeated again and again. "In me you
see a dog's life. Go to school. Even if it kills you. With the pen
and with books you have the chance to live like a man and not
like a beast of burden."

I was seldom absent from school and never late. Geography
and history I mastered easily. I memorized with facility. I more
than held my own in spelling and widened my English vocabulary by working diligently at the daily exercises and homework which the teacher called "meaning and use." This expression baffled me for a long time. We used to walk along the
street, saying, "Hey, I gotta go home and study 'mean 'n

yourself'!" I did not worry about what the expression meant. I simply learned how to do it. The exercise involved a dictionary and a speller. We had to take five or six words from the speller, hunt for them in the dictionary, and then write a sentence illustrating their use.

Spelling bees were common in those days. The speller was graded with such words as "Mississippi" and "isthmus" in the lower classes and topped with words like "obliquity" and "Aix-la-Chapelle" and "aberration" and "capstone" in the upper class.

We memorized suffixes and prefixes, Latin and Greek roots, and we were required to give the meanings of words as they are used as well as their etymological meanings. Also each group of words had to be illustrated with "promiscuous examples." According to modern methods and educational theories, it was rough fare. But it had its values. It may not have been the best way to train the mind, but it did teach you to concentrate on mastering difficult jobs.

During the last year of grade school we had a period of German on Friday afternoon. As Professor Hoffstadter, the German teacher, stepped into the classroom, our regular teacher, Mr. Rosenthal, stepped out, and the fun began. Tall, slightly stooped, Professor Hoffstadter, like Mr. Casey, the principal, wore a beard and a Prince Albert coat, but Professor Hoffstadter's beard stuck straight out and came to a point and wagged up and down as he talked. For us it was the end of the week, and we waited impatiently to be off and away from school. For the itinerant professor it was the last of a long series of German lessons given day in and day out at various schools in the city. For both students and teacher there was only the desire to get it over with as quickly as possible.

Amid guffaws of laughter we sang

O Tannenbaum, O Tannenbaum
Wie grün sind deine Blätter . . .

After the song we had several German declensions of the definite article and a few German words to the question of:

"*Was ist das?*"
"*Das ist ein Bleistift.*"
"*Das ist der Kopf.*"

Only when Mr. Rosenthal sat in the classroom busy at some of his own work was it possible for the professor to do some teaching—usually what he had been trying to pound into our heads for some weeks.

"You are a rambunctious bunch of bums!" he would shout, his beard sticking straight out at us like the point of a rapier. We had no notion of what he was saying but the sound delighted us. "Rambunctious bums!" we yelled to each other. One boy, I remember, was so amused by the sound of German that he leapt out of his seat and into the aisle, holding his belly, convulsed with laughter, while poor Hoffstadter blustered and turned red in the face.

When I graduated and went to Morris High School I again found German on my school program. Who put it there I never knew. At that time I did not know that I could have chosen Latin or French. I just accepted the fact that I had to take German and that was that. Nor did my parents or the parents of other students question the choice. No one said, "If the German language is taught in the schools, why not Italian?"

During this period the Italian language was completely ignored in the American schools. In fact, throughout my whole elementary school career, I do not recall one mention of Italy or the Italian language or what famous Italians had done in the world, with the possible exception of Columbus, who was pretty popular in America. We soon got the idea that "Italian" meant something inferior, and a barrier was erected between children of Italian origin and their parents. This was the accepted process of Americanization. We were becoming Americans by learning how to be ashamed of our parents.

One of my favorite teachers, Mr. Carlson, gave me a nickel one day and asked me to go to the bakery shop to get him a Napoleon. I looked at him dumfounded but, having learned to do what I was told, I went off. In the corridor I ran into my friend. "Hey, Vito," I said, forgetting that in school I was supposed to call him Victor. "Know what Mr. Carlson just did? He gave me a nickel to buy him a Napoleon. Napoleon was a general!"

"Sure, he conquered half the world."

Vito walked over to the bakery with me and waited outside while I went in and placed the nickel on the counter. I felt that Mr. Carlson, whom I respected, was playing a joke on me. I could hardly bear the thought of it, expecting at any moment that the woman behind the counter was going to laugh in my face. "Give me a Napoleon," I muttered through my teeth.

When she reached under the counter and took out a piece of cream-filled pastry, I felt a tremendous relief. My faith in people was once more reaffirmed.

And then at Public School 83 there was a Miss Quigley. She offered a prize to the boy who would do the best work in class. I was that boy, and the prize was a beautiful illustrated edition of the life of Abraham Lincoln. I read it again and again and cherished it, because in those days books were very precious. Miss Quigley lent me others and told me how I could borrow books from the Aguilar Library at 110th Street.

Today the library is housed in a beautiful multistoried building. At that time it was in a small store and there were not many books. Still, to those of us who never owned any, it was a fascinating and wonderful place. From that day on, hardly an afternoon passed that I did not go there to pick up a book.

Now I was living what seemed like fragmentary existences in different worlds. There was my life with my family and Aviglianese neighbors. My life on the streets of East Harlem.

My life at the Home Garden with Miss Ruddy. Life at the local public school. Life at whatever job I happened to have. Life in the wonder-world of books. There seemed to be no connection, one with the other; it was like turning different faucets on and off. Yet I was happy.

5 / **W**hen finally, after much delay, work on Jefferson Park was begun, those of us of the Aviglianese colony moved to tenements several blocks away. Instead of kerosene lamps, we now had gas light and a gas stove and a meter which kept us constantly scurrying for quarters. In the middle of a meal or at night while I was reading, the gas would lower under a boiling pot of spaghetti or the light would dim, and the meter would have to be fed. My father said it was like having an extra mouth in the family.

Instead of one toilet, there were now two toilets on each floor, serving four families. It was a definite improvement over our first home in America, but it also meant more rent to pay. And there were more mouths to feed and more clothing to buy, because now there were five of us children. The youngest, my sister Clementina, had just been born. In the end we were not much better off.

My mother was always tired now. We helped her as much as we could but she never seemed to get caught up with her work. There were times when she would sit with her hands folded in her lap, an air of weariness upon her. She lost all desire to go out into the street or to see anything new, as if just keeping alive was problem enough in itself. Often Mary would say to her, "It is beautiful in the park now—grass, trees, flowers. You can sit in the sun on the new green benches."

My mother would only smile and perhaps touch Mary's hand in a gentle caress. "Run along. Today, I cannot. Tomorrow. Tomorrow when I will have more time. . . ."

Povera Mamma! The time she waited for was fast running out.

I remember in those days how we used all our resources to keep our parents away from school—particularly our mothers, because they did not speak English and still dressed in the European way with the inevitable shawl. We didn't want these embarrassing "differences" paraded before our teachers.

But the circle was widening. At first there were only Italians and Americans. The distinctions began as we from Avigliano started to differentiate between Aviglianesi, Neapolitans, Calabrians, and Sicilians. Then we came in contact with the Irish and the Germans and the Jews and the other nationalities outside the immediate borders of the Italian community. Our knowledge of the world—and, I'm afraid, our prejudices—spread out to embrace the enlarging borders of our experience.

Our teachers impressed us mainly because they did not live in the neighborhood. They dressed better and spoke differently and seemed to come from somewhere beyond the horizon. Somehow we tried to measure up to this outer world which we knew as American, though we had no conception of what it was. Only its people had a life far easier and with greater luxuries than ours. But in trying to make a good impression on our teachers, it was always at the expense of our family and what was Italian in us.

Whatever problems we had at school or in the street, we never took up with our parents. These were our personal problems, to be shared only by companions who knew and were conditioned by the same experiences. How could parents understand? Parents belonged in one of the many separate watertight compartments of the many lives we lived in those days.

This fear of ridicule, constant with us of foreign birth, was further aggravated when we went to Morris High School, which was coeducational and where practically all the girls came from a wealthier and older environment. We were not used to girls, and having to associate with them filled us with uneasiness. When we went anywhere or did anything, it was always with boys. This was the way we had been raised. In Italian families, practically from infancy, the girls are always separated from the boys.

That first day, four of us from East Harlem walked over to the annex in the Bronx where we were supposed to report to a special room. We found the room all right, but when we approached and saw some girls standing in the doorway, we drew back. "Girls!"

We went outside again. "Say," I said to Emil Panevino, one of my group, "did you know there were girls in this school?"

"No one said anything to me about girls."

"And American girls, too," my friend Victor commented. "What are we going to do?"

We stood there huddled together, trying to gather enough courage to go back inside, when a gruff male voice said to us, "What's the matter with you boys? What are you standing there for? Don't you belong in school?"

At Morris High the pressure of work and study was much heavier, but the greatest obstacle was to establish any feeling of identity with these new students. They came from better homes in better sections of New York, and they possessed greater self-assurance—particularly the girls. Also they were well dressed and had spending money. They had a social life which we did not share and little gatherings to which we were not invited. In fact, we did not want to be invited for fear that in some way we might have to reciprocate. We did not want them to see our homes and our parents and how we lived. The circle widened only in the sense that we were thrown into contact with a larger community. We still kept very close to our own little East Harlem group.

Another thing which astounded me in those early days of high school was the tremendous emphasis placed on sports. The greatest prestige did not come to those who got the highest marks but to the athletes. They were the leaders. How many times I wondered what my uncle Zio Prete would have thought of such frivolity.

At first I was hesitant about taking part in athletics or striving to make one of the school teams. It seemed a strange way to spend one's time and energies—at play! Yet greater than all else was the desire to excel in the accepted way, to show that you were just as good as the next fellow no matter what the difference socially. Growing up in the rough-and-tumble life of East Harlem had given me certain physical advantages. The test came during a school-wide chinning contest. I was small but wiry. My arms were strong from pulling dumbwaiter ropes. I placed second in the entire school. This spurred me on to make one of the school teams so that I could proudly display the school emblem, a huge maroon "M" on a white sweater.

The excitement about the chinning contest was more than I could keep to myself. I had to tell the family about it, and it happened to be one of those rare nights when my father was home for supper. To the delight of my younger brothers, I explained the mechanics of chinning. My mother and father listened with interest for a few minutes. They looked at each other. The expression on my father's face changed from mild bewilderment to utter bafflement as I continued. I realized that I had made a tactical blunder but there was nothing I could do about it. Finally I blurted, "I was second! Second best in the whole school! That's something!"

My father threw down his napkin and pushed away from

the table. He paced across the room gripping the back of his head. "There is hardly enough to eat in the house. We kill ourselves. We work so that he can have some future—and he spends his time at school playing!"

"It is not play!" I argued. "It is part of the school work. We have to do it." This only made my father angrier, and now my mother was upset.

"Then stop school and go to work. You do not have to waste money and time to be a strong man. A jackass is strong and he never went to school. The ditch-digger is strong. The man who cleans the sewers. Only they get paid for being strong while you get nothing. . . ."

It was no use. I should have known better. It was one of those times when ordinarily I would have resorted to the old standby, "You will never understand." Instead I said nothing, simply grabbed my school books and walked out of the flat.

I went to the Accurso home. Mary was now going to college and majoring in mathematics. I was having some difficulty with algebra, and once or twice a week she spent half an hour helping me. The minute she saw me she knew that something was wrong. "I'm going to quit school," I said. "I'm going to go to work and earn money. I've had enough of this stuff."

She was sitting at a little desk in a corner of the parlor where she did her studying while her mother, Carmela, tall and strong and dominating, was in the kitchen with her younger children around her. Mary told me to sit down. As I related the story of the chinning contest and its angry reception at home, she quietly opened my book to the algebra lesson.

"You are right. They are right." Mary laughed. "It's a case of two rights meeting and making two wrongs. Anyway, I'm glad you won the chinning contest."

"Second," I corrected. "The other boy just beat me out. But I got up there twenty times. Next time. . . ."

"That's the spirit. Now you know you're not different from anyone else—unless you think you are. It's not important how many times you can chin. The important thing is that it makes you feel better. You're just as good as the next fellow. That's what you should have explained to your father and mother."

I listened without looking at her, watching the toe of my shoe, conscious of the fact that Mary's younger sister Rose was peeking at us from around the kitchen door.

"You should try to make them see," Mary went on, "that here in America where everything is so different from Italy, a person must at least try to understand the differences. Unless he does this, he cannot get along. If you had taken the time and the patience you could have explained. Isn't it so?"

I shrugged.

"Look at me. Am I right?"

I didn't say it, but I looked at her and managed to smile, and it was the same thing. Nothing more was said and we got on with the algebra lesson. I felt better.

The threat to quit school that I had expressed to Mary in a moment of anger became a reality. At the end of my third year at Morris I decided to leave, and neither Mary nor the entreaties of Miss Ruddy could make me change my mind. The decision was solely my own, and I arrived at it one night after hours of wandering about the streets in the rain. Eventually a policeman, seeing me drenched and standing under a gas light, sent me home.

Whatever I could earn after school was not enough, despite the fact that my father was working and my two younger brothers were also contributing. The helpless attitude of my mother, the despair always in her eyes, her failing health, the medicines and the necessities we could not afford, were more than I could bear. I had to take a full-time job.

Where was I getting in school? I argued with myself. What was I going to become and how was school helping me? I was old enough now to work as a man. I had to work. In work I might be able to find the answer.

My parents were by this time so far removed from my multitudinous worlds that they no longer questioned my decisions. If I wanted to leave school now it was my own affair. No one would interfere, especially if it was to help the family. As always, the family came before other considerations.

What stands foremost in my mind concerning this decision was the indifference and the lack of guidance at the high school itself. I simply turned in my books at the school office and went away. That's all there was to it. No one spoke to me. No one asked me why I was leaving or discussed my problems with me.

Outside the school building I was met by Vic Salvator, Emil Panevino, and another boy by the name of Joe Parish, all of whom had already quit school. We walked down the street together. I was still swinging my book strap, the last evidence of my school days. Parish was puffing on a cigarette butt just to show he was grown up. Vic, Emil, and I had given Miss Ruddy a rash and solemn promise *never* to touch alcohol or tobacco. ("No alcohol or tobacco?" my father, who loved both his wine and his twisted Toscano cigars, used to say. "This is carrying religion too far. Nobody can be that good.") This time, however, Joe's bravado made no impression. Apart from the drinking and smoking, we were now all a part of the crowd that had thrown over the drudgery of learning to go out into the world to earn money—a part of that free-and-easy world of self-decision where no one told you what to do, where you earned and spent your own money, hung around the street corner in your spare time, and went to bed whenever you felt like it.

"Hey, Len," Joe pried, "how'd it go? What'd the old man have to say? You just knock off like that?"

"I just tossed my books onto the desk and that's all there was to it."

"Just like that," Vic intoned.

"Did you expect the principal was going to come out and

kiss me?" I asked. "He doesn't even know I'm alive. Nobody knows we're alive inside there, except maybe one or two teachers. They don't even know when you come and when you go. They should worry if I ever come back."

"Come back?" Joe gasped. "You crazy or something, Len? Why would anyone wanna go back? Does a jailbird wanna get back to prison?"

"I'm finished once and for all!" I said, lashing out at a lamp-post with my strap.

"Yeah," Emil Panevino agreed.

I started to walk faster, away from them. "I'll never go back. *Never!*" There were tears in my eyes that my friends would not have understood, that I did not understand. Behind me I could hear Parish say, "What a crazy guy!"

6/ $\mathbf{I}$ loaded and unloaded crates for a company that manufactured brassware on Murray Street in downtown Manhattan. From the street level the crates were hauled off the horse-drawn wagons and up to the second story by means of a hand winch which it was my job to operate for five dollars a week, including Saturdays. The first couple of days my hands became so sore and blistered that at night I could hardly open them, and my mother made me soak them in warm salt water.

We sat there together in the kitchen, the basin in her lap and my hands in the basin, and we didn't say much, but all the time I knew what she was thinking. She was thinking that I was a man now like my father and the others. I was working as they were working. Perhaps she was thinking that if I had stayed in school it might have been different. She looked at my hands and shook her head, saying *"Figlio mio!"*

The money I earned helped to make things a little easier at home. But the compensations were not nearly so great as I thought they would be. The things I had learned at the Home Garden kept running through my mind. "Man does not live by bread alone. . . ." What else, then? I had tried living without bread for a while and see how far I had gotten. I stayed at home nights and Sundays. I borrowed books from the Aguilar Library and slept near the window so that in the morning, with the first rays of light, I could prop myself up on one elbow and read without disturbing my two brothers who were in the same bed.

I was restless, brooding. I hated the job and the winch and the packing cases and my callused hands, because I could see nothing beyond. My father had said, "A jackass is strong and he never went to school." Now my father was silent. I was working and earning money. That required no comment. The work was torment, he knew that. But this was a deep and personal problem which a man had to solve for himself—a problem my father had always had and had never solved.

For a time I stayed away from the Home Garden and Miss Ruddy. I took to wandering the streets when I wasn't trying to lose myself in books, but at the same time I could not rid myself of an overpowering sense of boredom and uselessness.

"You can't keep it up like this," Mary said one day. She was teaching now in one of the elementary schools in lower Manhattan. Of all the girls I knew in that period, when education was not considered necessary in the life of a woman, she was the first of the Aviglianese group who went to college. This was because of her aptitude for study and her mother's determination to see her educated regardless of precedent.

Mary met me one evening while I was standing in the entrance of the tenement building, hating to go upstairs, and watching the drizzle of rain on the cobblestones. I heard her footsteps as she came hurrying down the street from the el, her slight frame almost hidden behind a huge, black umbrella. "Hello! How is the working man?" she asked, as she caught sight of me.

She had been to a matinee performance of the Metropolitan Opera, standing room, to hear *Aïda*. Her dark eyes shone with enthusiasm as she spoke about Caruso and Giuseppe Verdi and the magnificent settings. "You will have to come with us sometime, Leonard. You simply must." Then she said, "You haven't been at the Home Garden. Miss Ruddy keeps asking for you. Everybody asks for you, even the children, Leonard."

"I work and I'm tired nights."

"Everyone works, but there's always time to do the things you like to do. You used to like Miss Ruddy. You used to like school and now you've quit and you're tired and you don't do anything any more. You can't keep it up. You're not happy. You've got to give up working and go back to school next term. You've got to . . . ."

"I can't. They need the money at home."

"They'll manage. They've always managed. And deep down I know it would make the old people happy. Promise you'll go back, Leonard."

I wanted to say "yes." Instead I said, "I'll think about it." But now I knew, come what may, I had to go back.

That year away from school had its value. I was out in the working world, mingling with all kinds of people of different nationalities and learning my way around. I lost a great deal of my shyness. I found out that although the Irish drank a little more, they were just as warmhearted and friendly as I considered the Italians. While the Jews liked business and trade, they would give you the shirt off their back if you needed it. While the Germans were sometimes overly self-assured and even pompous, it was to cover up their own feelings of inferiority or strangeness—just like the other immigrant groups.

Cranking the winch and attacking packing cases with my baling hook, traveling the elevated trains and eating in nickel joints, I found out that New York did not consist of merely Americans and Italians, but rather of people in varying stages of the thing called Americanization. While I could not have put these thoughts into words, I began to find myself reacting differently toward the bustling humanity around me.

When I returned to Morris High School, it was with a greater assurance and confidence. I no longer shied away from strangers, sticking to my own particular group, except when the day was over and I headed back to East Harlem. I no longer avoided the glance of a girl because her eyes were blue and her hair blond and her clothes expensive.

The infamous chinning contest that had plunged me into such trouble at home led me to enter sports in a big way. I was on the soccer team. I became captain of the senior basketball team. Proudly I wore my white sweater with a larger maroon "M" on it. Like a gray flannel suit on Madison Avenue today, it was my badge of belonging. I was accepted. School became different somehow. Even the teachers and the principal seemed closer to me than before.

But always, in unsuspected flashes, I became conscious of wrongdoing, of wasting precious time in frivolous sports. The admonition returned to me "The student must suffer to learn." I remember the so-often-repeated story of the Aviglianese who became prime minister and who as a boy was so poor that he used to study under the street light because his parents could not afford oil for the lamp.

I began to acquire a feeling for the English language and its sound and flavor. I knew many words I never dared use in conversation or in class, but which were there and fixed in my mind from reading and from constant use of the dictionary. I joined the literary club and wrote for the school paper. Then I became an active member of the debating society.

During this period I was fascinated by the struggle of the Russian people to achieve some measure of freedom from the Czarist rule. For the debating society I wrote a speech defending the nihilists and their methods. "Why, you can't give this speech, Leonard," my teacher said. He was a quiet, soft-spoken man with a special knack for handling pupils. "You can't defend murder and bombing and bloodshed."

I grew hot under the collar. "The Czarist regime was all bloodshed," I argued. "Slavery and Lincoln and the Civil War. Mazzini and Garibaldi and the liberation of Italy. All blood-

shed. Does justice begin where bloodshed leaves off, or does
bloodshed begin where justice leaves off? Who knows, except
there has never been any great movement for the liberation of
a people without bloodshed."

I never made my high-school speech in defense of the
nihilists. At the time I could not understand why I was not
allowed to speak on the oppression of people. This, too, was
an invaluable part of my education—that two wrongs don't
make a right, that oppression can grow out of a revolt to over-
throw oppression. But my intense interest has never wavered
in the problems of social justice and minority groups, in the
painful situations which we as immigrants had to face and
which are faced today by Negroes and by those newcomers
so often and disdainfully called "spicks" instead of Puerto
Ricans.

At home I gave English lessons to Italian immigrants and
charged from fifteen to twenty-five cents a session, depending
upon the affluence of the student. Twenty-five cents for the
man of private business and fifteen cents for the pushcart
peddler and wage earner. "Maestro Professore," they would
call me and bow respectfully to my mother and father, though
neither of my parents ever had the patience to let me teach
them more than a dozen English phrases. My mother would
shoo me away with a tired gesture: "Don't bother me." My
father would say, "In fifteen years I have not been able to
make peace with that infernal language and you expect me to
begin now? They call you 'Maestro Professore'? Good. I am
happy. Happy for you and happy for myself. What little
English I know is enough for the work for which I am paid."

With my father's pay, the money from my evening and
weekend teaching, and what my brothers were earning, we
were managing to get by. But my mother's health was no better. She had settled into a permanent kind of languor which
slowly ate away the very life of her. The doctor prescribed

iron injections, liver pills, one thing after another, but none of them seemed to do any good. After a while she could no longer bear to have the doctor around, so we stopped calling him. We became accustomed to her pale, drawn face, her emaciated body, and her perpetual weariness. We became accustomed to the idea that she could not live very long.

Near the end of my last term at Morris High School I tried not to think about what the next year would bring. I closed my ears when my classmates mentioned the word "college." It was the promised land—college—but not for the likes of me. A friend, Harold Zoller, inadvertently made me face up to the idea. I'll never forget the day. At the high-school field day we had won a crazy three-legged race together. Arms locked about each other, my left leg strapped to his right, we hopped along leading all other contestants by several yards. We were both short—in fact, very similar in many ways, except that Zoller had blond wavy hair and a face made for easy laughter. We got along well together. He was the first of my close companions who did not live in East Harlem and who was not of Italian origin. He was the first non-Italian whose home I visited, a lovely brownstone house on 136th Street and Seventh Avenue. There I went through the gymnastics of trying to balance a teacup on my knee while his parents went out of their way to show their cordiality. In turn, I gathered up enough courage to ask him to our house for a spaghetti dinner. I also invited Mary, to weight the conversation a little more on the English side.

Zoller had a wonderful time in our dark, cramped rooms. It was his nature to enjoy himself no matter what the surroundings or circumstances. His frank, direct manner led him into any topic of conversation that came into his head. To him all people were alike, especially his friends, and he expected they would do pretty much what he was going to do himself. It was while Mary and I were walking him back across town to the streetcar that he stuck his hands, thumbs out, in his jacket pocket and, grinning to show how wonderful he felt with a mountain of spaghetti inside him, said, "Now what, Len? Have you made up your mind yet? Come to any decision?"

"What decision? What are you talking about?" Just the same I was sure of what was coming. I could feel it by the tightening of my collar and by a sudden desire to run away, though the subject had never been mentioned or discussed between us in any way.

"College, of course. What else did you think? Columbia is my choice." He laughed again. "I mean to say, my Dad's choice. But it's a great college, Len. You couldn't do better. Make up your mind, boy. How about Columbia?"

We were standing on the street corner waiting for one of the new and glittering electric trolley cars. I could see it in the distance, between the traffic of horses and wagons and bicycles and pedestrians. I prayed it would come fast. "I–I don't know," I said, looking down at the pavement, at the hem of Mary's skirt, at the buttons on her shoes, aware of mounting anger toward Zoller because he couldn't sense that he was talking about an impossible subject.

"Try to make it Columbia, Len. We'll try for the soccer team together—and make it, too!" The trolley was coming to a stop now. Zoller turned to Mary and shook her hand. "It was very nice meeting you, Miss Accurso. And you convince him. Columbia or nothing!"

"I'll try."

He swung up and into the trolley car and waved as it moved away down the avenue. I stood for a moment while Mary looked at me, her eyes questioning, waiting for the answer I hadn't been able to give Zoller.

"Don't you understand!" I said. "He's talking about college! Not high school. College costs money. Money I haven't got. Money I will never have. Money. Money. Money. I'm so sick of the sound of that word."

"People with less money and fewer qualifications than you have gone to college. It's all in how much you want to go."

"Let's not begin that all over again."

We walked along in silence. I was tired of hearing about what people with determination could do if they made up their minds. At this moment I didn't care. I was only concerned with the fact that my mother was sick and I had part of the responsibility of a family on my hands. I would go back to a full-time job and forget all about it.

"I suppose you've given up?" Mary said.

"There's nothing to give up. A simple fact. I can't go to college!"

"Have you ever heard of the Pulitzer Scholarship?"

I stopped and faced her. "What do you know about the Pulitzer Scholarship?"

"What everyone knows—that it is open to any high-school student who needs it and can pass the examinations. I also happen to know that your English teacher has already spoken to you about it. Miss Harding, that's her name. Isn't it so?"

"Have you any idea how many applicants there are for this scholarship from all over New York? Hundreds! I'd never make it."

"Miss Ruddy would even write a personal letter of recommendation to the Pulitzer Committee."

"It's no use," I insisted. "Besides, it's too late."

"It's not too late. Speak to Miss Harding."

I didn't want to build up impossible hopes. "I won't!" I kept repeating. "I can't go to college and you know it."

Mary looked at me. Without another word she turned and walked off, leaving me there, repeating to myself, "I can't!"

I had no belief in my going to college. I could see the long summer stretching ahead of me and the job I would have to find as a clerk or manual laborer. I thought about it all night and in the morning I still felt the same way. Think about a job, I said to myself. Nothing else.

During the English period I waited for the bell for us to change classes and then walked over to the desk where the teacher was seated. "Miss Harding," I said.

"Yes, Leonard."

"Is it too late—too late for the scholarship, I mean?"

Miss Harding rose from her desk. "I don't think so. We can call up the World Building from the principal's office and find out." She smiled and took hold of my arm. "Come on." As we went down the corridor she added, "I'm glad. I'm glad that you decided to take a chance."

7/T he American doctor was tall and gaunt and he stooped. With his pointed gray beard and black leather satchel he looked impressive. Miss Ruddy had sent him to us, and he had an excellent reputation. After spending an hour with my mother he came out, shrugging his shoulder. He glanced at my father, then at me, and moved slowly over to the window, looking down at the sidewalk four stories below. "I could guess. I wouldn't be sure. In a hospital we might be able to find out. Even then, I'm not sure."

"To an Italian, a hospital is just the same as a grave," I said.

He nodded. "She would never survive it. And here, her death is just as certain as if she were to jump out of this window. Anyway, keep her quiet. Rest as much as possible, and . . ." he cleared his throat, ". . . wait, that's all. Just wait."

When the doctor had gone I started to explain to my father, speaking in a whisper so that from the bedroom my mother could not overhear. It was hard to put into words the idea that for her it was all over. With a gesture my father motioned me to be quiet, as if to say that what the doctor had told us he had known for a long time. We sat together in silence. Then my father shook his head and let out a deep sigh. "For what?" he said. "For what? Leave home. Come to a strange land. All the suffering. To what purpose? For an end like this?"

This was in 1907—fifty-one years ago. My mother was dying. It was a sad summer for all of us at home. I had taken the college-entrance examinations for the Pulitzer Scholarship. It provided twenty-five dollars a month and free tuition in any school at Columbia, from engineering to medicine. I had taken the examinations but did not want to build my hopes around what seemed to me an impossible outside chance.

The dreary summer wore on. I worked down in the basement of the American Express office, where my job was to search old files for the originals of remittances which somehow had never reached their destination. The hours were long and the pay low, but it was not this which troubled me most. It was my reaction to the job itself—the same as to the other jobs I had had: treadmill, mechanical work, the monotonous day-in-day-out routine without any hope of change or hope for the future, without any sense of accomplishment. In combination with my mother's illness, the general depression at home, and the uncertainty of my future, it made for one of the most disturbing periods of my life.

From the basement of the American Express office I used to carry my information upstairs to a barnlike room where some hundred employees worked, typing and sorting and filing papers under the watchful eye of a supervisor. I remember this supervisor well. Although he seemed aloof and remote from the people who worked under him, he somehow took a liking to me. "Leonard," he said, taking in the whole floor with a sweeping gesture, "I wouldn't give a nickel for the chances of anyone in this place. Maybe one or two might advance to a little better job with a little higher pay. That's about all. This is no place for you. Get out. Go to college. Go to college!" His advice was like a thorn in my flesh.

One evening toward the latter part of August I returned home from the Express office to find great excitement at the house. My brother Joe, babbling incomprehensibly, greeted me at the door and rushed me into the bedroom, where my mother was sitting up in bed, smiling happily. She reached to grasp my hand. "Narduccio, my son. It has happened. You will go to college. You will!"

For a moment I thought she was feverish, but the faces around me, even that of my little sister Clementina, told me that something had actually happened—something that I could begin to believe in.

"They were here today," my mother went on in a breath. "An *Americano*. Very polite, and La Signorina Ruddy. Through her he asked me all kinds of questions about you and the family. He will let you go to college, this man. I am sure of it, Narduccio. He was a good man. I could tell by his eyes. God has favored you at last. I am so happy." She kissed my cheek and then lay back against the pillow, completely exhausted.

I moved out of the bedroom to let her rest, taking the children with me. An uncontrollable elation began to take hold. I tried to be calm, to reason things out. Nothing really portentous had occurred. A representative from the Pulitzer Committee had called to inquire into our economic situation, and had brought Miss Ruddy along as interpreter. But try as I might to steel myself against disappointment, I could not quell the growing certainty that I would go to college.

I rushed from the tenement flat and downstairs, hurrying along the street to the Home Garden. It was the hour before the evening's work in which Miss Ruddy snatched a quick supper. She was seated at the simple rosewood desk in the room which she used as her study, munching a sandwich and sipping a glass of milk, at the same time reading from a book at her elbow. When I walked in and stood before her, excited, unable to think of anything to say, she simply removed her reading glasses, held them poised between her fingers, and waited.

"Miss Ruddy!" I blurted. "My mother. You were there to-day. I mean . . . the Pulitzer Scholarship. Is it true?"

Miss Ruddy smiled and motioned me to sit down. "So now you believe there's a chance? You're no longer my Doubting Thomas?"

8 / **M**y mother died just before I entered Columbia. We buried her in the Calvary Cemetery in Brooklyn.

The situation at home became more complicated than ever with six boys, a young sister, and a father who was away at work most of the time. Something had to be done. My brothers Ralph and Michael were contributing, but this left two brothers and a sister, all of school age, and a three-year-old child. The problem of my sister Clementina was solved by the ever-helpful Miss Ruddy, who found a wonderful family in Long Branch to look after her as one of their own. My brother Frank went to live with the Salvatore family, and my brother Joe went to live on a farm in the Catskills with the parents of Michael Scilipoti, one of my close Home Garden friends. The rest of us moved into a flat close to our lifelong friends, the Accursos, where Mary's mother could run in and out and keep a watchful eye on things.

In September, 1907, I began my studies at Columbia College with great expectations. I had been building in my mind what giant intellectual strides I would take in this famous institution of learning, how much knowledge I would acquire, how I would probe all resources and seek universal truths—the grandiose kind of ideas most boys have at this age, I suppose, except that my background and early training tended to make my dreams even more gigantic.

I was immediately jolted from my idealistic conception of a university by a battle between the freshmen and sophomores. The campus tradition was that a freshman's cap would be placed atop the flagpole. The sophomores would muster around the flagpole while our job as freshmen was to rush the pole and try to recover the cap. In this melee we punched and wrestled with each other until the upper classmen intervened, putting an end to the battle. We did not recover the cap and we were all pretty well roughed up on both sides. This was my introduction to Columbia. I remember limping from the campus with Garibaldi Lapolla, another East Harlem student who enrolled with me at the same time.

"Man alive!" Lapolla said, tucking in his torn shirt. "If the old folks could see us now! They'd think the whole bunch of us should be locked up in an asylum along with all the professors and the dean."

"Don't tell them," I advised. "Keep quiet." Experience had taught both of us that the spreading chasm which separated us from our parents could never again be bridged and that what happened to us in the outside world belonged to us alone. The challenge of newness and strangeness had to be met.

Perhaps it was my fault that I did not reach out and completely absorb what this great university had to offer. Columbia was a disappointment to me in many ways. I concentrated on romance languages, with French as my major. Natural inclination urged me to Italian, but these were still the days when it was fashionable to forget Italian. To have prepared myself to teach Italian would have seriously limited my possibilities of earning a living. Already the idea of teaching in some form or another had begun to formulate in my mind.

We rushed around the campus from one class to another. Science. Mathematics. Philosophy. Chemistry. Spanish.

French. History. And a class in Dante in which I was the only student. There were many courses but with no unifying principle about which we could center our attention. The courses were, for the most part, easy—too easy. The demands upon us were high-schoolish for the most part, not mature. There were lectures and quizzes, but not enough real teaching and little rapport between student and instructor. In short, the idea of the dedicated life of the student which I had learned as a boy in Avigliano was not met by what I was receiving here.

I tried to explain it to Mary. "There is no contact of minds. You feel that the professor is niggardly about the knowledge he hands out—as if he were afraid he might give too much at one time. You go to a lecture and listen and simply accept. What kind of education do you call this?"

She hesitated a moment. "It's education to prepare you to live in a competitive society, I suppose."

"But you can be a dope and still be a gentleman," I said. "That is, if you make one of the varsity teams. You learn history. You reach back into the civilizations of the past. What for? Where is the relationship with the present, with the problems of the world today, with the life here in East Harlem, with the things which concern you and me?"

"You've just got to make the connection yourself," Mary said. "The student who can't surmount these difficulties is not cut out to be a scholar."

I smiled. "The trouble with you is you never attack—you're always defending everything."

I was the student, she knew, who wanted to be the scholar. Within me too was the desire to be accepted and to form a part of the world in which I found myself. In spite of my Italian origin and the place where I lived, I felt I deserved to belong.

So when the captain asked me to try out for the varsity soccer team because of my record at Morris High, I consented, in spite of my feeling that it was much more important for a student to devote himself to his studies.

That afternoon as we were going down the long steps leading from Morningside Drive in the direction of East Harlem, Garibaldi Lapolla said intensely, "You've got to make the soccer team, Len. Show them that we've got the stuff."

We were joined by John La Guardia, who used to walk with us. "What stuff? What are you fellows talking about?" he exclaimed, catching the drift. "Why should we have to prove anything? I'm sick and tired of making excuses for myself. Here I've been calling myself John B. La Guardia. What's this *John* La Guardia? Who am I fooling? John is not the name my father gave me. Beginning tomorrow, it's going to be Giovanni Battista La Guardia. On every examination paper and everything I sign, and the hell with what anybody thinks!"

Apart from the name changing, there was also a change in our feeling toward other things which were Italian—our attitude in connection with food, for instance. In the early years we were always ashamed of the bulky sandwiches of crusty Italian bread heaped with salami, cheese or Italian sausage. We used to keep them hidden or eat them even before we got to school, so that our friends of the white-bread-and-ham upbringing would not laugh at us. Now we began to delve back into the past for what was part of our heritage. When we did not bring lunch from home, we sought out the Italian restaurants, or even a good Jewish or German delicatessen, where the bread was honest flour and the meat spicy. And it became common to say not just "I'm hungry," but "Boy, what I wouldn't give for a great big platter of macaroni!"

The reaction was setting in. What at one time we were ashamed of, must now be brought into the open. How else could we make peace with our souls? Had it been in my power, I am sure I would have returned the "i" which Mrs. Cutter of the Soup School had dropped from Coviello. But names have strength and a character of their own and are not played with easily. Covello persisted, inasmuch as the dropping of an "i" in no way altered its Italian origin.

Through Harold Zoller I received a bid to join the Alpha Chi Rho Fraternity and for years I was the only Italo-American to belong to the Columbia Chapter. It was at this fraternity that I finally came into contact with men of true intellectual caliber. For the first time in my life I associated with young men of my own age from all over the United States. I began to get a clearer picture of the rich variety of American life.

I spent much of my spare time at the fraternity and at noon ate my lunch there. Some twenty of us would gather around a long table and while eating, discuss everything under the sun. Often we listened to a talk by some visiting alumnus who had already made his mark in the world. It was even possible with these people to discuss Italy and things Italian. They were interested and wanted to know about Italian immigrant communities and the reason for crime in these depressed areas. "We can talk with you; you're not like the others," they would say. Instead of resenting the implication, I would patiently try to put them straight. These were the peak years in immigration. I read everything I could get my hands on in order to understand and talk more intelligently on the subject.

"But why do they keep flocking over here by the thousands?" one of my fraternity brothers persisted one afternoon. "I've seen how these people live here. How are they any better off than where they came from? It would be so much simpler if they stayed where they were."

"Many of them wish they had, this I can assure you. But it seems that the idea of improving one's condition can't be killed. For the hundreds who live in poverty, there is the one who becomes a success. He is the one that counts. In Italy there is no chance for success, only hopelessness. That's why they come. That's why they'll keep right on coming, because if the success does not come to them, it will come to their children. Somewhere along the line it will come."

Someone else said, "But look at the way they herd together. What are their chances for success that way?"

"Success is relative. To be able to afford bread every day
is a form of success. When you can eat meat twice a week
instead of once every couple of months, that's success. Here
there are no traditions and barriers handed down through the
centuries which say a man must remain what he is born. Here—
well, the streets may not be paved with gold, but at least
they've got an opportunity."

"And they take it, all right," someone commented. "The
jails are full of them. Some of them seem to feel that opportunity means grabbing everything they can lay their hands
on."

"But just imagine," I said, "what it means to struggle to
make a living in a society that you don't understand—and that
doesn't understand you. Under such conditions crime can become a form of revolt. It even gathers to itself an aura of success." (Later this idea was more perfectly expressed by the
man who stated, "Society has just the amount of crime it de-
serves.")

Across the lunch table the ideas flew. What had been private
thoughts and unexpressed ideas in me for years now found
words. I could talk with non-Italians about being an Italian,
about being an immigrant in America. Something in me was
being set free.

9 / After my mother's death, my father withdrew into himself for a time, even losing that spontaneous humor which had always been so much a part of him. But living close to the Accurso family helped a great deal to rouse him from the feeling of loss and of the pointlessness of life associated with such a loss.

For some time now, despite the fact that putting words to paper was difficult for him, my father had been corresponding with his brother Domenico Canio, the master shoemaker, and with my mother's brother Zio Prete. Envelopes postmarked from Italy were not unusual about the house now, but it never occurred to me to look into them. I had other things to think about. Some of my father's old humor returned, and once more he began to find relish in his wine and twisted Italian cigars. It was enough for me simply to know that he was enjoying the correspondence. As far as Avigliano was concerned, I would find time to inquire, "How is Zio Canio?"

"Fine," my father would say. "Fine."

"And Zio Prete?"

"Fine. Wonderful. Everything is fine."

I should have known that something was taking place, if for no other reason than that a new and confidential note had crept into the relationship between my father and the Accurso parents.

But I was taken completely by surprise, one Sunday afternoon, when my father asked if I would walk down the street with him. He was dressed for the monthly meeting of the Aviglianese Society, of which he was president, wearing his good suit, his heavy gold watch chain spread across his vest, and his black derby hat. There was a jauntiness to his manner and a tenderness as he took hold of my arm. "It is early for the meeting, Narduccio. Let us go over to the park for a little while. The air is better there. We can talk. We never talk, Narduccio. Ah, that is the American disease! In no time at all a father becomes a stranger to his children. *Beh, la volontà di Dio!* Perhaps somewhere, in another world, we will understand. . . ."

At Jefferson Park we found a secluded bench and sat down. I waited while he nervously relit his Toscano cigar. I could sense that he was stalling for time. Finally he said, "Narduccio, this is what I want to talk to you about. You are the eldest. I am sure you will understand. It is almost two years now since your mother passed away. There is no one in the house any more. It is lonely. Even with my friends the Accursos it is lonely, because friends have their own worries and cannot share ours. . . ."

I could feel discomfort and embarrassment creeping over me.

"I have been in correspondence with Zio Prete and Zio Canio." My father continued, "There is a widow. A good woman whose husband the Lord decided to take before his time. Her only daughter is now married. The mother remains alone. She is willing to come to America. I am thinking of marrying her."

My father sat there, waiting for me to answer. My fists clenched. Thank God I could not put my resentment into words!

"It is because I am your father that all this seems strange to you. You feel that I am betraying your mother. That is because it is possible for a man to have only one mother and he cannot conceive of another taking her place. But it is possible for a man to lose his wife and take another. Even religion does not speak out against this. In fact, your Zio Prete advises it. . . ."

We sat together on the park bench for some time. My father waited for me to speak. After a while he looked at his gold watch and got up. "Have you nothing to say, Narduccio?"

I struggled to answer, but the words would not come. My father got up and started away across the park. The light and sun had gone out of him and he looked old. I wanted to run after him, take hold of his arm, tell him I was sorry. Instead I sat there, victim of that disease of mountain people and of the Aviglianese in particular—the inability to display emotion.

While I was in my sophomore year at Columbia, the Young Men's Christian Association started an Americanization drive, the main feature of which was the teaching of English to foreigners. I was called by the director of the campus branch and asked if I would volunteer my services in East Harlem. I readily agreed and was sent to the Aguilar Library, which now occupied a beautiful new brick building on 110th Street.

I had taught Sunday School at the Home Garden. I had given private lessons in English to Italian immigrants of the neighborhood. But here began my first opportunity to teach a class. Armed with a textbook furnished by the YMCA, I went two nights a week to a room just over the library itself, where I faced some fifteen or eighteen Italian men who did not speak a word of English and who, though much older than myself, insisted on calling me "Mista Professore."

I started teaching in the prescribed manner, thumping my chest and enunciating slowly, "My—name—is—Leonard

—Covello. My—name—is—Leonard—Covello." Then I would walk around, touching each one on the shoulder, "My—name —is . . . My—name—is . . ." and wait, hoping for the idea to sink in.

"My—name—is—Giuseppe Malatesta," grinning.

"Good! Good!"

The idea was that you should not speak to them in their own language. Speak only English. Make them forget their native tongue. Thump an object, shout the word, and make them repeat after you. It was difficult. They could not get into the spirit, pronouncing words which meant nothing to them. Finally I became impatient and let out a tirade of Italian. "What is the matter with all of you? Did you come here to learn English or to sit like a bunch of cabbage heads? *Questa è una tavola*. This is a table! This is a table!"

They stared at me and at each other. They were like children making a sudden and wonderful discovery. A voice whispered, "Pasquale, *il professore è italiano!*"

"Why not," I said. "With a name like Covello, what did you think I was—an Egyptian?"

After that it was easy. They lost their fear of opening their mouths and making mistakes. They joked and laughed as they followed the lesson. They enjoyed coming to class. Many of them would even linger on afterwards to talk to me—but always respectful and keeping their distance and never forgetting that I was "Mista Professore."

Occasionally they would talk about their parents and I would suggest bringing them to class to learn English. "You know how it is, Signor Professore," they would explain in Italian. "They are old. They have known only the little village. It would be embarrassing. They do not even speak the same Italian as you."

"Then I will go to your home and talk to them in the dialect," I answered.

"And the door will be open and the glass of wine and the plate of spaghetti always waiting."

The learning of English progressed satisfactorily. Attendance was good. They wanted to learn English so they could understand what the people around them were talking about. They wanted to learn English so they could understand the "boss on the job" and possibly earn a little more money.

I began to take immense pleasure in these evening sessions, particularly when some of the men brought their children with them, to ask my advice about a school situation or problem concerning them. It was then that I realized how little these parents understood about school conditions and regulations affecting their children. Not knowing the language, they were reluctant to make any attempt to straighten out a child's difficulty outside the home. I came to the conclusion that while it was important to teach English to immigrant people, it was equally important for me to find out about the problems they were unable to solve in becoming adjusted to a new way of life in a new country. And I could only do this through the use of their native language.

While my father tried to ease the blow of his remarriage by taking me into his confidence, the real decision—following the age-old Italian pattern—remained in the hands of the elders. What Zio Prete and Zio Canio and the Accursos approved was accepted without question. In the summer of 1909 my father remarried.

As was natural, we boys did not warm up to his new wife at first. We resented having another woman take the place of our mother, but as time went on, we realized that it was the only possible solution, and the woman who had come as a stranger became indeed a second mother to us. The only one who took to her from the very beginning was my youngest brother, Frank. He was the first to call her "Mamma-Nonna" and that was what we all called her from then on.

Where my mother had been slight of build, of dark complexion, and had jet-black hair, Mamma-Nonna was square-set and had red hair and light skin, despite the fact that she had spent most of her life working in the fields outside the walls of Avigliano. And where my mother had been shy and not too communicative, Mamma-Nonna was voluble, bubbling with conversation, overflowing with health and good humor. And she was interested in everything new. Almost upon her arrival, she started to fumble with English. She possessed an insatiable curiosity which made her go out into the streets and into the neighborhood stores, to mingle with the world outside her door and even beyond her street.

When I came home at night she would sit there at the kitchen table while I ate and ask questions about my studies and what I had been doing that particular day. In the beginning, I sought to put her off. But with Mamma-Nonna, it was impossible to tell her that she would not understand. "You must explain," she would say. "If you take the trouble to explain, sooner or later I will begin to get the idea of what it is like to live in a country like America."

At mealtime, I found myself talking about my courses, my new friends, my attempts to teach English to immigrants, while she sat with her chubby hands folded in her lap, nodding or shaking her head. Before long she knew more about my affairs than my father. In fact, she soaked up information so quickly that often, when my father argued with her, he would say, "You're as bad as Nardo. You know everything about everything."

10 / The long hours of work, the hastily nibbled lunches, dinners consisting of a sandwich with a cup of tea or a glass of milk, the financial worries about keeping the Home Garden operating—all of these things began to tell on Miss Ruddy. The need for rest became greater than a few weeks of vacation could satisfy. She had to go away, the doctor advised, far away, where none of the problems of immigrants or East Harlem could touch her—preferably back to Canada where she could be with her father.

That it would come to this, Miss Ruddy had known for a long time. I think that Mary and I and Victor Salvatore, his brother Mark, Michael Scilipoti, Louis Ferrarini, and others also sensed that the days of the Home Garden we once knew were forever behind us. So long as Miss Ruddy fought her battle to hang on, we continued to go there, teach Sunday School, and take part in the various activities. But when Miss Ruddy left, she took our hearts along with her. Another woman replaced her. It didn't matter who she was or whether we liked her or not. For us, the time of the Home Garden was past.

My experience as an English teacher at the Aguilar Library had given me the feeling that I wanted to do more than teach children in a Sunday School, important as that was. It was characteristic that each of us at the Home Garden carried something of Miss Ruddy away with him—the desire, the obligation almost, to teach others. I wanted to work with young adults, with growing minds, with the older boys and young men of East Harlem who didn't know what to do with themselves and hung around candy stores, street corners, poolrooms, and dance halls. I could not believe that, shown the way, these young street-corner boys would not try to reach out to better themselves.

After considerable difficulty and petitioning a group of us from the Home Garden, led by Michael Scilipoti, convinced the board of directors of the Young Men's Christian Association of the need for a YMCA branch in East Harlem. Four thousand dollars was made available to us with the stipulation that we match this figure with a thousand dollars in neighborhood pledges of our own. We worked night and day, going from house to house and from store to store, speaking to merchants and business and professional men, trying to raise the money; generally we faced the argument, "If the young people want a club, let them pay for it themselves."

We managed to get the money after great difficulty, some of it in cash, most of it in pledges. Actually, we were able to raise only eight hundred dollars, but the project went through just the same. We rented a brownstone building at 322 East 116th Street and the work of reconditioning began. Gradually, as a result of our day-and-night labor, the back yard began to look like a handball and basketball court, as well as a place for gymnastic drills. The kitchen was transformed into a dressing and shower room. The dining room on the ground floor was converted into a poolroom, on the theory that if young men had to play pool it was better for them to play it in wholesome surroundings. On the main floor there was the secretary's office, which was also used for small conferences, and there was a large conference and recreation room.

In September of 1910 we officially and proudly opened the

doors of the East Harlem YMCA. Membership was three dollars a year with nominal fees for educational classes, gymnasium, and other special activities. We had a dramatic club, a music club, and a literary society. On Sunday afternoons there were lectures and concerts and intellectual discussions. We got the traveling branch of the New York Public Library to lend us hundreds of books in all fields, but particularly books on Italy. By now we had come to the full realization of how important it was to learn about our Italian culture and our place in American life. First of all we needed to know as much as possible about ourselves before we could feel that our people and their culture were not inferior—only different.

It was in connection with my work at the East Harlem YMCA that I came in contact with two men who were to have a decided influence in my life—an Italian immigrant by the name of Leone Piatelli, and an American-born New Englander named John A. Shedd. Piatelli was a poet who earned his living as a bookkeeper; Shedd, secretary to an American millionaire, had fallen in love with Italy and was doing volunteer religious work among the Italians of New York City.

Lost and wandering in the intellectual void of East Harlem, Piatelli was instinctively drawn to those of us who were going to college and could converse in Italian. It was after one of my English classes he was attending that he waited for me in the reception room and we walked down the street together. His manner was vibrant, alive. "We must teach Dante!" he exclaimed. "We must. There is an historical parallel between the development of Italy and the development of America. In his *Divina Commedia*, Dante lit the torch of civil liberty and national consciousness in Italy. The universality of his dream asserted itself in Italy through such men as Giuseppe Mazzini —and in America through Abraham Lincoln. The two seem to have been fashioned by the same hand."

I left Piatelli, my mind tingling. I could not sleep. I knocked on the door of the Accurso flat, where I knew Mary would still be awake, reading or correcting the papers of her students at the grammar school. Together we went up to the roof of the tenement where the night was a deep blue-black with pin-pricks of stars. Below and around us were the lights of the city, and over on the river the tugs and barges and smaller moving craft.

"You must meet this Piatelli. You'll like him. With mind and instinct he touches the truth. Dante, Mazzini, Lincoln! I never thought about them together before. Why? And now a casual meeting with a man who is almost a perfect stranger has given me a new feeling of direction. How I like this man!"

"I'm glad," Mary said. "You need friends like him—men who will excite you."

It was true. Leone Piatelli fired me with the desire to know more about the world of poetry and art and literature and to bring it all into relation to my own life. *"Il mistero della vita,"* as he phrased it in Italian. "The riddle of existence."

Mary and I stood together, silent for a time, looking over the rooftops of East Harlem. Both of us wondered, I am sure, how out of these tenements and the turbulence of human existence could emerge beauty of mind and spirit.

It is a strange coincidence that John Shedd, whom I met just a short time later at the YMCA, was an ardent admirer of Abraham Lincoln and over a period of years had acquired an extensive personal library dealing with Lincolniana. Shedd was the exact opposite of Piatelli. He was nearly twice Piatelli's age, close to fifty, heavily built, and in appearance much like G. K. Chesterton, with a massive head, flowing gray hair, straggly mustache, and bushy eyebrows curling out over the edges of the thick lenses of his pince-nez. His laughter was a hearty bellow that shook his whole frame. He loved people and living and had to be in the center of things.

John Shedd and his wife had been teaching Sunday School

in a little Italian Protestant mission on Cherry Street downtown. They helped out financially by their own donations and by soliciting funds from the St. Paul's Methodist Church at 86th Street and West End Avenue, just a few blocks from their home. His interest in Italy and Italians brought him to our branch of the YMCA.

Like a big, overgrown sheep dog he began poking around, wanting to know all about our program and activities. Almost before anyone realized it, he was on the board of directors and closely identified with every aspect of our work among the Italians. He loved pithy sayings, used them often in conversation—in fact wrote a little book of aphorisms called "Salt from My Attic."

"Leonard," he would suddenly say, "when we act the clown, we ought to be sure that we have a clown's audience"; or "Your man with downcast eyes forever sees dirt. There are no stars in the heavens for him"; and "Tell me what you love, and I will tell you what you are."

"I have never been in Florence," he told me at one of our first meetings, "but I know it as if I had been born there. The *Arno*. The *Ponte Vecchio*. *Gl' Uffizi*. *Piazza della Signoria*. Michelangelo's David. The beautiful bronze doors of Ghiberti that Michelangelo said could be the doors of Paradise. I can close my eyes and see it all. I can smell the odor of chestnuts and bread baking in the ovens. All—all there in the back of my mind like the little New England town where I was born."

He'd slap us on the back, his brain bubbling with ideas. "We'll get out a pamphlet and circularize all the Italians in the neighborhood. 'Friends unknown to you invite you to be their friends at the East Harlem Italian YMCA!' Splendid! We'll have dinner at my house and go over the details. You'll meet Mrs. Shedd. Neither of you is married? Too bad. 'Unmarried men and women escape many troubles, but they also miss earth's greatest joy—a home.' Will you come?"

"Of course." I no longer hesitated to accept an invitation to an American home.

Piatelli was hesitant. He kept to the business of the circular. "We shall call it, *Una Porta Aperta*. The Door Open. Right?"

"You mean, The Open Door. You must come, Mr. Piatelli. After all, you have to help with the Italian writing. I'll show you my edition of Dante and my Lincoln collection. After dinner, with coffee, you will recite Dante for us."

Piatelli smiled. "*Bene*."

It was the first of many evenings we spent together, and the first of hundreds of evenings I spent with each of them separately. Poet. Extrovert. School teacher. All of us different. All of us the same. The turbulent soul of Leone Piatelli searching for the purpose of his existence. John Shedd overflowing with life and an ungovernable will to live and help others. Myself, somewhere in between, at the threshold of the adventure, trying to find my way.

11/At this time it occurred to me that one solution to my future might be to become a professor of French. One of my Columbia instructors, John Gerig, suggested that I spend a summer in Paris studying French. He also showed me a photograph of himself and some students who had made their way to Europe on a cattleboat.

"It's hard work on the boat taking care of the cattle," he said, "but you get free passage. You land in Liverpool and from there make your way to Paris. This way it does not cost much. For anyone who wants to specialize in French, it's almost a requisite."

I was captivated by the idea. Still I did not see how I could make it. My summers had been spent augmenting the twenty-five-dollar stipend I received monthly from the Pulitzer Scholarship, which ceased during the vacation months. I had a few dollars saved from my private teaching, but hardly enough to make the trip and take care of my obligations at home. I was almost ready to abandon the project when Mary came to my rescue. She insisted upon advancing me some money. "Professor Gerig is right. You should go to France. As far as the money is concerned, consider it an investment. I am investing in your future."

The cattleboat job failed to materialize. Once more I was

about to give up the whole idea and once more Mary insisted
that I go. I finally took steerage on a German passenger ship
which landed me at Cherbourg. From there I took the train
to Paris, where I spent four months devoting myself to the
serious business of absorbing all I could of the French language.

In Paris I was thrown once more into the great tradition of
my boyhood and of European learning. *Lo studente deve soffrire.*

At college, with all the athletics and other activities, I had
lost sight of what basically should be the life of the student.
Here again was direction, seriousness of purpose.

There was an old Abbé—Abbé Rousselot. The course he
gave in French phonetics started at eight o'clock in the morning. When the bell sounded for the beginning of the lecture,
the doors were closed and no one could get in or out.

"When I am speaking, I will not tolerate an intrusion. If
you cannot be on time or have more important things on your
mind, do not come to my class. I am a teacher of French.
Nothing more and nothing less."

When L'Abbé Rousselot lectured or answered a question
you could hear the breathing of your companion. No one even
whispered. What you heard you carried away and remembered all of the days of your life, for such was the power and
dignity of this man. He was not the college professor who,
outside of class, wanted you to slap him on the back as if he
were one of your comrades. He was friendly and kind—but
always superior and beyond you in a way that was almost an
inspiration.

The students were mostly Russian women, studying to
qualify to teach French in their own country. This, of course,
was during the Czarist regime, when it was fashionable to
converse in French and to use Russian only when speaking
to servants.

There were other nationalities, including a few Italians. I
made particular friends with a young Greek, partly because

of his appealing manner and partly because we could only speak in French to each other. We walked all over Paris together and spent a great deal of time at the museums and at free concerts. Once in a while we spent a few centimes for the concert at the Tuilleries Gardens. We even hired a woman to give us private lessons in French so that by the time we were ready to leave France we had attained a degree of fluency obtainable only by serious concentration and by getting away from the use of one's own language.

As a result of this experience, when much later I took the examinations to teach French in the New York City schools, I came out high on the list. I was well prepared. The Paris experience had done much for me. But best of all was the memory I took away with me of L'Abbé Rousselot and the knowledge that between student and instructor there must exist dignity and respect, as well as understanding.

In February, 1911, I graduated from Columbia and in June of that year, I received my Phi Beta Kappa key. To earn extra money that spring I worked in the registrar's office, the registrar at that time being my German professor. One day he called me in to tell me that a certain Mrs. Johnson wanted someone to tutor her son Clarence, who lacked the necessary credits to enter Columbia. In the course of flitting from one private school to another he had acquired only three points, while he needed at least fourteen.

"During the summer months you will travel back and forth from their summer home on Long Island," I remember my professor saying while I listened in a daze. "You will receive twenty-five dollars a week and expenses."

"Twenty-five dollars a week!"

"And traveling expenses. Not one penny less. You will earn it, I can assure you."

"Yes, sir."

I received my money all right. And he was right—I earned

it. Sometimes I would stay over the weekend without any extra compensation to batter the lessons into young Johnson's head.

What was most interesting to me was the way of life of these people. The Johnson home was a spacious colonial structure with terraced lawns and gardens where workmen were forever busy. There were countless bedrooms, it seemed, and each with a private bath. My feet sank into oriental rugs. My wide eyes took in maids, a butler, and in the garage an automobile for each of the three members of the family.

"Incredible," I told Piatelli as we walked along the streets of East Harlem. "No one can have any conception of the luxury. You say to yourself, 'Is it possible? Can it be that there are people with so much when there are so many with so little?'"

"The stirring of the social conscience," Piatelli laughed. "Better not think too much about it, Leonardo."

I was only able to do something for Clarence Johnson after his mother agreed that I was to have complete control of him for at least eight hours a day. Otherwise, when confronted by the least mental effort, he would rush off in his automobile, or go boating or swimming rather than face the task at hand. I made him buckle down to work. His difficulty was not lack of brains. He had a good mind and could study when compelled to. It was only that he had been so demoralized by a life of over-indulgence that he was nothing more than an overgrown child. This age of irresponsibility had stretched out to his eighteenth year.

Shortly after Clarence had gotten into college, I received a frantic telegram from his mother: PLEASE COME IMMEDIATELY TO HELP CLARENCE. They had moved from their summer residence to their city home on Madison Avenue. Clarence had the entire upper floor of a four-story building to himself. It was fantastic—and only three members of the family in the entire house! "I don't understand what power you have over

Clarence," Mrs. Johnson went to great length to explain when I arrived. "I just can't seem to make him study the way you can."

I had no trouble pummeling Clarence into shape once more. He needed someone to enforce discipline, to show him how to study, to pin him down. Often I did not even know the subject very well. It did not matter. My main function was that of academic policeman.

The most important lesson I learned from the Johnsons had nothing to do with their wealth or position. Clarence was the antithesis of what had been inculcated in me in my childhood in Avigliano and in my early years in East Harlem—a child cannot be left to his own devices. He must have discipline, must be given responsibilities. He is a part of the family and the community and must be made to feel from the beginning that he has a duty toward that family and that community.

My eyes were also opened to the gulf which existed between people of various levels of American life. There was equality of opportunity, it was said, but in practice it did not seem to work out that way. I began to question why this had to be so. While I was never much interested in politics, I found myself now arguing social problems at college or with Mary or Leone Piatelli or John Shedd. I lingered on the street corners and in the parks, listening to the soap-box orators, particularly those of the Socialist Party. I read their literature. I kept seeing before my eyes the Johnsons, with their home in the country and their mansion in town, and the people of East Harlem who worked all day long and were barely able to fill their stomachs and clothe their children.

"Better not think too much about it, Leonard," Piatelli had said.

While working for my master's degree, openings to teach French occurred at Wesleyan and Syracuse Universities. Here was an opportunity to realize my goal—a professorship. Yet

the pay was such that I could not possibly afford to take either
of these jobs. To do so would have meant leaving New York,
where I could augment a modest salary with outside work.
Besides, I still wanted to contribute financially to my family.
Instead, I took the examinations of the Board of Education
and qualified as a teacher of French in the New York City
public schools.

Meanwhile, along with teaching French several nights a
week at Columbia Extension, I became involved in several
amusing jobs which gave me interesting glimpses into the
broad panorama of life in a great metropolis. During the holiday seasons I was employed as a store salesman for a Greek
who owned a florist shop near Columbia. His instructions were
always the same. "Water keeps flowers alive. That's all you
have to know to sell the customers who come to this shop.
The rest depends on your personality. Charm them into buying—and then tell them to use water."

Another job I held for several months paid the fantastic
sum of five dollars a day because of the bodily risk involved. It
also served as a practical introduction to the greatest of all
democratic institutions—voting. An organization called the
Honest Ballot Association recruited students for work during primary and election days. Two of us were assigned a
polling place at a barber shop on the corner of Amsterdam
Avenue and 61st Street—a section so renowned for its bloody
neighborhood battles that it earned the name of San Juan
Hill.

Here we sat at the polls during the primaries and jotted
down the name, address, and a brief physical description of
each person who registered. Then we had to go out and verify
that the registrant actually lived at the address given. The fact
that the neighborhood did not vary too much from our own
East Harlem gave us the confidence to go poking into dark
alleys and forbidding tenements, inquiring after people, often
finding that they had been dead for years. One of us would

enter a building while the other remained outside, ready to run for the cops. Then on election day we sat with our cards before us, challenging any voter who did not coincide with our information.

Lastly, there was my job as a whistle counter for John D. Rockefeller. The Rockefeller-endowed hospital on the East River in midtown Manhattan had just been completed. Three of us from the college were given work, in eight-hour shifts, to count the whistles and tugboat tootings which drifted up to the hospital from below. I worked from eight o'clock at night to four in the morning for fifty cents an hour, a midnight snack, and a breakfast. I sat comfortably in the tower of this hospital, watching the lights of the river boats, noting down each whistle and indicating whether or not it was necessary. Just how valuable this information turned out to be, I have no idea. What I did find out, however, was that the variations which existed between steamboat whistles were subtle in kind and infinite in number.

12/A

classmate of mine at Columbia, Angelo Lipari, was teaching French as a substitute at De Witt Clinton High School and the job seemed too much for him. Ordinarily of even temper, the last few months had made him very nervous. One night when we were sitting around at the YMCA, he blurted, "Confound those brats. As much as I like to teach, I can't stand them any longer."

"What? What's the matter?" I said.

"What's the matter? You never had to teach roughnecks like this. A different bunch every hour. Six hours a day. Monsters, planning and scheming how they can torment and tantalize you!"

I laughed and scratched my head. "You're making a mountain out of a molehill. You can handle them."

"You don't get it," Lipari insisted. "You don't understand what it is because you haven't been through it yourself. *No one can teach them.*"

It was only a few weeks later that Lipari came to me bubbling with excitement. An opportunity had come at last for him to teach at one of the New England colleges. He wanted me to take over his classes at De Witt Clinton. He had even arranged an interview for me with the principal, Dr. Tildsley. This was in December, a month before the end of the fall term. I was at Columbia working for my master's degree. Here was an opportunity I could not afford to turn down.

The next day I met Dr. John L. Tildsley, who for the next quarter of a century—first as principal of De Witt Clinton and later as Assistant Superintendent of the High School Division—was to exert a great influence on my academic career in the New York City schools. Stocky, square of jaw, as determined as he looked, Dr. Tildsley, after examining my credentials, asked me only one question. "Where did you go to high school?"

"Morris High."

"Then you know what a high-school job is like. Go upstairs to the lunchroom. Your class is waiting there."

Upstairs I found some forty teen-age boys sprawling around on tables and benches, yawning, bored, waiting for amusement. Obviously, because of the shortage of classroom space, the lunchroom was also to be my classroom for the time being. While the students sized me up, I selected a table and made it my desk. Before they could come to any conclusion, I folded my arms and, staring straight at them said, "My name is Leonard Covello. I'm your new French teacher. Now get out your books and let's get to work."

While we were conjugating French verbs, a teaspoon came sailing through the air and landed at my feet. Out of the corner of my eye, I saw where it had come from. "You," I said to the boy, "what's your name?"

There was a silence. "You, I said," taking a step toward him.

The boy muttered something under his breath.

"I can't hear. Speak louder."

"Jerry," came out, sheepishly.

"Jerry what?"

"Jerry Gilmore."

"All right, Jerry. Pick up the spoon. Put it back where it belongs."

He did not move. There was a hushed silence. I placed my

hand on Jerry's shoulder, exerting pressure with my fingers. "Come on, Jerry," I said. The pressure of my fingers increased slightly. I was acting instinctively. I gave no thought to what I would do next. I only knew that this boy was going to pick up the spoon. Jerry moved to do what he was told. When he sat down again, I turned to the class. "Now that we have this off our chests, let's get down to business."

I had no further trouble with that class or any other class. Word got around.

Angelo Lipari achieved an excellent reputation as a professor of romance languages. His was the quiet, rewarding life of a university town and campus and library and ivied walls. I thought about him often in those early days at De Witt Clinton, just as I thought about the many other teachers who seemed to have difficulty in handling adolescent boys. It seemed to me that no matter how they tried they always remained strangers to their pupils. I could rationalize their problem and put it into words but my heart could never fully understand.

It has always seemed to me that discipline, at least in part, depends on the attitude the teacher brings to the classroom. My attitude—whether good or bad, sound or fallacious—might be paraphrased as follows: "I am the teacher. I am older, presumably wiser than you, the pupils. I am in possession of knowledge which you don't have. It is my function to transfer this knowledge from my mind to yours. For the most efficient transfer of knowledge, certain ground rules must be set up and adhered to. I talk. You listen. I give. You take. Yes, we will be friends, we will share, we will discuss, we will have open sessions for healthy disagreement—but only within the context of the relationship I have described, and the respect for my position as teacher which must go with it." This attitude was instinctive with me. It was not until late in my teaching career that I ever thought to put it into words.

Unfortunately for my early days of teaching, I had taken no

methods courses, so that my main trouble was not learning how to handle the boys so much as learning how to teach. My first lesson plan seemed to me long enough to cover several forty-minute periods. Before fifteen minutes had elapsed I had covered the lesson and found myself trying to figure out what to take up next.

I then began to plan lessons more carefully, slowing the tempo, allowing time for things to sink in, encouraging questions, and giving the student's mind a chance to work.

Also, in the beginning I was too severe in assigning homework. I tried to formulate a system of teaching based only upon knowledge of myself as a student. In each class there were forty different temperaments and personalities, as well as forty varying degrees of intelligence and ability to absorb knowledge. As a student in college, I would cover about twenty pages of translation a day. I thought I was giving an easy assignment if I assigned half that amount. I soon found out that if a student translated two pages well, it was all I could expect.

My pupils in those early years at De Witt Clinton were of many nationalities, with just a sprinkling of Italians. I quickly realized that there was more to teaching than the mere business of memorizing verbs and doing translations. There had to be interest. The boys must be made to feel a rapport between themselves and their teacher and what they were learning. Now and then I found a few minutes to digress from the study at hand to other subjects and problems which interest boys. I would talk about baseball or wrestling or even current news. When we returned to the lesson there was a freshness, an eagerness, a desire to please.

Six months after I had begun teaching at De Witt Clinton, Dr. Tildsley called me into his office. He wanted me to stay on and coach the soccer team as well.

I was pleased by what took place in Dr. Tildsley's office, though I still had no intention of spending my life in the New

York City public schools. When I had my doctorate and could command a decent salary, I was going to become a professor of romance languages at some university and share the gracious life of a scholar with such as Angelo Lipari.

Nevertheless I had to tell Mary of Dr. Tildsley's approval. After school I rushed down to the Metropolitan Opera House and bought two tickets for *La Boheme* for that night. It was an occasion, so I splurged and paid two dollars for each seat. However, I have absolutely no recollection of the opera. All I remember is standing under the marquee during intermission, oblivious of all the finery of jewels and evening dress, of the sleek-groomed horses and carriages and motor cars parked along the curb, talking excitedly to Mary about what I was going to accomplish at De Witt Clinton now that my status was assured. I must have raised my voice because Mary said, "Easy, Leonard. Everyone will hear you."

I realized I was acting foolishly. "But you can't blame me for being excited," I said. "A steady job and steady pay. It makes a difference, all the difference in the world." Then I said what had been in my mind for months, for years, in fact. "Now we can get married."

Mary smiled. She took my arm and we went back into the theater.

As a boys' high school founded in 1897, Clinton had made a reputation for itself. Students flocked to it from all over the city. A restless crowd they were—so many eager to learn, and at the same time so many others with heavy obligations of working after school that made it difficult for them to cope with the many and stringent academic requirements. There was a steady flow of failures and drop-outs.

When I started at De Witt Clinton there was a large German Department, a large French Department, and only one teacher of Spanish. There is no question but that Clinton gave the best that a public high school could offer at that time in terms of mass-production education. However, there was one aspect of public-school learning which very early began to trouble me. Perhaps the root of it went back to my early work with the Italian immigrants at the Aguilar Library.

I was in the habit of arriving early at the school. I used to stand at the window before classes started, watching the boys pour into the building, conscious of an uneasiness, a feeling of disturbance. I remember talking about this to Shedd and Piatelli one night at the YMCA, at about the time when Piatelli was beginning to organize his Dante Club and Shedd was writing a play which he later called *Up at Abe Lincoln's*. We were sitting in the lounge, Shedd sprawling comfortably in an armchair, Piatelli pacing up and down giving us one of his inimitable renditions of the great poet:

> *Temer si dee di sole quelle cose*
> *C'hanno potenza di fare altrui male;*
> Of those things only should we be afraid
> Which have the power of doing others harm;

As Shedd read the translation, Piatelli looked at me. "Leonardo, you do not listen. We give you the beautiful Dante and your brain is far away. You are in love. Yes, that it must be."

"That it must be, yes," John Shedd mimicked. "But he has two loves, this fellow—a girl and a high school. Our friend has not much time for us these days."

"You worry too much for the boys, Leonardo. For the whole world, one man cannot worry. They will live and they will grow up and they will die. You can help them a little, perhaps—that is all." Piatelli touched his hand to my shoulder and sat down. "What is the problem?"

"Well, this is the problem," I said. "I instruct about one hundred and forty boys every day, but what exactly do I know about them? I watch them. They're like shadows as far as we, the teachers, are concerned—coming out of nowhere every morning and at three o'clock going back into nowhere. How can we really do our jobs as teachers unless we know something about the pupils we are trying to teach?"

Piatelli listened with interest. John Shedd could not see how one teacher could cope with the individual problems of all of his students.

"The teacher can't," I explained. "He can only try. He can open his eyes to the fact that not all students are alike because of factors over which the student himself has no control—his home life, the neighborhood he grew up in, his companions, where his parents came from. Yet these students are all thrown together into one class and expected to conform or react in the same way to set academic standards. I'm not saying that the problem is a simple one or that a solution is even possible. I only say that the teacher who is aware that the problem exists and somehow gets closer to his boys becomes a better teacher."

It was the beginning of countless discussions on the subject of schooling as only one aspect of a child's life. What of the others? The subject both fascinated and tormented me. Without being quite sure of what it was, I began to sense a purpose in life which transcended the simple business of teaching the rudiments of a foreign language.

Little by little other problems in education began to press upon me. I grew painfully aware of the formidable job of the teacher who has to face thirty-five to forty boys in five different classes every day, five days a week—thirty-five to forty boys in rows of seven, blackboards all around and a platform in front for the teacher to stand on. The actual instruction—the conveying of knowledge from one mind to another—began to seem like almost a secondary problem. The teacher's main task was to control these boys at the most restless period of their lives, to channel their boundless energy as they move *en masse* along corridors every forty-five minutes from teacher to teacher and from class to class but with the same blackboards all around, while outside the sun is shining, the air is brisk, and the river glistens.

Somehow during the educational training of my later years, I had forgotten what it was like to be a boy in high school. Little by little I began to relive my own youth in terms of the students before me. I tried to analyze the process of education from their standpoint. What was it all about? Here we were seeking to impart information and to train the mind. However, to the student it seemed a delayed-action process. What he studied now would be good for him later on, he was told. The student became confused. When? How, exactly? No one had the answer. Or the answer was vague, projected somewhere into the distant future. But the boys were vitally alive now, concerned only with the present.

Then there was another problem, the unavoidable fact that not all students were book-minded. This was hard for many of us to understand in those early days. Our being teachers in itself suggested a certain fondness for books and love of learning. We found it difficult to believe that not all people are born this way, that there are those who experience great difficulty in learning from the printed page. Yet all teaching was based on the principle of book study. Students who were not book-minded simply failed. It became evident that they had to be treated in some special way.

"Who is responsible for these failures?" I asked Mary in a despondent moment. "For that matter, why should there be failures at all?"

Mary said, "I've often struggled with the same problem and have never come to a solution."

"There must be some solution," I argued. "Maybe it's not the teacher so much as the system which is wrong. Apparently the school is set up with only one purpose—a terminal goal, college entrance. Everything is cut and dried. The only trouble is that the student is far from being cut and dried. He is an individual, with individual needs and abilities."

Not long after this another teacher of French and I got permission to organize a special class for the failures in our department. We tried to find out as much as we could about
each student and sought to awaken in him a response to our
special efforts. We were moderately successful. At the end of
this special session, three-quarters of these students were able
to return to the regular class and take their place again among
their companions. There remained those who could not or
would not make it. Some of these were children of Italian immigrants. They had no interest in learning French and only
took it because of the requirements. "What do I want to learn
French for?" they would argue, "when I can't even speak the
language of my parents? Why don't we learn Italian? You're
an Italian—why don't you teach Italian?"

It was another question to which I had no answer.

13 / J

ust before Easter, 1913, at the Presbyterian Church in East Harlem, of which at that time Norman Thomas was pastor, Mary and I were married. It was inevitable. From that first moment when she taught me to say "yes" in English on the ferry-boat ride from Ellis Island our lives had been bound together. She was both an inspiration and a source of strength to me. She counseled me when I needed advice. She helped me with my lessons when I was going to school. She lent me money when I needed it. She shared my joys and my disappointments. And when my mother died and it seemed that the void could never be filled, Mary became the bridge between the gloom and the sunlight.

We had rarely spoken of marriage, yet by some unspoken agreement we knew that one day it would happen. We both had our responsibilities to our families. When I became assured of a permanent position with the Board of Education this problem was solved. With both of us working, there was now enough to take care of our obligations and set up a little home of our own. Amid the rejoicing of all the Covellos and the Accursos, we rented a small apartment near Columbia, where I was still teaching an evening class in French as well as taking courses to complete my master's degree.

The world was beautiful that year—as it should be for young

married people with the future filled with the promise of dreams and ambitions yet to be realized. Ahead of us stretched long years of adventure and happiness, or so we thought. For our honeymoon we went to Toronto and spent a week visiting with Miss Ruddy. She was living with her father, a wiry octogenarian who had migrated from northern Ireland as a boy and had helped pioneer the Canadian wilderness. Though he was bent with age, his gray eyes were vital and alive. "Ah, it was God's work she did in New York City," he said, referring to his daughter, "but it was her health He also took."

It was true. Miss Ruddy was thinner and had even less color than when we had last seen her. Perhaps separation from the work and life she had come to love had smothered any serious effort to get well. Back at the Home Garden an entirely new group had taken over. Religious instruction had been abandoned. The little Protestant mission gave way to a settlement house, later called the Haarlem House. Miss Ruddy took this hard. "Young people need spiritual guidance," she remonstrated sadly. "Children must be given early in life the foundations of a faith which will sustain them in later years. Any community gathering place must base its work on the teachings of Jesus Christ and the Holy Bible."

Both Mary and I agreed. In fact, our choice of the Presbyterian Church of Norman Thomas for our wedding came as a result of our having left the Home Garden in order to continue the Sunday School teaching we loved. This meant shifting our activities from one location and church to another, but continuing the same work. The consideration of sect hardly entered our minds. Methodist, Baptist, Presbyterian, what difference did it make, so long as we had our work to do and our young people to teach?

Miss Ruddy gave us her blessing. She felt pride in us as her spiritual children, and this strengthened our faith to continue her work.

"The satisfaction, the joy for me," she told us in parting,

"is what I have bequeathed to you of myself. In both of you I will continue to live after I am gone. It is as if God had given me children of my own to remember and to perpetuate the life I passed here on this earth."

We returned from our honeymoon—and plunged into trouble.

Our YMCA branch, now in the third year of its operation, was finding it increasingly difficult to fulfill the yearly pledge of a thousand dollars to the central board. Despite the excellent work we were doing, the active interest of the young men of East Harlem, our increasing membership, and, above all, the great need for such work, it looked as if we might have to close our door. The fact that all of our services were voluntary and no salary was paid except to the secretary, Lawson Brown, who received the niggardly sum of seventy-five dollars a month and gave practically twenty-four hours a day to his work, did not make any difference. We still had to meet a pledge of a thousand dollars. As usual, the merchants and people of means would not come to our rescue. It was the same old story. If the young men of East Harlem wanted a recreation and educational center, they could pay for it themselves.

Also it became apparent that the state YMCA board was concerned with large projects which handled young men by the thousands and whose buildings would be landmarks in a community. In vain we pleaded that the work of our little center be continued, citing the case of Miss Ruddy and the Home Garden and the contribution she had made to a whole neighborhood with what in the beginning had been a one-room mission. We felt that a more effective job could be done in small units where greater attention could be given the individual. But we lost our case. The YMCA of East Harlem was closed.

John Shedd, Piatelli, and I transferred our activities to the Jefferson Park Italian Methodist Church. There we organized

the Young Men's Lincoln Club of Little Italy. We met every
Friday night and discussed the boys' problems—how they
could stay in school, how they must learn to understand
their parents' problems. Using the life of Lincoln as our moral
basis, we talked about some of the great Italians and what
could be learned from their lives. The idea was to acquaint
these young men with their Mediterranean culture and give
them an appreciation of and a pride in the country of their
parents. "If we know intimately the giants of the past," I
can still hear Piatelli's mellow voice saying, "we can build
our own lives and our own nation on firm foundations."

We studied the accomplishments of such men as St. Francis,
Savonarola, Galileo, Garibaldi, Da Vinci, Mazzini. We took
up great events in American history: the discovery of Columbus, the landing at Plymouth Rock, the signing of the Declara-
tion of Independence, William Penn and the Indians. We were
striving to give these young men something more than they
were getting from their teachers in the day school: an understanding of the relationship between these two cultures. And
we tried to impress upon them that, instead of being ashamed
or confused by the duality of their background, theirs was an
especially rich heritage, of not only one culture but two—the
old and the new.

Late at night, tired but happy with the sense of accomplishment which comes in working with growing minds, I would
go home to Mary in our new little apartment, there to sit up
for a while longer, sipping a cup of coffee, each of us talking
over what we had done that day. Mary was now teaching in
a school in the lower east side of Manhattan—and thus we
were earning our livings in exactly the same way. Unlike a
great many people in similar situations, we made no agreement
never to talk "shop." "Shop talk" was our life. We had already
spent years telling each other what we were doing, sharing our
every teaching experience. It was an important part of our ever-
growing love for each other.

However, this deep happiness of my personal life was not to last. Viewed from this distance of forty-five years, it almost seems that it ended really before it began. In the spring of 1914, shortly before the beginning of the First World War, Mary became ill. As in the case of my mother, it was a sickness difficult to diagnose. We were still not the kind to call a doctor at the first sign of a headache. When finally we did call a physician, we were no further enlightened than before.

From here on, my recollection of Mary's illness becomes jumbled and vague. One doctor followed another. One said one thing, another said a second. Diseases I no longer recall were named—always tentatively. Now I know it was a form of nephritis, although I do not remember this term being used at that time. Mary grew weaker by the day while I stood helplessly by, unable to assist her in any way. She never went back to her class at Public School 91 and the children sent notes to find out how she was coming along. After a month spent in the Catskills, where it was thought the fresh air and sunlight and milk might do her some good, Mary returned to her mother's home. There she went to bed and never left it again. In the month of August, just a week or so after the outbreak of the First World War, Mary died.

I was left with the intolerable anguish of her death. And somehow it lay heavy not only on my heart but on my conscience. As in the case of my mother, I never got over the feeling that, in some way I could not define, this death might have been averted.

I went back to live with my family again—with my father, Mamma-Nonna, and three of my younger brothers. I plunged headlong into a frenzy of activity which occupied every moment of my waking day and dropped me exhausted into bed late at night. In this way I kept myself from brooding over a loss which could have driven me out of my senses.

"You will end by ruining your own health, Nardo," my father said. "Nothing is worth this. There must be moderation,

moderation." As always, my ways and the ways of the New World were strange to him. I can see him sucking his pipe and pausing from reading *Il Progresso,* while Mamma-Nonna nodded her head in agreement. "God decides," she would say, "what has to be and then brings it to pass. For a man to kill himself with work is taking on a responsibility which does not belong to him. This is not right. And more, I am sure that tonight you did not eat any supper."

"I ate a ham sandwich and a cup of coffee."

"How can anyone live on food like that? Come, I will cook a nice plate of spaghetti."

"I can't, Mamma-Nonna. I don't feel like eating."

With the war continuing in Europe, the outside world seemed turned upside down, too. The war's initial effect on me was a bizarre one. England and Germany were cut off from their South American trade, and it seemed as though everyone in New York decided that here was an opportunity to deal with Latin American firms. Spanish, always a minor language in the high schools, suddenly was in great demand. At De Witt Clinton the only Spanish teacher was a man by the name of Lawrence Wilkins, while in the French Department we had a dozen teachers. When the new fall programs were being prepared, Wilkins came to me in desperation.

"Covello," he urged, "you've got to help me. You've had a couple of years of Spanish at Columbia. You must take over one of my first-term classes. I just can't handle them all."

And that is how I started to teach Spanish. It was curious. Here I, an Italian by birth, having spent years to perfect my French because it was not possible to earn a livelihood teaching the language and culture of my parents, now was called upon to teach Spanish. But I was beginning to learn that logic very often has no bearing on the direction one's life takes. Anyway, I reasoned, my business was teaching, no matter what the subject. Armed with a beginner's textbook I went to work.

If I had had only a few years of Spanish, my pupils had no knowledge of the language at all.

While teaching, I devoted myself to a serious study of the language. The next year found me with several new classes, with the demand for teachers of Spanish increasing every day. I taught evening high-school classes at Clinton, where fifty to sixty people were crammed into a room meant for thirty-five. Almost before I knew it, I had given up entirely the teaching of French—the language I had struggled so hard to acquire. Everything was topsy-turvy. But it was the war and nothing seemed to matter or make much sense. For once in my life I did not try to seek direction in what I was doing. I only wanted to work and keep busy.

Occasionally some of my students of Italian origin would stop me after class. Their numbers now were increasing with every new term. East Harlem's Irish and German groups had been absorbed and were dispersing. Now it was the Italian's day in this melting-pot area of the world's greatest city. "Hey, Mr. Covello," they would say, "first it's French. Now it's Spanish. When are you going to teach us Italian?"

Still I had no answer for them. How could I answer when I could not even understand the pattern of my own behavior as a teacher of languages?

14/I

t was an odd thing that while Italian was not
taught in any of the city high schools, it was still possible to get
credit for it if a student could pass the New York State examinations, known as the Regents' Examinations.

One day while I was on lunchroom duty, three students approached me. Two of them were former pupils from one of
my French classes—Hannibal De Bellis, who later became a
physician, and Steve Calarco, who first went into law and is
now in the wholesale fruit business. The third I knew only
by sight and because of his reputation as an athlete and his
participation in various school activities. His name was Benny
Segreto. Only about five feet six inches tall, he had rugged
shoulders and powerful arms. His face was full, and an exceptional strength and determination showed in it in the rare
moments while he wasn't smiling and joking. I had heard him
speak with considerable force at meetings of the student
council, and his accent tagged him as coming from the island
of Sicily.

He stood there now, his hands in his pockets, listening
politely while De Bellis and Calarco explained that they wanted
to take the Regents' Examinations in Italian and needed extra
coaching.

"Hannibal and I were both born in Italy," Steve explained.

"What we're trying to find out is if we know enough to pass this examination. You're the boss."

We all laughed. Benny Segreto now spoke for the first time. "They know very much, Mr. Covello. I speak with them. I have studied Italian in Palermo."

The tenor of his voice had nothing of boastfulness. Here was a simple statement of fact. Immediately I was curious as to the ultimate purpose of his schooling. Despite his genial smile and warmth of manner, there was a boundary beyond which intimacy was not invited. In his glance one could almost sense the pride of people who have both Mediterranean and Arab blood in their veins.

"Let me consult my schedule," I said to De Bellis and Calarco, "then I will let you know when I can fit in the time. It may have to be at night."

After they left, I picked up a cup of coffee and sought a vacant table. Benny Segreto followed. "If you will permit me?" he said, in Italian.

"Sit down. It's a pleasure."

"I have been thinking," he began, "there are many of us now at De Witt Clinton—some like me who were born in Italy and those who were born in America. We are many, but there is nothing which holds us together. We need a club—special for those who are of our blood."

Here was a student in the very school where I was teaching who at the age of seventeen or eighteen had already grasped the problem which I and many of my colleagues were fumbling to solve. "Why?" I asked in order to draw him out. "Why do you feel that such a club would do any good?"

He took some scribbled notes out of his pocket and smoothed them on the table in front of him. "*The Circolo. Il Circolo Italiano*, we will call it. We need a club like this to make the Italian-American student understand that he does not have to be ashamed that his mother and father are Italian. He will find out that friends all over New York, who live just like him, think just like him, come here to school for the same reasons. He will learn that instead of belonging just to the block or the neighborhood, he belongs to something much bigger—much, much bigger. . . ."

I was very much impressed by Benny Segreto.

In my years as a teacher, I was to experience similar admiration at contact with the exceptional student, but never in quite this same way. "And how far along have you gotten with the organization of this club?" I asked.

"We have already talked about it to our principal, Dr. Paul," Benny Segreto said. "He likes the idea very much. That is why I am here. For the club to be organized there must be a faculty advisor. We have decided that the faculty advisor shall be you."

That night I had dinner at the home of John Shedd, and he was to read to Piatelli and me the second act of the play he was writing. For the first time since Mary's death, I felt a purpose in being alive. "For nothing is really dead (I picked up the thread of Miss Ruddy's belief), but continues on in the memory of those left behind." If the memory of Mary was to live, I had to live. Strange that an apparently unrelated conversation with a high-school student should begin to clear my brain and reaffirm my faith in life.

I remember the wonderful dinner we had that night at John Shedd's home—a brace of grouse and wild rice served by a maid who responded to the tinkle of a little bell at Mrs. Shedd's elbow. Our hostess was a tall, dignified woman, who always made us feel at home.

I began talking of Benny Segreto. As we left the dinner table and followed the rotund figure of John Shedd to his study, I was still on the subject of the proposed *Circolo Italiano*.

"As I understand this idea for a *Circolo*, it must not be an isolated island interested only in the social or intellectual activities of a group of students of Italian parentage. No. This would defeat the purpose. The *Circolo* must keep in mind that its members are American citizens in an American school and soon to be active citizens in an American city."

"Excellent," Shedd commented, sitting behind his ornate writing desk and shuffling the pages of his play. "Such a group could help create a sympathetic bond between the parents and their children, as well as between Italians and non-Italians."

"It is like we will build a bridge from Italy to America," Piatelli interrupted. "This will be the *Circolo*. At both ends people will learn from each other. It is what we have been trying to do for a long time. This Benny Segreto has been taking our ideas from us."

I remember that we expressed ourselves that night in high-flown phrases, making beautiful plans and resolutions for many hours before we finally got around to listening to the second act of John's play. An outsider would have smiled at our idealism and optimism in those days of the First World War. But the fact remains that as a result of such thinking on the part of boys like Benny Segreto and adults like ourselves, the *Circolo* was born. It was to have a decided influence upon thousands of De Witt Clinton boys in the years to come.

Though basically a club for Italian boys, the *Circolo* also enlisted the interest of members with such names as Styler, Solomon, Murphy, Oltarsh, and Ocker. It even published a magazine called *Il Foro* or *The Forum*, a combination literary publication and review of club activities. It was written in both English and Italian with Piatelli as our foreign-language advisor and John Shedd as our American expert.

I remember *Il Foro's* special Dante issue, commemorating the 65oth anniversary of Dante's death, which was awarded a bronze medal by the Casa di Dante in Rome. The editor-in-chief of this issue was Salvatore Cutolo, one of our outstanding students. Today Dr. Salvatore Cutolo occupies the position of

Deputy Medical Superintendent of Bellevue Hospital in New
York City.

Through the untiring efforts of Benny Segreto, the *Circolo
Italiano* extended its influence to other high schools in New
York City and ultimately it attracted considerable attention
even outside educational circles. "While they themselves are
learning the language of Italy," wrote the *New York Evening
Mail* of that period, "the students of De Witt Clinton High
are endeavoring to teach the immigrants of that country the
language, customs, and ideals of America."

15 / War came to us in April, 1917. Woodrow

Wilson excited us with his idealism. The air rang with slogans one wanted to believe in—"The war to end all wars!" and "Make the world safe for democracy." Older students dropped out of De Witt Clinton to enlist. Benny Segreto, who had already graduated but continued active participation and interest in the *Circolo*, volunteered for an artillery unit and was sent to Sandy Hook for training.

No matter how I reasoned, I felt that I had to participate in some way. I joined the Columbia Volunteer Unit and spent Saturday afternoons in training. It was laughable, this citizens' army we were supposed to represent. We provided our own equipment, learned the elements of squad formation while marching around Columbia's South Field, and took long hikes into nearby Jersey. We were rugged Americans, we felt, a match for anybody, even the seasoned veterans of the German Army. We believed in our superiority then as we believe in it now. It is an American characteristic to believe we are superior, whatever the facts or experience actually reveals.

Then another, odder opportunity to be of real service presented itself. The fruit and berry crop of New York State was threatened because of a shortage of labor. Appeals went out to the schools for student labor and for teachers to supervise.

Here was a problem, directly related to the war, that I could understand and in which I could be of help. It meant giving up the summer job I had counted on to augment my teacher's salary and also my activities with the Lincoln Club and the Presbyterian Church, but it was the least I could do.

Along with three other teachers from De Witt, I was assigned to the fruit country of the Hudson Valley, about seventy-five miles from New York City. My particular area was in the neighborhood of the little village of Milton. I found myself in an abandoned farmhouse just a few miles outside the village, guiding thirty-two teenage charges, the vast majority of whom had never even seen a cow and were only vaguely aware that strawberries did not grow on trees.

There was no furniture of any kind, except a long plank table, improvised benches, and a wood-burning kitchen stove. Each of us had two blankets and a bed tick which we filled from a pile of straw. We each ate a sandwich that first morning, and by ten o'clock I had the boys hard at work in the neighboring strawberry fields.

The serious business of preparing food fell to my lot. For the first two weeks I was the cook, using the Boston Cook Book as guide. One or two of the boys took turns helping me. The routine was to look up recipes intended for four and then multiply by ten: meat balls, stews, fish, eggs, baked beans, and occasionally steak, together with loads of bread and butter and milk, and ending in generous helpings of prunes, pie, or cake.

It was a fascinating summer for me. The city boys all had a wonderful time in the country and actually looked forward to returning the following year. Some, after paying board of $3.50 a week, sent home as much as forty dollars from their earnings in fruit and berry picking. Sunday was parents' day, and the "farm cadets" enjoyed touring the fields and quiet lanes with their folks. I even had visitors of my own. On several occasions Mary's younger sister Rose came with a group of her friends. She was now working as a stenographer in a downtown business office in New York and beginning to take an interest in the things I was doing. We had been seeing quite a bit of each other. She was a good listener, always cheerful, and she had a way of making me see the brighter side of things, no matter how down I felt.

One Sunday we had a picnic under the trees, down by the creek, and it was there that the idea came to me of buying a place in the country someday when I could afford it, where my father and Mamma-Nonna could pass the remainder of their days and where I could go for a visit and rest from the city pavements once in a while.

I learned an important lesson from this experience at the Farm Cadet Camp—a lesson which became the nucleus of my thinking about the education of adolescent boys and which remains unchanged even in this day of child psychologists and the cult of self-expression. Hard work, especially in cooperation with his fellows, provides a growing boy with a feeling of accomplishment, recognition, acceptance, and responsibility. There is no quick road to manhood. It is a slow process of development which begins at the cradle. A human being is not born with his duty clear to him. A sense of duty must be acquired. A boy must be taught how to contribute, through his labor, to the society in which he lives. What I had been taught in the little mountain town of Avigliano applied to the America of the twenties, and still applies today.

In the fall of 1917, just before I enlisted to join Benny Segreto and some other De Witt Clinton alumni at an artillery unit at Sandy Hook, New Jersey, I had a memorable conversation with Rose. I had come to rely a great deal upon her judgment and understanding. Partly by virtue of her boundless energies and good humor, her approach to life was direct and practical. Early in her high-school years she had been thrown into contact with the commercial world of downtown Manhattan. She liked her work as secretary in an export firm and was fascinated by the business world. To her all things were of interest and no one particular way of life more important than another. "Heavens, Leonard," she would say, "a Wall Street broker or a college professor, what difference does it make? The important thing is whether or not you are happy. And to be happy you need money. Without money your chances for happiness are lessened."

"It's that dollars-and-cents mentality you've acquired downtown," I joked. "You don't believe a word you're saying."

She laughed her easy, tomboy laughter which had warmth and frankness in it and somehow told me of the years she had skated along the sidewalks, her school books dangling from a strap, her whole manner proclaiming her self-assurance and sense of belonging. "It's a fact and you know it. Who should know better than we immigrants the importance of money!"

I believed her but did not like to have it expressed so bluntly. I preferred the intellectual approach—the statement with qualifications, the subtleties, the varying shades of meaning and awareness of another side to the discussion.

The day I decided to enlist I met Rose downtown and we had lunch together. I was excited. The evening before I had spent with John Shedd and Piatelli, discussing the motivations of patriotism. I told Rose what I was going to do. She answered simply, "If you feel you have to go, nothing I can say or do will stop you. But I believe that you can do much more by remaining where you are, teaching at De Witt and helping in the war jobs which have to be done right here in New York."

It was hard to put it into words without making it sound sentimental—hard to express in any fresh way that in war people get killed and that no man has the right to expect another to take this risk of death for him. What I was trying to express had been said a hundred thousand times before and would be again. It was still something personal and individual that had to be lived and experienced within one's self. "I have thought about it a great deal," I explained to Rose. "If I sat back now and did not enlist I would not be living up to what I was taught to believe. What I want to teach others to believe, I have to go."

After a pause, Rose said, "I sensed it was coming, and I really did not think I could talk you out of it. I only hope. . . ."

I looked at her.

"I only hope that you'll come back."

I was in training at Sandy Hook. I remember Benny Segreto with a heavy military pack strapped to his back, doggedly fighting his way through an endurance contest against men much bigger and stronger than he—the perspiration oozing from his forehead, his shoulders hunched and his teeth clenched in the painful determination to be up there in front.

Benny had always been this way, caught up and carried along by an overwhelming desire to excel in whatever he undertook, only in him the motivation was tempered by a fundamentally gentle nature and a sense of humanity and justice. What might have made him objectionable to his companions, turning him into a bully or a braggart, only endeared him all the more to those of us who knew him. Though he stood head and shoulders above others, he never seemed conscious of being above their level.

"Benny," I said to him after he had won this race and was in a state of near exhaustion. "You are foolish. It was only an exercise. The winning or losing is not this important."

When he had caught his breath, Benny answered, "To me it is very important, Mr. Covello." Though we had known each other for a long time now, were in the same army unit, headed for the same uncertain future in a war overseas, he never called me by my first name—never broke down the barrier between pupil and teacher. I was always "Mr. Covello" to him.

After a shower we headed away from the barracks in the direction of the ocean. Benny said, "I was thinking about what you just said. My brain tells me that it is not very important to win a pack race, or even the racing I used to do in school. But

that does not change anything. Inside there is something else
which is stronger. I cannot be less than the best. It is foolish.
It is vanity. Very often I am ashamed, but I cannot help it."

We moved along in silence for a time. "Do you feel," I
asked, "that it would have been different had you been raised
in Italy instead of America? Would the compulsion to win
have been less?"

"I am sure of it," Benny said. "It is maybe because I was born
in Sicily and still do not speak like an American that I have to
show that I am good for more than hanging around street
corners. It is something as childish as this."

It was not long after this that Benny told me of his ambition
to do some sort of cultural work involving both the United
States and Italy—an enlargement of his original *Circolo* idea.
"I do not think I will go to college," he said. "I will try to get a
job where I can work with both Italians and Americans—some
kind of work that will keep me in contact with the two countries." He turned to me, laughing. "How I will do this I have
not the least idea. And you? You will go back to Clinton after?"

"I don't know. I always wanted to teach in a university.
Sometimes I even think I might take up medicine. My father
always wanted me to become a doctor."

Benny Segreto was silent.

"You don't approve?"

"It would not be right for me to criticize," Benny said. "You
are older. We must do what we have to do. Only it will be sad
for me to think that you are not at Clinton. You have done so
much there."

"Nonsense. I haven't even gotten Italian accepted in the
school."

"It will come," Benny said. "Because of you and a few
others, it will come."

It had never occurred to me that I should have joined up
as anything other than a common soldier. I did not believe in

special privileges and I can truthfully say, looking back over a span of forty years, that I would not have felt right using the advantage of education to obtain rank over men like Benny Segreto or Charlie Bonanno or any of the enlisted men I knew.

While I was completely aware that in an army there had to be officers as well as enlisted men, I was totally unprepared for the sharp distinctions. It was a bitter cold winter. Food was terrible. The barracks were poorly heated, and we had to scrounge around the beaches of Sandy Hook for driftwood to keep warm. We were not unaware that the officers' quarters were comfortable and warm, their food specially prepared and served to them.

This sort of thing has been the gripe of soldiers ever since the very first war. I knew it and my companions knew it. Still, it did not help matters any or make the injustices easier to swallow. The classic example came on the day I was summoned to the adjutant's office on some routine matter. As I walked into the room, I caught sight of a familiar figure seated behind the desk, wearing lieutenant's bars. It was a fellow I knew from Columbia. We were not friends exactly, but we would say "hello" and chat whenever we met on the campus and we had sat next to each other in a Comparative Literature course. However, seeing him again suddenly in the strange, impersonal atmosphere of the army was like coming upon a bosom pal.

"Hello, Larkin!" I greeted him.

His body straightened in the swivel chair. He glared at me. "You're out of order, soldier!" he said, as if I had uttered some blasphemy, and he was telling me that this was heaven and he was God.

I don't remember much after that, except trying to cover my embarrassment as I stood there muttering, "Yes, sir," and "No, sir," to questions he flung at me. Then I was walking away from the drab building which was the adjutant's office to my own barracks with a feeling of humiliation inside of me such as I had rarely experienced before.

16/ I

nasmuch as we were headed overseas, I organized some classes in French. Our captain liked the idea. It gave prestige to our unit, so much so that in keeping with military procedure I was made a corporal. It was unseemly that an instructor should have the same rank as his pupils. When we arrived at Brest, I was made "morale officer," to act as interpreter between the soldiers and the French population and settle differences which might arise.

Volunteers who could speak French were requested for special intelligence work. After talking about two minutes with an examiner, I qualified and also managed to have Benny Segreto transferred along with me. We spent a month in Bordeaux. Then, because of my knowledge of Spanish, I was assigned to an American captain, Luis Careaga, to establish an intelligence unit on the Franco-Spanish frontier at Hendaye.

For the first time since my enlistment I was beginning to have a feeling that I might be serving some purpose in the war. I wrote to Rose, "There has been a definite turn in the order of things. It might be that I am going to be able to contribute something to this war, after all. How much, exactly I do not know. No matter. Over here it is enough just to have the notion that your special qualifications are being utilized."

We worked in close cooperation with small British and

French intelligence units. Our object was to feed back to head-quarters information about what was going on in neutral Spain with respect to the political sympathies of the people, German propaganda activities, and information on U-boat traffic in the northern waters. At first, it seemed somewhat ridiculous that we should have to risk internment while stealing across the border when there was the American Embassy still functioning in Madrid as well as an occasional consulate here and there. Then we learned that these offices were not only understaffed, but their personnel were watched closely, not only by the Spanish authorities but by German agents as well. The routine reports they could send were of no great value from the stand-point of military intelligence.

Pretty soon I got the flavor and feel of the language, so that no matter where I found myself I could pass for a Spaniard from another region of Spain. Captain Careaga held the fort at Hendaye while I, dressed in the traditional beret, baggy pants, shirt, and loose-fitting jacket thrown over my shoulders, wandered about Spain for the next ten months, journeying from Barcelona to Madrid to Zaragossa—all over Spain wherever our contacts led us. I read all the newspapers I could lay my hands on, attended political gatherings and pro-allied meetings in the wine cellars of cafés. One Señor Hierro in Bilbao referred me to a Señor Melendez in Zaragossa and so on. I learned not to refuse a glass of wine, and because there were occasions when my nerves needed quieting, I learned how to smoke. The ultimate value of the information I passed back to Paris I shall never know.

Though the Armistice was signed in November, 1918, our unit was asked to continue its work until the peace treaty in June, 1919. I enjoyed that period in Spain, traveling from one little provincial town to another, doing pretty much as I pleased, resting now and again in a gnarled and twisted grove of olive trees—trees already old when Goya was young—

sipping wine from a goatskin, traveling dusty roads, sometimes on a bicycle, sometimes on foot, the quiet landscape that time and the sun had bleached, all around me, the soothing, restful colors of Spain and of my childhood just across the horizon.

The world of East Harlem and New York public schools was far, far away, a part of the distant past, almost like somebody's life I had read about. I felt at ease among the provincial Spaniards. In this country where life was hard but laughter came easy, a meal often consisted of no more than a chunk of bread, a glass of wine, a few olives, and a piece of cheese. It was, in a way, like returning home.

It was in Spain that I made the acquaintance of Captain Easton, an American intelligence officer. He claimed to be impressed by the work I had done there, by my facility with languages and my ability to get along with people. When he found out that I came from New York he made me a proposition to work with him in the foreign advertising business. Several large eastern and midwestern agencies had pooled to establish a central clearing house in New York for all of their foreign advertising. He needed someone like me for what he called "media analysis, contact, and promotional work" dealing mainly with South America. The pay was a thousand dollars more than I had been earning as a school teacher. "And that's only the beginning!" Easton said. "You can't afford to say no!"

Here was something so removed from anything I had ever thought about that I did not know what to answer.

"I'll have to think about it," I said finally.

I remember writing to Rose about Easton's offer and her reply: "Of course, you'll accept. How can you go back to teaching school and spend the rest of your life wondering what might have happened had you gone into advertising?" That was Rose, all right. The direct approach, practical, hitting right at the heart of the matter.

My last night in France I had dinner with Benny Segreto in Bordeaux. He was going to remain in Europe, intending to work his way to Italy to contact some American firm doing business there. We went to a little café and I ordered a special bottle of *vin rose* to toast the occasion. I told him about Easton's offer. "Benny," I said, "I'm not sure but I think I'm going to give it a try. After all, nothing says I have to remain a school teacher forever."

"*Niente*," Benny agreed.

"It's not too late to have a try at something else."

"Of course," Benny said.

An old battered victrola with a horn was playing "Roses of Picardy." Couples were waltzing. Now and then the voice of an American soldier mixed with that of the French. I was excited by the thought of my return, of seeing Rose and our families again, excited by the prospect of the future, and yet I hated to leave. There was a kind of romantic sadness about saying good-by to a time and a place and a slice of myself which could never be the same again. At my elbow a cigarette burned in the ashtray. I raised my glass and gazed through the wonderful rosy wine and I thought of Miss Ruddy and the pledge I had taken as a boy never to drink or smoke. Dear Miss Ruddy, I thought, forgive me. With the wine and a cigarette perhaps I understand you even better than ever—your goodness, your worthiness, the sacrifices you must have made. Aloud I said to Benny, "It's not as though I had gone into the ministry or priesthood, is it? I'm not a dedicated man. Nothing ever told me as a child that when I grew up I had to be a school teacher. Anyway, you can barely live on a school teacher's salary. Is it so surprising that I should want to try my wings in the world of trade—in advertising?"

"Not at all," Benny laughed. "*Pas de tout*." He could hardly control his amusement at what must have been my fiercely defensive attitude.

An entire year of my life went into that spectacular, bubble-blowing game called advertising. I made more money than I had ever made in my life. I had a beautiful, glass-partitioned office on 43d Street just off Fifth Avenue with an excellent reference library and a secretary to open my mail, type my letters, and transcribe all of the materials I dictated concerning South American newspapers and periodicals in order to persuade firms to spend United States dollars in advertising there. I met publishers, editors, and business people. I was given an expense account and became adept at explaining why a swamp-root manufacturer who "absolutely guaranteed" to rid you of kidney disease would find it more profitable to advertise in Lima, Peru, than in Mexico City, bringing to the argument all the statistics, data, and information which modern research could supply.

For a time I was very much interested in this new work, every day unfolding a bright new adventure, another glimpse into that many-faceted carnival of ballyhoo. I was intrigued. But after a while, a sort of monotony set in. No matter where I looked the picture was the same—money—only clothed and veiled in a different way. Money—and how we could squeeze more of it out of our clients.

I found myself more and more in East Harlem, dropping in at the Boys' Club at the Jefferson Park Methodist Church, seeking again the companionship of John Shedd and Leone Piatelli.

"Our friend has deserted the luxuries of expense-account living," Piatelli joked in Italian. "He returns to the peasants. Perhaps he has come to study us as a vehicle for experimentation in the use of some new laxative or cough syrup."

"Where else is the advertiser to experiment? Is not this the purpose of slum areas?"

John Shedd's belly shook as he laughed. "Our Leonardo returns to us. Finally he learns it is the sick oyster which possesses the pearl."

Later when we were alone, Piatelli asked me if I had been back to the school.

"I went back for a visit."

"They have a class in Italian now. It was organized by Anthony Cipollaro, the student you placed in charge of the *Circolo* when you left."

I nodded and changed the subject. "Have you heard, Benny has a job now in Naples with the American Express?"

"He wrote us," Piatelli said shortly. "Tell me the truth, Leonardo. How does it go in the merchandise-selling business?"

"You put it crudely."

Piatelli hunched his shoulders while his face assumed an air of pained concentration. "How else? Your business now is to sell merchandise. This fact does not change no matter how you twist it around."

"I am called a media analyst."

The first part I said in Italian. "Media analyst," I repeated, rolling the words around on my tongue. We looked at each other and burst out laughing. There was no need to say anything further. I could not fool Piatelli.

My dissatisfaction was noticeable to Rose from the beginning. As usual, she came right to the point. "It's a mood," she said. "It will pass. No matter what a person does to make a living, there are bound to be times when he will get discouraged."

At home they noticed the change in me too. My father was all gray now, but he went to work every day at the tavern on 22d Street, and his eyes were bright and he smoked just as many twisted cigars and drank just as much wine as ever, despite the admonitions of Mamma-Nonna. "Woman," he would fume, "my father died at eighty-eight and my mother at ninety-three. I do not remember that there was any shortage of wine or cigars in Avigliano."

One Sunday afternoon, while I was getting dressed to go

out, my father sat on the edge of the bed watching me. As I knotted my tie I could see him in the mirror. He fingered his luxurious mustache and kept shaking his head.

"What is the trouble?" I asked at last, knowing very well that this was exactly what he was waiting for me to ask.

"I do not know," he said in the Aviglianese dialect. He bunched his fingers and poked them against his forehead. "It is almost a year now and I cannot get it through my skull. What is it exactly, this kind of work that you are doing that pays so much?"

"I've only explained it a dozen times."

"Then explain it again. Are you in a hurry? Where are you going? Five minutes sooner or later, the world will keep spinning around. '*Adavatisin*'?" he repeated in English. "It is honest, this work? Do you like this work? This is what I ask, Nardo."

"Of course, I like it," I said in exasperation.

He got up from the bed, came closer to the dresser, suddenly and dramatically breaking into his own kind of English, which he rarely ever used with me. "You can't fool me! Then why for you not so happy no more? You no joke the same. You no laugh the same. Is not worth make more money if you no happy. Better the doctor if you no like the teaching."

It was ironic that this talk took place at just about the time the larger agencies were considering doing away with this foreign office in New York. Somehow this centralization hampered the healthy competitive spirit which was the life blood of advertising. "Nothing to do with you, Covello. Nothing at all," Mr. Easton assured me. "In fact, the Rankin Agency phoned. They want to see you on a proposition of their own."

The upshot was an offer from the Rankin Advertising Agency to go to South America as their contact man and special representative at a salary of thirty-six hundred dollars

a year and expenses. My head whirled. In less than a year I
was being offered well over a thousand dollars more than the
maximum pay of a teacher in the city schools—plus expenses.
At the same time I could not be rid of the sensation that somehow fate was tricking me. I was caught, against my will,
trapped, because I would never have the courage to turn
down such an offer. I told Rose about the new job. I told
Shedd and Piatelli. I told my father. Always I had the impression that the words coming from my mouth were not my
own, that I was talking through someone who was a stranger
to me.

One afternoon I had to go over to the main library on Fifth
Avenue to look up Spanish periodicals. It was summer and a
beautiful day. For a long time I wandered around Bryant Park,
examining the pleasant green of the shrubbery, the pigeons
flying, the people scattered around on the grass. I found myself wishing for the war again and Spain and the simplicity of
the life I had known there. "Leonard," a voice called. I turned
to see Dr. Paul, the principal of De Witt Clinton.

We sat down on a bench and talked. I can't exactly say
what we spoke about. It does not matter, except that it had
to do with the school and the boys and the work I loved. After
a while we rose and walked around to the front of the library.
In the main hall we shook hands, each to move off to the task
he had come for. Dr. Paul hesitated. He looked at me closely,
unable to make up his mind. "I don't suppose you ever thought
about coming back, Leonard?" he said. "I don't suppose you
would come back in September?"

I told Rose that night. I tried to control my excitement. We
were having dinner in a little Italian restaurant before going to
the theater. Rose did not say very much. Once every now and
then she would turn her head to smell the perfume of a gar-
denia I had bought her, which she had pinned to her blouse.
"He asked me to come back," I said. "He wasn't just talking.
He really meant it. He wants me to come back."

"And what did you say?"

"I was so surprised I did not say anything."

"You told him about South America, of course?"

"Of course. But he kept talking about the school and all. . . ."

The faint trace of a smile hovered on Rose's lips. I stopped talking, feeling a little foolish.

"Go on," Rose said.

"There's nothing more. That's it."

"What you're really trying to tell me is that you don't want to go to South America. Isn't that it? You want to go back to De Witt Clinton." Her smile broadened into open amusement. "Now I understand what is meant about leading a horse to water."

"Then you would not care? You would not mind if I gave up advertising and went back to teaching?"

"I wouldn't care if you became a street cleaner so long as you were happy. But it looks like you really were meant to be a school teacher."

17/ I

n September, 1920, I again stepped into a classroom and looked into the faces of about twenty-five boys who formed my first class in Italian at De Witt Clinton, perhaps the only Italian class in any public school in the country at that time. Our efforts and struggles prior to the war had succeeded, and there was a deep satisfaction in this achievement. Surely the language and culture of Italy held a place beside that of France, Germany, or Spain. Surely the student from the lower or upper East Side had a right to that spiritual lift that comes from knowing that the achievements of one's people have been recognized.

For this basic belief those of us who espoused this simple cause were often criticized by fellow teachers and by the general public. They argued that we were keeping the boys "foreigners." The boys were in America now and should use English exclusively. I was myself accused of "segregating" my students, and more than once by Italian-Americans themselves. The war had strengthened the idea of conformity. Americanization meant the casting off of everything that was "alien," especially the language and culture of national origin. Yet the amazing paradox lay in the fact that it was perfectly all right for the Italo-American boy to study Latin or French, German or Spanish.

Fortunately, at De Witt Clinton, we had the approval of Dr. Francis H. Paul, the principal, who was sympathetic with our point of view. It was he who had made the *Circolo* possible in the first place and who had later approved the introduction of the teaching of Italian.

Dr. Paul called me into his office one day not long after my return and spoke about the problem of the rapidly increasing number of students of Italian origin now coming to Clinton from all over the city. "These boys are not easy to handle," he said, sitting on the edge of his desk. "To put it bluntly, it will be your job to look after these boys. I will see to it that your schedule is changed so that you will have time to take care of them. In short, Leonard, from now on I want you to be the father-confessor of these East Side boys."

In an out-of-the-way corner of the old De Witt Clinton building, I found a small room that was being used as a stock room. Together with some of my students I spent several Saturdays cleaning and painting and putting it in shape for an office. The room had a very narrow window and just enough space for a desk, a few file cabinets, some chairs, and a mimeographing machine. It wasn't much of an office, but it was good enough for a beginning. It was good enough for the first office of the first Italian Department in the public schools of New York City.

In this two-by-four office I held conferences, handled disciplinary problems, interviewed parents, and planned our work. For the very first time in my experience as a teacher I began to have a feeling of inner satisfaction which rose from the knowledge that here was a job that I really wanted to do. All my thoughts about a professorship or becoming a medical doctor faded, never to be revived. No longer was I merely teaching a language or a subject. Here I was grappling with *all* the problems affecting the boys coming to me for help.

Often I would be working in my office, late in the afternoon, and a knock would come on the door, hesitant, re-

luctant, and I would know at once that it was another of my
boys coming to me for help or advice. When the knock came
during school hours I could almost be sure it had to do with
a school problem. But when it sounded out of the stillness of
the deserted corridors, I could be equally sure that the problem was a personal one.

At this moment I can still see Joe D'Angelo sitting in the
chair near my desk. He was a tall boy, weighing about one
hundred and eighty pounds, dressed in a new suit and carrying
a derby. To make it easier for him to talk I kept my eyes on
the narrow knot of his tie while he fumbled to explain why
he had come. He was going to a party. His companions were
waiting for him outside the school. "I had to see you first, Mr.
Covello. I gotta get this thing off my chest. It's the old man.
He keeps hittin' me all the time. No matter what I say or do
he's gotta start cloutin' me. He's a big guy and he works on
the docks, and it hurts, and I can't stand it no more."

"If he really hurts you. . . ," I started to say.

Joe D'Angelo shook his head. "That's not it." He held out a
bony fist across the desk for my observation. "What he don't
know is I've been fighting around the Jersey clubs a lot under
the name of Kid Angel. I'm pretty good. That's what he don't
know. If I hit him I could put him in the hospital. That's what
I'm scared of. It's gonna happen and it would kill my mother."

After a silence I said, "How is it you never told them at
home about the boxing?"

"Because ever since I was a little kid my mother has been
telling everybody that I was going to be a lawyer."

"While you want to be a fighter?"

"No. I want to be a lawyer. But I make a couple of bucks
in these club matches. I get a kick out of it, and I don't have
to work in a store or a factory after school. Only thing is, I
could never make them believe it."

I sent Joe off to his party and told him to spend the night
with his uncle who lived in the Bronx. Then I took the sub-

way downtown to the "Little Italy" of Greenwich Village.
The D'Angelo family lived in one of those red brick tenements on MacDougal Street. As I entered the downstairs hall
and caught the odor of garlic and tomato sauce, I felt right at
home. Pappa D'Angelo himself, clad in his undershirt, answered the door. He was short, with heavy shoulders and a
gray mustache, and an iron-gray stubble of hair covered
his head and became a mattress of gray on his chest. He looked
at me, wiped his mouth with a bright, checkered napkin, and
was about to slam the door in my face. When he caught the
name De Witt Clinton, his manner changed.

"*Perdona!* Scuse me, please. I think you was selling piano
or something." He gently took hold of my arm and ushered
me inside, directly into the kitchen. "Ninitta," he said to the
middle-aged woman seated at the table. "Get up. Get one
more plate. Is the teacher from the school where Joe go.
Clintona." Suddenly he stopped dead. "Is Joe?" he shouted.
"What he do? He do something bad? That why you here? I
kill him! I break all the bones in his head!"

The mother started to cover her face with her hands in
anticipation of some terrible calamity. I took hold of the
father's arm and, wagging my free hand in a characteristic
Italian gesture, at the same time speaking in the Neapolitan
dialect, said, "Who said anything about Joe being a bad boy?
Joe is a good boy. He is a very good student."

When both father and mother got over the staggering fact
that I could not only speak Italian but could even speak their
dialect, they made me sit down and eat a dish of sausage and
peppers. "It is an honor. You will do us a great honor, Signor
Maestro," Pappa D'Angelo insisted, in the most flowery language at his command. "Also a glass of wine. A gentle glass of
wine made with my own hands. So he is a good student,
Giuseppe? And good he should be." He extended a massive
paw. "With this instrument I have taught him right from
wrong. Respect for his elders. For those who instruct him

in school. In the old tradition. In this way he will become educated and become a lawyer and not work on the docks like his
father."

"Exactly," I agreed, rolling a mouthful of wine over my
tongue. "It is just this that I have come to see you about.
Giuseppe is getting too big. You have to handle him differently, now."

"I have been telling him this again and again," the mother
broke in.

"Quiet," Pappa D'Angelo said. "Where is the harm in a
father correcting his son? This is something new. Something
American. I have heard of it but I do not understand. Only
this very evening I had to give Giuseppe a lesson in economy.
A derby! Imagine, a boy buying and wearing a derby. To go
to work in a factory!"

"With me," I said, "it was shiny shoes with buttons. Besides it was his own money—money that he earned with his
own hands."

"Which changes nothing at all."

"But which makes for impatience and loss of temper. He is
getting too old for you to knock him around. He is afraid
that one day he is going to forget himself and hurt you. That
is what he is afraid of."

It was a joke. Pappa D'Angelo started to laugh. He downed
a full glass of wine and heaved his powerful chest. "Ha, ha.
Now he thinks he can lick his pappa." He slammed his fist
down on the table. "Wait he come home, I show him. I show
him who the boss in this house, lilla snotnose!" All of a sudden he was so mad at his son again that he could only talk the
language of the docks.

"Wait a minute," I said. "Calm down. Do you know what
kind of work your son does when he is not in school? Do you
know how he makes the money that he gives you here at
home and that paid for the derby?"

I told them then as simply as I could that their son was not working in a factory but was making money as a prize fighter.

The father did not get it right away. "A fighter," he asked, "with the hands?"

"With the hands. A boxer. I have been told that even though he is very young, he is good. He would have a future as a fighter. But Joe does not want to be a fighter. He fights so that he can earn money to be a lawyer. But he is afraid when you beat him that someday he is going to forget you are his father."

"*Madonna!*" the mother breathed.

Pappa D'Angelo rocked his head. After a while, as if this were not enough, he scratched it furiously. He looked at me sheepishly. He started to smile. The smile broadened into a grin.

"That lilla sonamangonia!" he said.

That was my encounter with the D'Angelo family. There were so many others in those days that sometimes it seems as if I spent almost as much time in the homes of my students as I did at the school. There was Nick Barone, who didn't show up in class for a couple of days. He worked on an ice wagon after school, and one of the big ice blocks toppled over and smashed his hand, landing him in the hospital. Nick had spoken to me about his parents. They could speak no English at all and both mother and father worked at home doing stitching and needle piece work for the garment industry—the common exploitation of the time. They had little or no contact at all with the outside world.

The Barone family lived in the Italian section around 28th Street and Second Avenue. I went there after school and found the small tenement flat in a state of turmoil—crowded with neighbors, and the mother and father carrying on so that I thought for sure that Nick had passed away. When I was finally able to make them understand who I was, both parents grabbed my hands, imploring me to save Nick before it was too late.

"He will die there," the father lamented. "Everyone knows what goes on in a hospital—the last stage before the grave. A soul could die in a torment of thirst and no one would lift a finger to bring you a glass of water."

"Old superstitions about hospitals," I sought to explain; "stories from the old country when distances were great and knowledge of medicine limited and the patient almost always died before reaching the hospital. It is different now."

"But we could take such wonderful care of him at home here," the mother entreated. "I could cook him a chicken, make him broth and pastina and food to get well. The good Lord knows what they will feed him there, if anything."

After I had managed to calm them somewhat, I had both the mother and father put on their best clothes and I took them to the hospital, where up until now they had not dared to go. We found Nick sitting up in bed, joking with a nurse and having a gay time with his companions in the ward. When one of the internes even spoke to them in Italian, their attitude changed to one of great wonderment.

On the way home from the hospital the father turned to me with an expression of guilt and deep embarrassment. "You must forgive us. There are many things here we know nothing about. It is hard to change old ideas and the way we think even though we see the changes every day in our children." He shook his head. "If only everybody in the world could speak the same tongue, then perhaps things would not be quite so hard to understand." And the more I came into contact with the family life of my boys, the more I became aware of the vital importance of language in the double orientation— to family and to community—of the immigrant child.

Though Italian was now being taught as a first language in De Witt Clinton, it was not being taught as a first language in other high schools. A student could study Italian only after he had had a year of Latin, French, or Spanish. We determined to do what was necessary—have the Board of Education of

New York City pass a by-law placing Italian on an equal footing with the other languages.

The campaign to accomplish this involved civic leaders, interested citizens, and members of the Italian Teachers Association, particularly Professor Mario E. Cosenza of City College, who was president of this association for many years.

We invited parents to entertainments at which our students put on plays in Italian, we publicized the campaign in
the Italian newspapers, and we had conferences at the Board
of Education. The most effective part of the campaign was
the home visits that we made—speaking to the individual
parents about signing petitions to introduce Italian in a particular school.

How many homes I entered at this period where I had to
guide a trembling hand in the signing of an "X"! How many
cups of coffee I drank, jet black with just a speck of sugar,
while explaining our purpose. The parents were usually
astonished that they should be consulted in the matter of what
was to be taught to their children. They couldn't believe the
schools were really interested in their opinion.

"Signor Maestro, we are people who never had any education. In Italy we worked in the fields from when the sun
came up in the morning until it went down at night. In America we work, but we hope that with our children it will be
different. That is why we came to America. But do not ask us
to decide things we know nothing about."

Our visits usually turned into lessons in democracy, trying
to make the immigrant understand his rights and privileges.
"Would you prefer your son to study Italian, or some other
foreign language?"

"What a question! Naturally, we prefer him to study our
own language. But *real* Italian. Italian as you speak it, Signor
Maestro—the Italian of our great men, of Garibaldi."

In May, 1922, through our work and the help of Salvatore
Cotillo, New York State Senator elected by the East Harlem

community, the Board of Education placed Italian on an equal footing with other languages in the schools of New York City.

I had longed for the day when I would have just one class in Italian to teach. Never did I imagine that in the space of a few years there would be hundreds of boys studying Italian at Clinton—and that there would be five teachers in the Italian Department.

18 / The days and nights at Clinton made me welcome the approach of summer vacation; and thinking about summer I found myself overcome by a longing that I had not experienced in many, many years. I longed for the mountains and the clear air and simple life of a rustic community. Specifically, I longed for the touch of my uncle's hand against my forehead, and a glimpse of the land whence I had come. My mind stretched back to my childhood.

"Twenty-five years," I said to Rose, on an evening when I got away from school earlier than usual and Rose and I went to a concert. "In that time I was able to go to Paris to perfect my French. During the war I spent, on and off, about a year in Spain improving my Spanish. But I never returned to the place where I was born. I wanted to, and I never did. Now I feel a little ashamed. I feel I must go back to Italy."

"Then go," Rose answered.

I made plans to leave as soon as school closed. Just before I left I remember my father talking to me, a light in his eyes. "So many of us left Avigliano and so few of us ever returned," he remarked. "For me the time is past. I would never have the courage to go back. You will embrace my brother for me. Embrace Zio Prete, your mother's brother, for me too. Tell them that if there is such a thing as another world, I will see

them there. Only," he added with a smile, "with the priest you
would do better to put it in some other way."

Mamma-Nonna's apron found its way to her cheek. "You
have never known any of my people, Nardo. They all lived
outside the walls of the town. See them for me. Talk to them.
Let your lips carry my happiness across the ocean to them."

It had been my intention immediately upon arriving in
Naples to contact Benny Segreto at the American Express office where he was working. However, I had to rush to make my
train for Potenza. Almost before I knew it, I found myself
traveling along the circuitous and dusty route still vivid in my
mind from so many years before. Perhaps the train was a bit
more modern; but the soot was no less, and the seats were just
as uncomfortable, and the interminable tunnels gouged out of
the mountains were as terrifying as ever.

Suddenly it was as if my mother were there, seated again
at my side. I could see the mute resignation in her eyes and the
mingled emotion of horror and relief when the black ordeal
of tunnels was over and we emerged into sunlight, gasping
and choking for breath.

The torment of what is past and gone forever! *Cara Mamma*,
what I would have given to have her beside me on that return
journey!

At Potenza I was greeted by the official reception committee
from Avigliano, selected, I am sure, by my uncle the priest and
my uncle Domenico Canio, the master shoemaker. It consisted
of a dozen men, most of them related to me in one way or another, and included Mingo, who as a boy had been my companion when we sneaked into the church and washed our hands in
Holy Water to cast a spell over the schoolmaster's heavy,
black ruler. All of them were dressed in their black holiday
suits and, even as the train came to a standstill, I could see that
they felt awkward, ill at ease, self-conscious at finding themselves surrounded and gathered up by the confusion and
activity of a city.

The station platform at Potenza was crowded, but the moment the train stopped and I stepped down from my compartment, the committee surged toward me and in the midst of an overpowering welcome both I and my luggage were gathered up and swept off to a nearby café where, over coffee spiked with *anisette*, we awaited the bus for Avigliano. I could not get over the fact that they had recognized me so quickly. But, in the breathless flow of conversation which followed, I noted that twenty-five years in the lives of people did not make the changes I had imagined. It seems that only when you are young, people change. What I expected, I am not quite sure. But I was amazed that each one of these men, after such a lapse of time, would be so quickly recognizable to me.

"I will take you to the places where we used to play," Mingo said. "I will show you the things you have forgotten."

"You will show me? Put a blindfold over my eyes and turn me loose and I will take you to any place in Avigliano you want to go."

"Bravo, Narduccio! He does not forget. He remembers where he was born and those of us who stayed behind."

In Avigliano I found that the uncles were fine. A little old, perhaps, but good for another hundred years, as they say. But they were not interested in talking about Avigliano. They wanted to hear about America and New York and the people from Avigliano. "Is it true or just nonsense that Emilo Fava bought himself an automobile and rides to work in it every day, driving it himself?" "Is it true that Concetta Rocca married a man, who of all things, made a fortune selling pills through the mail, which were nothing more than bread dough? *Dio Santo*, I myself could have thought of that one. What a place this America must be!"

It was odd how the conversation twisted and turned and always came back to one thing—money, and after that the people who had made it, no matter how. The idea that a person could live in America and not be well off was inconceivable to them.

For instance, the fact that I had just gotten off the train from a second-class compartment indicated a personal idiosyncrasy rather than a reflection of my purse. It would have been the same had I informed them that I intended to spend the next month or so traveling around Italy on a budget of about a dollar and a half a day for meals and lodging. They were simply incapable of divorcing affluence from the word America. It was their way of hanging on to the slender thread of a dream that someday, somehow, they themselves would forsake Avigliano for that never-never land across the sea which, in no way, could be less than fabulous.

Often, during my trip, I sought to relate this conception of financial well-being with the actual circumstances back home. How devastating must be the disillusionment to the average immigrant, how difficult to face up to the facts of reality! Even I, as close as I was to the older people, could only imagine what it meant for them to leave the "golden years" behind to seek the elusive pot of gold at the end of the rainbow. No wonder the shrinking within themselves. No wonder the "living burial" in the graveyard filled with kindred spirits known as the slum area. Who but the few really bold and the reckless and the strong could survive? For the others, what was left of their bubble but the water which came at a turn of the tap, the toilet in the hall, the electric light, the subway that rattled them to work for a nickel—and their children? Their children! That was it. The rewards for all this sacrifice would come through the children.

It appeared that everything emanating from America reached these people as a distortion. The immigrants themselves were largely at fault. News was colored, success magnified, comforts and advantages exaggerated beyond all proportions. And even if someone occasionally did try to give an accurate picture of things, in the little Italian village or community they would say that he was being modest or unwilling to tell the truth for fear that a relative might scheme to get money out of him.

What were these simple mountain people to believe? They believed what they saw with their own eyes, what they read and what they were told—and, most of all, they believed what they wanted to believe: that if ever they were fortunate enough to reach America, they would fall into a pile of manure and get up brushing the diamonds out of their hair.

My stay in Avigliano was divided between the homes of my two uncles. Domenico Canio, the shoemaker, had retired and was now living with one of his married daughters, for it was tradition in our town that no self-respecting human being worked beyond his sixtieth birthday. If during all these years he had managed to set something aside, so much the better for his little addictions to coffee and tobacco and a thimble of *liquore* now and then. If not, the problem of his support was simply shifted over to his children and that was that—a fixed and changeless custom. Zio Prete, on the other hand, having made his arrangements with God, still continued services at the church, though he left the most strenuous ministrations of his calling to an assistant.

Between the two households, I spent ten days being fêted. The occasion of my visit coincided with several religious feasts. There were picnics and fireworks with the *piazza* festooned with electric lights and parades which wound in and out of the cobblestone streets from *Il Castello* to the lower reaches of the town, known as *Bassa Terra*. Donkeys wore ribbons, horses, straw hats, and the peasants put on gay colored costumes which were no longer in current use, though I vividly remembered them from my childhood. And, of course, the band. During all these festivities, I felt only a little less prominent than the President of the United States.

It was my last day. My two uncles and I left the uppermost wall of the town and were slowly ambling along the dirt road which led gradually up the mountain slope to the shrine of *La Madonna del Carmine*. It was the pilgrimage my mother had always loved to make, and we had saved it until the end, almost as a personal act of devotion in which only the three of us were to take part. Behind and below us the countryside stretched in symmetrical blocks of varying greens and yellows, marking the areas of cultivation, the stages of growth and harvest, interspersed here and there with the darker hues of orchards, vineyards, and olive groves.

Somewhat wearied by all the festivity, I found myself profoundly happy to be alone with my uncles on a walk which was also a tribute to the past and to the memory of one who was gone. Zio Prete, leaning upon his Malacca cane, his soutane gathered into his left hand, moved effortlessly up the slope, as did Uncle Canio, carrying himself very erect though his luxuriant square-cut beard had turned grayish and his eyes blinked in the bright sun.

"Ha, ha, ha!" Zio Canio laughed as I paused for a breath. "With automobiles and subways and paved streets, the legs lose their agility. That's your America. Feel this." He raised a leg and made me grip his thigh. It was like taking hold of a knotted rope. "These are legs as they should be—as the good Lord intended them in their service to man."

We sat on a boulder just off the side of the road, a grim reminder of some raging torrent in the ancient past. The priest tapped it with his cane. "Always the struggle to hold land. If it is not man, it is the mountain that steals it and carries it away." There was a silence. Then the priest asked, "I wonder, Narduccio *mio*, if you would have become a professor had you remained here in Avigliano?"

Zio Canio objected. "Did you have to go to America to become a priest? Or Don Salvatore Mecca to be a school teacher? Emilio Puglia to become a doctor? Vincenzo Tartuffo, a lawyer? Did not Emanuele Gianturco, doing his lessons under a street light right here in this very town, rise to become a minister of Italy? Why then, all this talk about opportunities in America?"

"For one who has never left his own doorstep you manage to say a great deal," the priest scoffed, thumping his cane on the boulder to punctuate his words.

"My dear priest, one of the world's greatest philosophers never went more than fifty kilometers from the town where he was born. Look at my brother, Narduccio's father. Tell me what America did for him? And his mother, your sister, buried in a cemetery God knows where among how many thousands of strangers. Will you tell me what is so wonderful about this? Yes—now that we are alone and there is no one else to hear, tell me."

Though Domenico Canio had talked to the priest, he turned to me for the answer. I was the American, after all. I did not know what to say. Over the years, both of them had learned a good deal about East Harlem, its tenements, its frightened Italians clinging together, the few who got out and went on to better things. It seemed absurd to rattle off the usual phrases about "equal opportunity" and all that. Yet I had to say something. "You have to live in America to appreciate the advantages of life over there," I muttered with a classic vagueness which made even the priest smile.

"You really are a school teacher, Narduccio," Zio Canio said, taking my arm as we continued toward the shrine once more.

"I suppose the answer lies much deeper than we are capable of grasping," Zio Prete commented. "But there is one undeniable fact. If you were to take all of the people who left Avigliano since the start of the century and bring them back, together with their families, where would you put them all? We would need three towns the size of the one we have now. Multiply this by all of the towns in Italy and the people would be pushing each other into the Adriatic or the Mediterranean. And that is a fact."

"Facts! Facts!" Zio Canio said, dismissing them with a

flourish. "The essence of the matter is whether or not a man is any happier because he lives in America?"

Zio Prete raised his finger. "*Caro* Domenico, the answer to that one lies with God and within the man himself."

At the shrine we knelt to say a short prayer for my mother. It was hot, the sun high, the breeze humid on our backs, coming over the mountain from the direction of Africa. As I gazed at the terra-cotta image of the saint, I stole a glance at each of my two uncles, thinking about their amusing arguments—the aging Catholic priest and the liberal-minded shoemaker. I thought about myself and how, hardly being conscious of how it happened, I had become a Protestant. I thought about the vast gulf which separated us, both in distance and in the way we lived. And yet, how at peace I felt with them on this ancient mountain slope of Southern Italy. I thought about my pupils at De Witt Clinton and wished they could have been there with me to feel something of what I felt about their own people and their past.

The next few days I spent in Naples with Benny Segreto. Benny had not changed much, though he was a trifle heavier; but he said he was going into training in preparation for a long foot race which was to take place in a week or so. The most amazing part of Benny Segreto was his exuberant good nature. It was sheer delight just to be with him, regardless of whether we were sipping a vermouth at the café and Benny was telling me about his girl friend "*mia debolezza*," or "my weakness" as he called her, who lived in Rome, or whether he was conducting me on a sightseeing tour of Capri or Pompeii or the Blue Grotto, or whether we were simply sitting under a tree on Posilipo with the Bay of Naples stretched below us, Vesuvius beyond, and he was telling me about his future plans. He never spoke ill of anyone. He had a word for the coachman, the waiter, the streetcar conductor, the boatman, and when he moved off down the street people waved good-by.

In honor of my visit, Benny took a few days off from the American Express office. "How often do I get the chance to be with a friend who was also my school teacher?" With Benny, you had the pleasant knowledge that he meant every word he was saying. Now he spoke glowingly about the work he was doing—work which to anyone else would have been a routine office job.

"It is wonderful!" Benny told me. "New faces coming in and out all the day long. One minute it is an American lady from Philadelphia who wants to know if she should trust Neapolitan tourist guides and if it would be proper for her to visit that 'you know which' room in Pompeii. Next it might be a peasant, a *contadino,* who wants to know what it would cost to visit New York for a month—he has a sister there who will not live very long. Sometimes sad. Sometimes funny. But always I have the satisfaction that I am helping somebody—the American to understand about Italy, and the Italian to understand America. It is what I want to do."

"Then you intend to stay on with the American Express?" I asked, recalling my own deadening experience as a boy with this company.

Benny winked at me. "That depends on my little 'Roman weakness.' After I am married I will decide the next step. For the time being I am happy because I feel useful."

When I left Naples for Rome, Benny rode in the carriage with me to the railroad station, giving me last-minute instructions about the rest of my travels in Italy. "In Genoa," Benny counseled, "you must stop at our office. I have already written to Dino Biondo there. He is another De Witt Clinton pupil, only a few years before you taught there."

We shook hands. "Take care of yourself," I said. And then for no particular reason that I can remember, I added, "Why don't you give up that long-distance race?"

Benny grinned. "Don't worry. Starting tomorrow I will get

back into serious training." Then the old fiercely competitive Benny reappeared. "I will win that race."

During the following month of my travels around Italy, whenever I sat down to take care of my correspondence, I was always sure to select a nice local picture postcard and send it off to Benny in Naples, with some amusing comment to remind him that I was following his sightseeing advice.

I arrived in Genoa just a few days before the boat was to sail for America. By this time I was heartily fed up with cathedrals and bell towers, cemeteries and museums, formal gardens and famous birth places. I just wanted to sit around with nothing much to do but smoke a cigarette, drink a glass of wine, and think my thoughts while watching the shipping in the harbor.

Several times I passed the office of the American Express Company without going in, putting it off because I did not feel in the mood for conversation, thinking mostly now of my return, of seeing Rose, of outlining work for the new school term beginning in September. At last I could put it off no longer. Benny had said that there was a former Clinton boy in the Genoa office and had actually written him of my arrival. The last thing I wanted to do was offend Benny by not following through.

Stepping into the office I asked one of the clerks for Dino Biondo. She pointed to a tall, elegantly dressed young man with dark wavy hair. I walked over to where he stood behind the counter, looking over some invoices. He nodded and said to me in Italian, "Is there something I can do for you?"

"I'm Leonard Covello," I answered in English. "Benny Segreto asked me to look you up."

The young man stared at me. At first I thought he had not understood. I repeated, "Benny Segreto sent me. I'm leaving tomorrow morning and I thought I'd drop in."

"I heard you," he said. Slowly he placed the invoices in a drawer beneath the counter. "Then, you have not had any news from Naples?"

"I've been moving around," I said. The young man's lips pressed together. His eyes turned from me. I grabbed hold of his arm. "What's the matter? What happened?"

"Benny is dead. He dropped dead at the end of a road race."

19 / T he sadness of the loss of my friend Benny
Segreto was buried under the activity of my next few years
at De Witt Clinton. The study of Italian snowballed from a
registration of about thirty students in 1920 to five hundred and
thirty-eight students in June of 1925. Rose and I had gotten
married and were now living in quiet contentment in a little
apartment near New York University. It had been a very simple
wedding. Neither of us believed in the complication and
elaborate fuss usually associated with marriage among the
Italians, where sometimes the family even goes into debt to "do
the thing right."

At Clinton, meanwhile, we were going through the period of
"intelligence-test insanity." The movement started at the beginning of the century when Alfred Binet, a French psychol-
ogist, devised a series of tests, with which he claimed he could
measure the intelligence of children. These were individual
tests. However, during World War I, the Binet tests, which had
already undergone improvements by other psychologists, were
utilized as the basis for group-testing soldiers for specific jobs.
These became known as the "Army Alpha and Beta Tests." It
was from the Alpha and Beta tests that still other psychologists evolved the group tests which were to plague so many of
us teachers during my years at De Witt Clinton.

I will never forget one of these testing periods. Several hundred boys were seated at the lunchroom tables. The tests all had a time limit. The examiner stood on a platform with a stopwatch and whistle, ready to signal the beginning and end of each test. There was the essay-type test, in which questions were answered in essay form and the result depended, at least in part, upon the examiner's judgment, personal views on the subject, and frame of mind. There was also the short-answer type of question and the true-or-false question, as well as the question to which the answer was selected from three or four alternatives.

Even to those of us without specialized training in psychology, it was obvious that these tests could not accomplish all that was claimed for them. There were students who could work under this pressure, but others were unable to concentrate, became panicky, and as a result got low scores.

I remember giving Rose, who had a penchant for statistics, a pile of these intelligence tests and having her make a graph of the scores. The graph showed that the boys of Italian parentage in general rated lower than the others.

"How is this?" I argued. "Do you mean to tell me that this is supposed to be conclusive evidence that my boys have less brains? I don't believe it! My experience does not bear this out. I'm not convinced."

"Don't get excited," Rose said. "I'm not the analyst. I only made the graph." Further investigation showed that tests made up for city children proved them smarter than children from farm districts. But when special tests were evolved for agricultural communities, the results were the other way round. In general these tests measured only the opportunity a student had had to learn. They proved that a boy from a slum area whose parents spoke broken English usually did not have the vocabulary to express himself and had not had the opportunity to absorb the fundamentals of education as thoroughly as a student from a better economic environment. In other words, they only proved what most of us already knew.

What the tests failed to take into account was the fact that students and teachers both are human beings—not a batch of questions and answers. Today, while intelligence tests are still used for placement and other purposes in schools, the claim is no longer made that they are an exact indication of native intelligence.

One of the chief problems in the early years of the Italian Department was the lack of adequate texts with which to teach the language. We found that existing Italian textbooks were too advanced for those of our students who had had no previous foreign-language instruction. And their limited knowledge of the Italian dialect heard at home was of little value to them.

Working with one of my assistants, Annita Giacobbe, I prepared a beginner's textbook. We started it in 1923. In 1927 it was published by The Macmillan Company under the title of *First Book in Italian*. It took us four years to get this book into its final shape, and it covered only the first two years of the Italian course. We spent a tremendous amount of time on each lesson to perfect it. Annita Giacobbe and I would outline a plan in my little office. Some of the older boys from the Italian Department would type the stencils and run the mimeograph machine which turned out the materials to be tried out in class. Then the lesson would be revised, the students giving their views, and the mimeograph machine started all over again. Without the help of the boys themselves, Annita Giacobbe and I could never have found the time or energy to complete this text which, we were determined, would attract and not repel the student. After many conferences, the publisher finally agreed to allow us illustrations for the book, which greatly enhanced its appeal and educational value.

If I had put the same amount of time and energy into the preparation of a French or Spanish text, I would have made a great deal more money. But I am sure that Annita Giacobbe, seated today in her little villa in Sicily, will agree with me that the satisfaction we derived in creating an Italian book for our boys was by far the greater part of the compensation we received for our effort.

The name of one of my East Harlem students was to become well known to New Yorkers. He was Vito Marcantonio. Marc, everyone called him. Short of stature and slender of build, Marc was a volcano of energy. He became involved in everything that had to do with the *Circolo* and the Italian Department. Some of the students called him a socialist, though I am sure that not many of them had any idea of what they meant by it, except that Marc was always discussing world affairs, politics, and labor conditions.

Once I unexpectedly came upon Marc, berating a group of fellow students. "You birds don't even know you're alive. I'll bet you that this very minute there's somebody, some guy outside there figuring how he's gonna make money off of your hides when you go look for a job. You don't even know that!"

There were enough students around who disliked Marc's off-hand oratory and "socialistic" tendencies to keep him from being elected president of the *Circolo*. This did not bother Marc. Instead, he managed to have the organizational setup revised and had himself elected chairman of the executive committee, with powers over the president himself. When he had accomplished this, he came to my office and told me about it, laughing for all he was worth. "Pop, you are now looking at the chief executive of the *Circolo*," he said. Marc was the first to start calling me "Pop," a name which my boys have used ever since.

This was when Fiorello H. La Guardia was President of the Board of Aldermen of New York. The war was recent enough so that everyone still called him "Major." Dr. Paul asked if I could arrange to have "The Major" speak to the boys at one of our assemblies. It was a good idea. La Guardia could be very stimulating, particularly to young people. They were attracted by his facial expressions and they loved his act—the way he would sputter and hiss and pound his fist into his palm—and they would listen to what he had to say.

I sought out La Guardia at his office, and he readily accepted the invitation. It was in the days when he would go anywhere and to any amount of trouble to make a speech. However, in order to give the occasion an added air of importance, we decided that a student speaker should precede La Guardia. As a graceful gesture toward La Guardia's background, Marc was selected.

It would be difficult for anyone to forget the startled faces of the students gathered at assembly that day when Marc stepped forward on the speaker's platform and said, "This morning I am going to talk about old-age pensions and social security."

I had known what Marc was going to talk about. Now I was hoping he would be able to put it across.

In a few moments, there was complete silence in the auditorium as Marc's impassioned voice pressed the argument for providing for the old age of people who with their labor had helped to build America but who had never been able to earn more than enough to feed their children and pay for the clothes on their backs. He spoke passionately, eloquently—and, I know, sincerely. ". . . for, if it is true that government is of the people and for the people, then it is the duty of government to provide for those who, through no fault of their own, have been unable to provide for themselves. It is the social responsibility of every citizen to see that these laws for our older people are enacted."

The applause which followed as Marc backed away from the lectern convinced me more than ever that adolescents are far more capable of serious thought and understanding than they are given credit for being. While other boys could poke fun at Marc and kid him along, when he spoke, they listened.

La Guardia shook Marc's hand, slapped him on the shoulder in a congratulatory gesture. Then, in his own inimitable way, he thrust out his chin and picked up the thread of Marc's speech and used it as the basis for his own talk. "Our neglected citizens. . . ." His audience howled.

Assembly that day was a huge success. The students, Dr. Paul, and all of the teachers were pleased, even excited. Most important of all, for La Guardia and Marcantonio it was the beginning of an association and friendship which was to endure for many years. Almost as soon as he had finished law school, Marc went to work in La Guardia's law office, became involved in politics, and managed La Guardia's congressional campaigns in East Harlem. When La Guardia was elected Mayor of New York in 1933, Marc was elected to replace him in Congress.

Despite my growing preoccupation with De Witt Clinton, I still managed to spend an occasional evening and to teach Sunday School at the Jefferson Park Methodist Church. I needed the boisterous generosity of soul, the good humor of John Shedd, and the incisive, sensitive mind of Leone Piatelli as sounding boards for my work and ideas. And now there was a third at the church who excited me—its pastor, Amadeo Riggio, a volatile, fiery Sicilian, afraid of nothing under the sun. In search of one of his flock, he would enter any dive in East Harlem at any hour of the night and turn the place upside down. It was Pastor Riggio who established a project we called *La Casa del Popolo* (The People's House), where Marcantonio and other De Witt Clinton students from the *Circolo* played an important role.

One of our convictions had always been that, in immigrant areas like East Harlem, the adult had to be educated as well as the child. We now decided to do something for the parents of the boys we taught daily in the public-school classroom.

Our object was to establish classes for the thousands of

Italians in the neighborhood—something on the order of what we had done before at the YMCA, only with a more definite scope and purpose in mind. We wanted to educate for citizenship, to make active, responsible, voting Americans out of these people who did not have the means or the knowledge to go about it.

At 118th Street near First Avenue, an abandoned Methodist church which Pastor Riggio managed to acquire for us from the City Missions Society provided the building for the *Casa del Popolo*'s activities. But a great deal of work was necessary to tear out the old pews and replace them with desks, folding chairs, and tables for our purpose. We organized classes, planned a special afternoon recreational program for children, and put out a weekly bulletin to point up neighborhood problems and topics of interest, which we ran off on a small printing press at the center.

At a meeting after class one day, I threw the problem at the boys. "We can't expect much help from the outside. After all, these are our own people. If we don't help them, who will? Are we going to allow them to be robbed of their rights as Americans simply because we are too indifferent to teach them English and train them to pass the citizenship tests?"

There was a spontaneous cry of approval.

I was not surprised at the outcome of this meeting. All along, deep down I had known that the boys would rise to the occasion. As I have stated so many times, the young adult is happiest when occupied at some task in the service of his family or society; it fills him with a sense of maturity. I am convinced that one of the weaknesses in the educational program of our schools these days is the absence of suitable activities to make the pupil aware of his positive value to the world around him. And out of this void in a boy's life come indifference, boredom, and insecurity, all of which spell one word—delinquency.

We had more volunteer help from our students at the *Casa*

del Popolo than we were able to utilize. And because their hearts were in their work, they turned out to be vigorous teachers. To make them feel they were earning as well as working, we gave them a payment of fifty cents a session. They were more than delighted. Marc was put in charge of the citizenship classes. There in the little room which used to be the rectory of the church, intent, but not without humor, Marc expounded the elements of American history to some twenty Italian workingmen.

"Pete Vannini," he would ask a mustached bricklayer about thirty years old. "Who was the father of our country?"

"What father? What you talk? Is people have a father, not a country."

There was another class of elementary English taught by Alfred Marra, now Director of Internal Medicine at St. Francis Hospital in the Bronx. I vividly remember a lanky, square-jawed northern Italian laborer trying to read from a textbook. The poor fellow struggled to get out, "And the bee said 'booze, booze.'"

Alfred Marra tried to keep a straight face. "Buzz, buzz," he corrected, "not booze, booze."

The lanky Italian grasped the back of his skull in an attitude of desperation and turned to the rest of the class. "What a cursed language! Letters which say, 'booze, booze' suddenly become, 'buzz, buzz.'"

How many immigrant Italians Marc himself instructed and took down to the naturalization center to obtain citizenship would be difficult to estimate. He would take them down periodically, in small groups, aided by other students who acted as coaches and witnesses and took care of other details. While working at the *Casa del Popolo* he was also leader of the East Harlem Tenant League, which conducted a successful strike against postwar rent gouging. Years later, when running for Congress, those who did not know him wondered at the

terrific plurality he always managed to pile up, no matter
what his political banner. These doubters never saw Marcantonio in his office, in shirtsleeves, the crowd milling about his
desk consisting of neighbors he had helped or was about to
help. They never saw him on a street corner making a speech
or listened to the comments of the crowd. They never saw him
walk along 116th Street, heard the old and young greet him.
If they had seen these things, they would not have wondered.

Our next step in the drive to educate the whole family was
to organize the Italian Parent-Teachers Association at De
Witt Clinton. Our first president, Michael Tucci, was an
importer of Italian foodstuffs. Some of the meetings of the
executive committee were held at his home, where, along with
discussing school and parent problems, we sampled choice
delicacies from his warehouse. Leone Piatelli was vice-presi-
dent, and our secretary was a widow and dress designer by
the name of Lina Cantu. Her son, Erminio, was one of the most
intellectually gifted boys I have ever known. A businessman
who had two sons in the Italian Department, Giovanni Sicili-
ano, became treasurer.

The Association held monthly meetings which, in addition
to the business aspects, planned conferences for the Italian
parents to acquaint them with the school program, with vocational opportunities for their children, and to stress over and
again the importance of continuing education if possible
through college. Nor was the social side of the picture neglected. Semiannually, in cooperation with the *Circolo* and
other students in the Italian Department, we held *Serate
Italiane* (Italian Nights) either at the school or in East Harlem
or on the lower East Side. There would usually be an Italian
play put on by the students themselves, followed by a dance
and refreshments.

Before very long the Association accumulated a substantial
treasury. This money not only took care of the needs of the

poorer Italian boys—a jacket, a pair of eye glasses, shoes, carfare, lunch money—but also allowed us to make a contribution
to the social-welfare committee of the school. In this way the
school itself came to realize that Italian parents were not only
interested in their own boys but were also willing to lend a
hand to help others.

Slowly we were beginning to understand that the unit of
education was not merely the child. The unit of education must
be the family.

My memories of that early PTA at Clinton carry with them
also the shadow of a tragic incident. I mentioned an exception-
ally gifted student who was the son of our PTA secretary,
Lina Cantu. His name was Erminio. Slender of build, with
delicate features, soft black hair, and musician's hands, Erminio
stood at the head of his class in all subjects. But his special interest was the study of French and Italian, in particular the
Italian poets. He could recite passages from Dante and had
read Carducci and other poets that were not ever taken up in
class. Though he had an aloof quality, all the other students
liked him. His father was dead and he lived alone with his
mother. He told me how he read poetry to her at night.

The custom in the Cantu household was to make coffee over
an alcohol burner. In the morning, Erminio would have the
coffee ready for his mother when she got up. Exactly what
took place on this particular morning no one ever did find
out. It seems that the burner was low on fuel. Erminio must
have reached for the alcohol container and uncovered it before
extinguishing the burner. An explosion was followed by
screams of pain. The mother rushed in to find her son en-
veloped in flames.

Erminio died in the hospital a few days later. I went there
several times before he died but he never recognized me. The
body was sent to Italy and buried in the family plot in Milan.
Several years later I took a bronze tablet there from his friends

and fellow students of the *Circolo*. Erminio's death—or perhaps it was his life—left a lasting impression. None of us at
Clinton ever forgot him. Nor was it possible to forget his
mother, Lina Cantu, because in a sense the alcohol lamp killed
her as well.

She no longer came to the PTA meetings. It was too painful
a reminder of life that was gone. I lost track of her for a time.
One day, quite unexpectedly, I met her on the street. At first
she did not recognize me. Then she smiled. "I am going to the
park," she said. "In the park the birds talk to me. They talk to
me of Erminio. I go there all the time."

Occasionally there were boys at Clinton with whom, try
as we might, we could do nothing. No amount of talking or
threats of expulsion or the reformatory seemed to make any
difference. They could no more avoid trouble or misconduct
than a fly could avoid molasses. While their thoughts should
have been occupied with study, their minds instead were off
in dreams of adventure and freedom from the drudgery of
school work. Teachers tried everything. Parents beat them.
Nothing availed. Their lives remained a constant turmoil of
perverseness with respect to the academic side of school life.
For such students the only solution was the workbench, their
time occupied from early morning until nightfall in the effort
to make a living.

But then there were the exceptions—students like Dom
Galdone and Pete Sicardi, who for all their inaptitude and
disinclination for school work had about them the suggestion
of promise if only they could be set straight. Some of these
boys we sent to the George Junior Republic.

The George Junior Republic was exactly what its name
implied. Founded in 1895 by W. R. George, a strapping, handsome, natural-born teacher and once an assistant of Miss
Ruddy's, it was located at Freeville, New York. Actually, it
was a little village similar to other upstate towns, except that

in the Junior Republic the voting citizens were young people of both sexes from sixteen to twenty-one years of age. The laws of the State of New York and such laws as the young citizens enacted in their own meetings were the laws of the Junior Republic. They had their own police system and their own jails. The motto was "Nothing without Labor" and, believe me, they lived up to it.

Applicants came to "Daddy George," as he was affectionately called, from everywhere—from city and country, from rich homes and poor homes, and often from no homes at all. There was a yearly tuition, but this was adjusted to the circumstances of the individual or his family.

About one-third of the population of the George Junior Republic brought it a bit of notoriety. These were the boys who had committed a serious offense, had been found guilty and sentenced to some reformatory or jail. Then, instead of sending them to the institution, the judge would announce suspension of sentence if the Junior Republic's administration would accept the offender as one of its citizens.

During my years at Clinton, I sent a number of intractable boys to the George Junior Republic, or rather I should say, made it possible for them to go there. I spent some time at the Republic myself, studying their strict but kindly methods in handling boys; and one of my earlier students, Sal Cimilluca, then studying biology at nearby Cornell, used to drop in to see them and keep me informed.

Dom Galdone was the one of my boys who probably profited the most by his year at the Republic. He was sent there in the first place because he was always getting into trouble both in and out of school and would never do any schoolwork. But he was a capable boy and his mother determined that he should have an education. This made him a logical candidate for the Republic. I happen to have in my hands one of the very first letters written by Dom to his mother. It was to me a particularly touching, if simple, document.

I got in jail again for smoking, but I will be out soon.
It is snowing out here and very cold. I get up at half-past-
four every morning and go down to the barn to work.
I feed the horses and take care of the cows. Let me know
if it is snowing in New York and also if the dog is still
living. I close my letter by giving my best regards to
everyone. Love and kisses.

The reason I did not tell you I was in jail is that I did not
want to hurt your feelings.

While Dom was still at the Republic we also sent up a boy
named Pete Sicardi, who had gotten into serious trouble for
stealing and whose parents were just about ready to give up.
Since Dom was now a veteran, I wrote him to look after the
newcomer. A few months later I received a message from
Dom.

Dear Pop: I shouldn't start the letter this way, but I
must tell you. Last Friday Pete and two other fellows
stole a car and when they got about 30 or 40 miles away
from the Republic they tipped over in a ditch and Pete
hurt his ear which is still swollen. He is in trouble. He
might even go to jail. Real jail in Elmira, I mean, not what
we have here. Please don't tell Pete's father. Pete is afraid
he might come up here and hurt him or something.

After more than a year at the Republic, Dom left. He
wanted to finish high school at Clinton and go on to Cornell,
where Cimilluca had shown him around. He also insisted that
he wanted to be near his mother. He had changed completely.
For days he helped me in my office, no longer dreading work
or study but, in fact, looking forward to it. The George Junior

Republic had given him what we had been unable to at Clinton —a sense of his place and responsibility in the world.

Though "Daddy George" has been dead for many years, his unique Republic is in operation today, working with those supposed "bad boys" and finding so much good in them.

20/ Not long after our marriage, Rose decided that she wanted to abandon the business world, complete her college education, and become a teacher. For, as she laughingly phrased it, "If teaching is to monopolize all of our waking moments and all of our conversation, I've got to do something to get a word in edgewise."

I was all in favor of this idea. I could see us drawn closer together than ever by the bonds of a common purpose and interest in life. But in order to achieve this objective, sacrifices were necessary. With Rose no longer working and both of us still having obligations "at home," I had to go back to private lessons and teaching evening school five nights a week. I stopped teaching at ten and never reached home before eleven o'clock at night and was out of the house in the morning again at seven-thirty. The evening-school check ("blood money," we used to call it) reached us in the middle of the month, at the opportune moment when the day-school check had been exhausted. Then for two summers I taught six-week stretches at the YMCA to further augment our income.

It was a deadening routine. Nor was I unique, or alone the victim of this maddening process of trying to make both ends meet as a public-school teacher. Most of my friends were in the same situation. A man teacher's salary never seemed to catch up with the cost of living. Ironically it was only during the depression of the thirties and because of the low prices that came with it that conditions brought about something of a balance between what we were earning and what we had to spend on food and clothes.

Our Teachers Union, of which I was one of the early members, could not do very much. Off and on since 1916 we had been fighting to achieve a cultural wage; but the gap between what we earned and the cost of living never narrowed. Gradually there began to be a noticeable decline in the number of male teachers in the schools. The public clamored for the best possible education for their children but they wanted it cheap—certainly at no increase in the salaries of teachers who, in their estimation, had it easy enough, working from nine to three and with three months' vacation every year.

These were the years of postwar inflation. The self-determination of peoples had been proclaimed at Versailles, and at home the Palmer raids on Socialists were taking place. Kids on the street sang "Avalon" and "Whispering" and on our public-school system the heavy hand of conformity descended. Freedom to teach became to a great extent a mockery, and such slogans as "Democracy in Education and Education for Democracy" that we had adopted in our Teachers Union seemed a far off Utopia.

In fact, to express one's political opinions was sure to result in reprisals. Obedience to authority—"unquestioning obedience"—was expressed by some as one of the goals of American education.

Something occurred, however, which marked the beginning of a new era in my career as a teacher. I was invited to teach a Spanish course at New York University. While I was teaching there I persuaded the Dean of the School of Commerce to allow me to start an elementary class in Italian. Before long the number of students increased to a point where I asked my assistant at De Witt Clinton, Annita Giacobbe, to take over some of the classes.

The room in which I taught at New York University was also used by Professor Paul Radosavljevich, a Yugoslav, who taught Experimental Education. Professor Rado, everyone called him. Often I would arrive early and sit in on his course while waiting for my own class to begin. Slowly I became engrossed, fascinated by this hulking, articulate European who had been so thoroughly and carefully trained as a scholar and could express himself with equal facility in English, German, and the Slavic languages. Often after our work we would stop at some little Italian restaurant in Greenwich Village and have a bite to eat and a glass of wine together. "Study for your doctorate, Leonard," Professor Rado advised after he began to understand something of my interest in immigrant problems. "In order to help your people you must advance in the educational system. Become at least a superintendent of schools. Concentrate on the ethnic factor in education. That is your field—the cultural factor in education—a subject a great many educators talk about, but very few actually understand."

Under the influence of Professor Rado I felt a new incentive to continue my education and began to take educational courses for my doctorate. Out of our talks the idea grew in my mind of doing a comprehensive study on the social background of the Southern Italian. In order to cope with problems dealing with the education of the immigrant and his American child, it was first necessary to have all the information I could accumulate. "For instance," I explained to Professor Rado, "in the mind of the average Southern Italian immigrant a constant tug-of-war takes place. I run up against it all the time. On the one hand he wants his son to have the advantages of an education never possible for himself, and on the other, centuries of tradition tell him that a boy must work, have responsibility, and contribute to the family. These are not easy to reconcile—

school and work. In the average family it leads to a great deal of friction."

In order to know more about our boys we devised a questionnaire for them to fill out. We wanted the usual information such as age, home address, subjects the student was taking, teacher's name beside each subject, recreational interests, but also other data—if he worked after school, success in passing subjects, cause of failure, details of home environment, and particularly in what way we could help him. Through this questionnaire and by means of personal interviews, we were beginning to find out what was happening in school and out of school and also getting glimpses of life in the Italian communities. "We want to know more—we have to know more about this thing everyone keeps referring to as the Americanization process."

Professor Rado agreed wholeheartedly. He was eloquent on the subject. The school set itself up as the most powerful Americanization force in the immigrant community, he said. Actually how true was this? Had this assumption been submitted to any proof? What if the school was not the dominant force and there were more potent forces shaping the lives of American-born children of foreign-born parents? Had the school the necessary resources to compete with and overcome these other forces—negative forces often giving rise to delinquency and crime in immigrant communities? Or to put it another way, was the American school welding together, culturally, the various ethnic groups that composed its population?

"And if the answer is yes," I said, "then I would like to know what it is that the school is attempting to weld together. What is going into this welding process? Does Americanization demand a renunciation of the culture of the immigrant or does it seek a fusion of his culture?"

"That is the question."

"Tell me, Paul," I added, "where is the source of cultural strength for the immigrant—any immigrant?"

"That is easy. The source of cultural strength for any immigrant must be the country of his birth. Until the immigrant can be assimilated to a point where he begins to draw from American sources, he must look backward into the past. That is why, Leonard, you must write your doctor's thesis on the cultural or ethnic factor in education."

True to the ancient Aviglianese custom, my father retired after his sixtieth birthday—that is, he retired from the daily business of going back and forth from his work at the café on 22d Street. Instead, he decided, he was going to do something more in keeping with his age and temperament—run a corner penny-candy store.

He lasted at it just about six months. At the end of that time practically every kid in East Harlem owed him money, while he owed the store rent and the candy-supply house. "What kind of business do you call this?" I asked him. "How do you expect to continue at this rate? The children certainly know where to come."

My father hunched his shoulders. "Narduccio, what would you have me do? These are little children. What do you expect from little children?"

It was the end of his career as a merchant.

Mamma-Nonna meanwhile had been after me for quite a while on a plan of her own. They were alone now. My sister and my brothers were all married, with the exception of Frank, the youngest, who was training as a cadet in the merchant marine. "Ah, how long it has been since I have felt the earth with my fingers," Mamma-Nonna sighed to me. "Your father does not know—he was from within the walls of Avigliano and his family the *artigiani*. But I am from the soil." As a little girl she had worked in the fields with her father and mother. She had heard that not far from New York City it was possible to buy a little house and a piece of land for not very much money. "Is this true, Narduccio?"

"I believe it is true, Mamma-Nonna." I had had the same idea in mind for some time.

"If we had such a tiny place, instead of paying rent here in the city and getting nothing in return, I could have a garden and raise all the vegetables we would need. I would have chickens for eggs and a goat for milk. Except for sugar, flour, coffee, we would have to buy practically nothing."

"All this means a lot of work."

But to Mamma-Nonna everything was work. She had never known anything else. Now that she was getting older she felt she wanted to enjoy the work she had known when she was young. She wanted to see things growing again.

When I questioned my father about this, he answered, "Perhaps Mamma-Nonna is right. For better than thirty years now I have been hiding from the sun. It would be good to walk in and out of a house without climbing a mountain of stairs. It would be good to walk on a piece of ground that you can say is your own and have room for a few barrels down in the cellar where you could make some wine."

About fifty miles outside of New York City, near the little town of Monroe and in the neighborhood of Bear Mountain, we found a small frame house with about ten acres of land. Here the old folks lived in perfect contentment for many years, Mamma-Nonna with her chickens, her garden, and her goat, and my father doing little odd jobs around the place and walking every few days to the village with a knapsack on his back to do the shopping. There was also a tumbledown shack on the place which, with the help of my brothers, I fixed over into a sort of studio and bedroom for Rose and me to rush off to on Sundays when we could spare a few hours from our work in New York.

Practically every Sunday there were spaghetti dinners under the trees on the back lawn—gatherings which in the city had

taken place only on holidays or special occasions. With the
first turning of the leaves in the fall, my father would arrange
for the delivery of a truckload of grapes and give us our working orders a month in advance. "On the weekend of the
twenty-fifth of October we will press the grapes. No excuses.
The wine must be made and everybody must help." By this
time I had an old Model-T Ford, and Rose and I would jump
into it and bounce all the way up to Monroe to contribute our
share in this annual wine-making ceremony. After a few
years, Rose's cousin, Dr. Salvatore, bought a house just a few
hundred yards away for his mother and father. Now my
parents had the companionship of old friends from East
Harlem. They visited back and forth, and it was as if the
friendship of the city had been transplanted in the green
earth and fresh air of the country.

So, in a way, the dream of a happy life in the New World
came true after all for my father and Mamma-Nonna.

21/O

n the lower East Side of New York City, around 10th Street, there was a large building known as the Boys' Club of New York. In 1927 its Board of Directors and other interested citizens created another branch and purposely located it in East Harlem, where there was a high incidence of juvenile delinquency. Several years later, a grant of thirty-six thousand dollars was made available to the School of Education of New York University for a study of the effect of a boys' club program upon a local community and its problems. This East Harlem branch at 111th Street near First Avenue, with its six thousand members, was elected as the laboratory for the study. The research project was headed by a Chicago sociologist, Frederic M. Thrasher, whose book *The Gang: A Study of 1313 Gangs in Chicago* had become a classic in its field.

Before the study, many striking claims had been made favoring the establishment of clubs for adolescents. Judge Arnold of Chicago stated that the Union League Boys' Club in that city caused a decline of 73 per cent in juvenile crime in the district it served, and that in the neighborhood of the downtown Boys' Club of New York 60 per cent less juvenile delinquency is found than in other similar areas on the lower East Side. It was to test the validity of this assumption that the study in East Harlem was undertaken. In order to secure complete impartiality, the Boys' Club of New York took the initiative in having a university, through its department of sociology, undertake the research project.

I received a note from Dr. Thrasher and went to see him at his office at the University at Washington Square. He was a rather slender man, casual in his manner, though his eyes betrayed a constant interest in life around him. He shook hands and motioned me to an armchair while he closed the door of his office, then leaned back against the desk, facing me. "Have you heard about our little project?" he asked.

"Some. I'm deeply interested."

"I thought you would be. This club is in the neighborhood where you grew up. Many of the boys are Clinton students. This will be the first research project to attempt a community case study of this type. We will try to evaluate scientifically the work of such a club and try to estimate its importance in curbing delinquency. Furthermore, we want to understand the educative processes that go on in such a community."

This project fascinated me. It fitted in very well with my idea for a doctoral thesis on the social background of the Southern Italian immigrant. We would be studying every aspect of the life of the community of East Harlem which at that time consisted of ninety thousand Italian-Americans—the largest community of its kind in the United States.

When the Boys' Club study got under way, De Witt Clinton High School was still located at 59th Street near Tenth Avenue. Since a large number of our students came from East Harlem, it was possible to get a great deal of our information right in the classroom by means of questionnaires, personal interviews, and individual case studies. Much of this material related to family background, leisure activities, and future plans, especially concerning their life work. These were highly personal questions that had to be asked with warmth and sympathy.

In this study I was aided, as always, by Annita Giacobbe.

Her natural understanding of the boys led them to an un-
burdening of confidences that would have been extremely
difficult with any other teacher. I was also helped a great deal
by my older students and a former Clinton boy, Salvatore
Cimilluca, who had graduated from Cornell and was working
for his master's degree as a participant in the Boys' Club study.
Sal could speak the Italian dialects as well as the English of the
streets. His easy, friendly manner gained him entrance into
any home. "Signora," he would say, bunching his fingers together, "you're talking to me, Salvatore Cimilluca. My father
came over on the same boat with you. Now then, what is the
real reason that the truant officer keeps coming after your son,
Mario?"

"The real reason, *figlio mio*, is that we need him in the vegetable store. And on top of that the real, real reason is that little
Mario has a better head for turnips than he has for study. That
even God himself would not deny."

The techniques, the methods of investigation, and the information when compiled and analyzed formed the basis of
new sociological thought and focus on the problems of
minority groups in high-delinquency areas. And the Boys'
Club study did a great deal for me personally. My association
with Dr. Thrasher and the other sociologists opened a completely new vista in the field of education for me. I was now
convinced that to achieve educational objectives, it was necessary to have complete and detailed knowledge of every aspect
of the lives of the people to be educated.

A few hours each week I had been going to The Hamilton
House, a settlement house on the lower East Side, and talking
informally to a group of social workers. They asked questions
about things they did not understand concerning Italian immigrant families and I answered these questions to the best of
my knowledge, drawing upon my own personal experience,
the contacts with my students, what I had read, and the con-
clusions I had drawn from my study of the subject. "Why is

it," one of these workers asked me one night, "that the Italian mother plays so unimportant a role in the household?"

"It merely appears so. Tradition has had it for countless generations that the woman shall be inconspicuous. On the surface it still seems so, but be assured that hardly any major decision takes place in an Italian home without the mother having a major part in that decision."

These sessions were stimulating for me because they made me think, made me remember aspects of Italian life I had forgotten, helped me in my sociological studies and with the material I was beginning to gather for my dissertation. By this time I had come to the belief that a regular course concerning the Italian immigrant should be given at the University. I spoke to Ned Dearborn, Dean of General Education at New York University, and a course called "The Social Background of the Italian Family in America" was approved. I repeated this course every six months, with the student body consisting mostly of Italo-American teachers, social workers, and graduate students. It was a course which for many years afforded me deep personal satisfaction.

The value and success of this particular course, revolving about one nationality group, resulted in the inauguration of another course involving the many racial and national minorities. I was one of the guest lecturers for this course, which included James Weldon Johnson, who lectured on the Negro. In 1938 we all contributed to a standard work entitled *Our Racial and National Minorities in the United States*, a book which served as the basis of many studies and courses on the subject of intercultural education.

As I look back to that period of my life now known for some reason obscure to me as the roaring twenties, I am impressed by how small beginnings developed, expanded, and gathered momentum. For instance, a casual talk with a student who was having difficulty maintaining himself in school because his father had died led to the creation of a Student Welfare Committee, and in turn, student scholarship aid. I relied upon the reaction of my boys to the problems they were facing to develop ways and means at Clinton to grapple with these problems.

Listening to the stories of the boys who were failures in the eyes of the school, and particularly in their own eyes, we tried to work out special programs for them. With a very devoted group of teachers, many of whom were not Italian, such as Dr. John McCarthy, Miss Catherine Griffin, Dr. Abraham Kroll, and Bertha Mandel, we used to meet during lunchtime and at times after school hours and discuss the problems of individual failure and what could be done. In his position as administrative assistant of the school, Abe Kroll helped many a difficult boy who found himself in a tight situation or was on the verge of expulsion from school.

To me, failure at any age, but particularly during adolescence, is something the seriousness of which cannot be exaggerated. Forcing a boy who is an academic failure, or even a behavior problem, out of school solves nothing at all. In fact it does irreparable harm to the student and merely shifts the responsibility from the school to a society which is ill equipped to handle the problem. The solution must be found within the school itself and the stigma of failure must be placed on a boy as seldom as possible.

Now the thirties were upon us, with their bread lines and apple vendors and the dole and what the cynics called the "alphabet soup" of the Roosevelt administration. Perhaps we as teachers were more fortunate than most of the population, in that our jobs were not dependent upon the ordinary economics of supply and demand. So long as children grew up and went to school there had to be teachers. Whether or not their parents could afford to send them to college was another matter. Our jobs were as secure as the government itself. But while the specter of the depression did not touch us personally, it was all around us, ever present in the faces of our pupils, who brought "the pinch" from home to the classroom.

The Boys' Club study and my research into the background of the immigrant pointed clearly to the necessity for a central clearing agency for all information concerning the Italian in America. I discussed the matter with Dr. Thrasher and some of my own associates. We decided that the most suitable location for such a project was the beautiful new Italian House—Casa Italiana—at Columbia University, the result of the efforts of a group of Columbia alumni under the leadership of Professor Peter Riccio, now the director of the Casa Italiana. Permission was readily granted for us to use the facilities of the Casa to undertake the work of the Educational Bureau. I was made executive director.

Although my own services were on a voluntary basis, there was still the problem of personnel and finances for this bureau. The financial question was partially solved by a small grant from the Italian Government and proceeds from social affairs we arranged. The personnel question was solved by the assignment of workers from the Works Progress Administration (WPA). Leone Piatelli, in the same situation as millions of other jobless Americans, came to work with us along with talented writers and newspapermen, while limited scholarships set up within the bureau itself attracted students interested in helping and learning more about the life of the immigrant.

The United States Census of New York City for 1930 emphasized the obvious but significant fact that Italians lived, for the most part, in heavily concentrated Italian communities, "little Italys" or "ghettos," as they were popularly known, "ethnic islands" in the fancy language of the sociologists. There were over twenty such communities in New York—communities in which 50 to 90 per cent of the people were of Italian origin. These communities lived their social and cultural life, for the most part, within the confines of their own borders. They were part of a great metropolis, but at the same time, not as yet an integral part of the greater cultural and social life. The participation of the Italo-American in the various activities of the city was mostly in its economic aspects—earning a living by working in the poorer paid and more onerous jobs available, while the few Italians in professional life for the most part had only Italian clients and operated within the Italian communities.

It became increasingly apparent that there was a pressing need for initiating and promoting educational programs within these "ethnic islands." There were hundreds of Italo-American societies in these communities—fraternal, mutual aid, sporting, professional, religious, and purely social. In characteristic fashion, each club or society worked within its own small circle. While they were aware and concerned about the problems that all Italians faced, they were ineffective because they had not learned to unite and to work as a group on a city-wide basis. This was one of the important purposes of the Casa Italiana Educational Bureau.

We compiled the names of all the Italo-American organizations in the metropolitan area and invited delegates from these societies to attend a monthly meeting at the Casa Italiana to discuss educational and social problems affecting Italo-Americans everywhere. We also created a speakers' bureau, with outstanding people in the educational field, to travel around and give lectures at various centers.

We were able to gather and publish valuable material on such topics as "Occupational Trends among Italians in New York City," "The Padrone or 'Boss' System" (exploitation of immigrants by their own kind), "Some Contributions of Italy and Her Sons to American Life," "The Italian Population of New York City," and the cataloguing of information which had never before been attempted with specific reference to the Italians as an ethnic group in America. This information was of great use to those of us seeking to penetrate the maze of rumors and contradictory notions concerning a particular people. It was as if we were fumbling in the dark until suddenly a crack of light entered and we began to see and understand and evaluate ideas and theories in terms of statistics and hard facts.

Because of my association with the Casa Italiana activities, I was asked to become a member of the Folk Festival Council of New York City, sponsored by the Foreign Language Information Service, which had been started during the First World War to work with immigrant groups. My job was to organize an Italian group to participate with other nationality groups in fostering native folk songs and dances. I remember the enthusiasm which greeted this project when I broached the idea to a number of my pupil-teachers at New York University and my associates at the Casa Italiana.

"What do you think?" I asked. "Are we capable of putting such a project across? Can we compete with the other groups?"

Elba Farabegoli, one of the group, looked at me in amazement. "What do you mean, can we compete? I know a great deal about folk music. And I believe we could even get Maestro Benelli, who toured the United States with the Florentine Choir, to be our director."

Miss Farabegoli put a great deal of time and energy into the formation of the Italian Choral Society, which is still functioning today as the Coro D'Italia. Through her efforts, we were able to secure the services of Maestro Benelli, whose musical knowledge and extraordinary ability enabled us to include in our repertoire a fine collection of folk songs that had their origins anywhere from Trieste to Sicily. We acquired authentic Italian costumes, and the interest of people who could instruct in the folk dances knew no bounds. Before long we were performing with other units of the Folk Festival Council at the International House, Town Hall, The Guild Theatre, Channon Theatre, and the mall in Central Park.

Here was another contribution of immigrant peoples to the cultural life of America. All these activities were a far cry from my initial plans. Where was the serious university professor who would dedicate his life to the romance languages? Where the calm, cloistered life of the college campus? My old friend Leone Piatelli, grown leaner and sadder than ever from his struggles with the depression, said to me, "Leonardo, you go rushing around as if you had been bitten by a tarantula. When do you ever find time to sleep?"

Actually, during this period, I had several opportunities for university work. One was a professorship in Italian at the University of Virginia. Also I was asked to become chairman of the Language Department at Townsend Harris Hall in New York. I turned these offers down. Attractive as they were, I was by this time committed to working with my East Harlem boys and bound in a thousand ways to the streets of New York City.

More than ever I had become attached to my boys. With experience I had learned things about my role as a teacher. I learned how much there was to know about the people I was trying to teach. I stopped talking at my students, lecturing to classes. I developed the habit of listening, trying to penetrate the inner world of the pupil facing me. When talking to one of my boys, the first question I asked was where he lived. I sought to project myself outside and beyond the walls of the school and visualize the block where he lived, the home from which he came, and the conversation that took place in the evening around his dinner table. Only in this way could I understand him better. And only by understanding him could I help him.

22 / East Harlem, known to its inhabitants in the days of Peter Stuyvesant as "Happy Valley," is one of the most heterogeneous and congested communities in the United States, with poverty and unemployment as its main character-istics and its atmosphere one of tension and struggle. Inter-estingly enough, its heterogeneity dates back to the time when the population consisted of only thirty to forty families. The historian Caldwell says, "It is an old error cherished in this lo-cality that the founders of Harlem all came from Holland. They came from various parts of Western Europe, from the sunny plains of France, from the fir-clad hills of Scandinavia. There were Danes, Swedes, and Norwegians of the Lutheran faith. A large proportion, however, were Hollanders and French Huguenots."

As late as 1854, Harlem was still a village of huts and very humble houses, with here and there a little farm, and milch goats all over the place. It was the period following the great blizzard of '88 which saw the beginning of the flood tide of immigration into the United States. The Jews were followed hard by the Italians, who poured into Mulberry Bend on the lower East Side of Manhattan and into East Harlem until there were about ninety thousand Italians in East Harlem alone. This

pressure of numbers was a thorn in the side of the older inhabitants, giving rise to tension and racial clashes.

During the last decade of the nineteenth and the first two
decades of the twentieth century there had developed in all
of Harlem a community of 175,000 Jews. By 1930 the rapid
infiltration of the southern and West Indian Negroes into Central and West Harlem and the Italians into East Harlem had
driven the Jews elsewhere and reduced their numbers to less
than 10,000. And between the Negro and the Italian communities there was a Puerto Rican community which, after
the Second World War, developed rapidly, until now it is the
largest concentration of Puerto Ricans in continental United
States.

Geographically, East Harlem is set apart from the larger
city by definite natural boundaries on three sides, and on the
south by a radical difference in the cultural composition of
the predominantly German Yorkville community, which
tends to set up an effective though intangible line of demarca-
tion. On the east there is the East River and to the north there
is the Harlem River, cutting it off from the Bronx, while Central Park on the west limits expansion beyond Fifth Avenue.

Even before the advent of the automobile these natural and
cultural barriers isolated East Harlem from the rest of the
city. And within the community itself cultural islands developed, separating the inhabitants from each other. East Harlem always has been and still is a "social frontier," in which
seethe the conflicts resulting from the penetration into an older
established community by one new and different group of
people after another. Verbal and physical aggression, distrust,
suspicion, nonacceptance are all a part of daily living. It is a
community always in transition, always on the move, its people ever looking forward to the day when they can break
away, shake off the stigma of being identified with it.

The movement to create a high school to serve the upper

east side of Manhattan got under way about 1931. Civic and political leaders both in East Harlem and outside of East Harlem urged the Board of Education and the Superintendent of Schools to make necessary provision in the budget for its establishment. Also actively involved were such educational leaders as Mario Cosenza, Angelo Patri, and Anthony Pugliese. Locally, the East Harlem Council of Social Agencies held meetings in the community, secured petitions, and took a strong stand for a general or cosmopolitan high school, in opposition to those who were advocating an industrial or trade high school.

"An industrial high school," I pointed out time and again at meetings, "presumes to make trade workers of our boys. It suggests that the boys of East Harlem are not capable of doing academic work. This is exactly the kind of school we do not want." Finally there was an agreement, and communications to this effect were sent to the Board of Education.

The thought of a trade school in East Harlem caused me deep concern. I stayed up late at night, preventing Rose from going to bed by my constant preoccupation with the subject. Rose, who was now teaching, listened patiently while I paced the floor. "The stigma attached to an industrial high school! The psychological effect upon the pupils and the community! Sure, people say on the outside, 'The proper school for them dumb immigrants. They don't deserve any better.' It's wrong, I tell you. Especially for East Harlem, especially for any underprivileged neighborhood. A high school here must have all the dignity of a seat of learning. It must reflect its influence into the community and be the center for its improvement."

"It all sounds wonderful," Rose said. "Now go to bed and get some sleep. High school or no high school, we both have to get up in the morning and go to work."

"You refuse to realize the seriousness here."

"I realize. I'm only trying to save you for tomorrow, that's all."

What was in the back of my mind was a neighborhood school which would be the educational, civic, and social center of the community. We wanted to go beyond the traditional subject-centered and the current child-centered school to the community-centered school.

The Boys' Club study we had made was a potent factor in our argument. This was an area of high delinquency. We now had data to prove that by working closely with students through the school, developing leadership, recreational programs, social awareness, we might be able to counteract disintegrating forces at work on the streets and even in the homes. We could keep boys longer in school, develop those who had college aspirations, and with greater individual attention alleviate many other difficulties which affect adolescents.

A committee of us headed by Fiorello La Guardia, then our East Harlem congressman, went to see the Superintendent of Schools at the Board of Education. Nothing much happened. No definite assurance was given for an East Harlem high school. We received promises of support, that was all. In fact, it is quite probable that pressure, political and otherwise, would have placed a new high school outside the East Harlem area had not the fortuitous election of 1933 made La Guardia Mayor of New York City.

Mayor La Guardia's approval was the deciding factor in the establishment of Benjamin Franklin High School and in preventing its being located on the West Side. Vito Marcantonio, then La Guardia's campaign manager, also played an important part. Owing to the efforts of these two men together with the East Harlem Council of Social Agencies, I was endorsed as a candidate for principal.

Still another man figured prominently in the establishment of the school. This was Dr. John L. Tildsley, who had given me my first public-school teaching job at De Witt Clinton. Dr. Tildsley, now Assistant Superintendent of the High School Division, called me to his office to prepare a statement indicating the scope of this new school. Despite his years and white hair, Dr. Tildsley was as energetic and determined as ever.

"I'm glad you will have a chance at this school, Leonard," he said. "Everyone agrees you are the logical choice for principal. I want you to tell me everything you have in mind regarding Benjamin Franklin. I want you to take me around East Harlem, acquaint me with the problems, let me see the neighborhood through your eyes and the eyes of the people who live there. . . ."

For several nights we walked around East Harlem together. We visited the Boys' Club, Haarlem House, churches, social agencies, social clubs. We talked with businessmen, with boys as we came upon them on the streets, ate dinner in the Italian restaurants, stopped in at some of the corner candy stores. Dr. Tildsley was tireless. He found out what he wanted to know concerning the neighborhood. Then he and I sat down together and framed the first statement as to the aims and the scope of the school for release to the press.

I was in my office at De Witt Clinton when I read the editorial comment of *The New York Sun:* ". . . this will be a 'fluid' school in the truest sense of the word; it will seize upon any interest discovered in a boy and endeavor to build his education on this basis; it will be an experimental school with its entire personnel saturated with the spirit of experimentation and willing to do anything and be anything for boys."

With such support as this, Benjamin Franklin High School left the dream stage and became a fact! When Rose came into the apartment she found me seated in an armchair in the living room staring at nothing. Without speaking, she placed her hand on my shoulder and smiled.

23 / For

For twenty-two years I was principal of Benjamin Franklin High School. During that time we moved from old buildings, originally annexes of De Witt Clinton, one of which dated as far back as the Civil War, to a large and beautiful red brick Georgian structure on the East River Drive.

For twenty-two years I served a school devoted to the education of boys who, in the estimation of the outside world, offered one of the greatest crime potentials of any section in the country. For twenty-two years I served a part of New York City which was looked upon by many people as a pariah community.

Now that I have retired, I look back upon these years as the most fruitful period of my life. I believe that to serve one's community and to be involved in the education of growing boys is the most rewarding task a human being can undertake.

One of the biggest problems in connection with the establishment of Benjamin Franklin was the staff. It was necessary to get good teachers, dedicated teachers, teachers who not only had the necessary scholastic background but who also understood growing boys. We had to have strong men and women, with feeling for and understanding of particular types of boys—boys from immigrant communities, whose parents often had very recently arrived. East Harlem spread itself over an area of one hundred sixty square blocks and had a population of over 200,000 souls—a city the size of Syracuse and yet lost and unknown except for those of us who lived there. Negro rubbed shoulders with white. Italians, Puerto Ricans, Jews, Germans, Irish lived down the street from each other. One of the first surveys made of the student body of Benjamin Franklin High showed that it included thirty-four different nationalities.

Quite a few teachers transferred from De Witt Clinton, among them Dr. Morris Deshel, Dina Di Pino, Annita Giacobbe, and Dr. Abraham Kroll, who came as my administrative assistant. A dryly humorous, pipe-smoking New Englander by the name of Austin Works, who was chairman of English in a New York City high school, also joined our staff. He exerted a great influence on our boys, who affectionately dubbed him "Mr. Woiks."

We had hardly settled in the old building on East 108th Street when Austin Works came to my office on the second floor to tell me how pleased he was he had made the decision to transfer to Franklin.

"I keep seeing before my eyes," he said to me, "some thirty to forty boys with potentialities for good and for bad. It is almost a certainty that some of the boys I am now teaching will come to a sad end, and the terrible part of it all is that nine out of ten of those who go wrong are decent human beings to begin with." He tossed a slip of paper over on my desk with a boy's name written on it. "Do you know this one?" he asked.

It was a boy whose father owned a penny-candy store over on Second Avenue. I knew them well, the mother, the father, three brothers, and an older sister. The sister had gotten married and left East Harlem.

"The father is as meek as a rabbit," I explained. "When things go wrong he shrugs his shoulders. The daughter was kept at home, but the boys never knew anything but the streets. The oldest drives a milk wagon. This boy, Nat, is the youngest. The middle one, Benny, is mixed up with the mobs."

"I've changed lodgings," Austin said, "moving closer to the school. This morning I came in lugging a heavy suitcase. When Nat saw me, he came running over and insisted on carrying my bag, all the way up to the fourth floor. He would not even take a tip. That is why I asked if you knew him. . . ."

A month or so later, Nat's brother Benny was shot down by rival mobsters in front of his father's store. I went to the funeral, primarily to express my sympathy to the mother and father, but also to keep an eye on the younger brother Nat during his ordeal. I was criticized by some of the people of East Harlem, who felt that I should not have attended the funeral of a hoodlum. Maybe they were right. Maybe it was not dignified for a principal to do this. Yet the fact remains that a few days later Nat came and thanked me personally for going to his home. He held his cap, twisting it in his hands. "I was gonna go after them myself," he blurted. "I'd a killed somebody. Then when I saw you there talking to my mother and father, I wasn't so sure any more."

I took Nat's arm and walked him down the hall to the office of Austin Works. Together we spoke to him of the futility of revenge which could only lead to disaster and further sorrow for his family.

I did not have occasion to see Nat until a few months later, when I came upon him in the lunchroom, laying down the rules of proper behavior in no uncertain language to a disreputable young student who looked pretty much the way Nat had once appeared to us. As my eyes sought his questioningly, Nat drew me aside and explained in a low voice, "Mr. Works had me assigned as a monitor here, Mr. Covello. This kid is one tough guy, but we'll straighten him out!"

All this happened a long time ago in the early days of Benjamin Franklin High School. I saw Nat a number of times after he left school. He had not forgotten his school or Austin Works or the principal who went to his brother's funeral.

Most of our ablest teachers were those who came to Franklin of their own volition. Among them was our Dean of Boys, Sal Pergola. Born in New York City of Neapolitan parents, Sal Pergola is a stocky, colorful, energetic man with an instinctive affinity for problems relating to tough East Side boys. He could throw an arm about a boy churning with resentment against some teacher and make him smile and feel ashamed, or he could berate another in a voice that could be heard halfway down the corridor; and the boys always had the feeling that he was one of them, trying to help them in his own way. They could no more think of hating Sal Pergola than they could think of hating an older brother.

By his amazing insight into the character of young men, he was able to penetrate the confidence of a youth who was the leader of one of the toughest neighborhood gangs in East Harlem. By long talks, Sal Pergola ultimately diverted this boy's interest from gangs and street fighting to an interest in his own future. He became one of the leaders in our civic projects and graduated with honors—all through the efforts of an understanding teacher and administrator.

Sal always likes to tell the story of his father, who in Italy had been an army officer and never lost his feeling for discipline. Sal could go out nights as a young man, but he always had to be back at a certain time. One night he returned about a half hour late. His father fetched him a terrific cuff on the side of his head. "This time I am going to forgive you," he shouted. He gave him another clout. "Next time I will not be so lenient."

Soon after my work at Benjamin Franklin High School got under way, Rose resigned from public-school teaching. As with any other high school of corresponding size, Franklin had its regular office staff. But once we started our community work, it was another matter. There was a shortage of help even though the Works Progress Administration assigned forty or fifty teachers, clerks and specialized personnel to help us in our school and community work. Without receiving compensation, Rose helped me in every way she could, revealing an outstanding ability to keep my activities in order while I plunged headlong into the intricacies of one project after another.

Before anything else, it was important to have on hand all available information about the community. A great deal of this information had already been procured through the Boys' Club study. But we needed more.

The antagonism of a public living outside the confines of East Harlem and the attacks of newspapers seeking sensational "blackboard-jungle" copy could only be countered by knowledge of the facts. I held frequent consultations with Dr. Thrasher and other sociologists at New York University, where I continued to teach the course on the social background of the Italian immigrant. For the purpose of attacking this community problem at Franklin, we began early to enlist the cooperation of churches, settlement houses, and civic organizations.

I walked into my office one morning to find a rather brash young man waiting for me. It was during Mussolini's Ethiopian campaign in 1935. Upon introducing himself as a reporter for one of the New York dailies, he asked, "Would you say, Mr. Covello, that there has been an increase in racial antagonism between the Negro and Italian since the start of this war?"

I looked at him in amazement. The reporter smiled. "This is a question of the black race and the white race. We know there have been incidents all over Harlem. How do you handle the problem at Benjamin Franklin?"

I tried to control my anger. Over at her desk, my secretary,

Marge Banzello, caught my eye as if she thought he was out of his mind. Instead of saying what I wanted to, I answered, "I don't know what you are talking about. There is no identification between my students and the Ethiopian War. I doubt if they feel anything at all."

"And I doubt if our readers would believe that."

"Your readers can believe what they want to believe," I said. "If they want to believe that the streets of East Harlem are running with blood, that's their business. And if your paper wants to help them believe it that's your business. But I can assure you that there is absolutely no truth in this rumor." A happy thought occurred to me. I conducted the reporter out of the office and downstairs to the gymnasium. There were a dozen or so boys practicing basketball, among them several colored students.

At the sight of us the boys stopped playing, one of the basketballs poised in the hands of a lanky Negro youth ready to shoot. I motioned to him, "Bob, come here!" Then I picked out the white boy nearest him, an Italian by the name of George Castelli. "You too, George."

"Now then," I said as both boys stood waiting, "this gentleman is a newspaper reporter. He wants to know if the war in Ethiopia has made any difference in the way you two boys feel about each other."

"Ethiopia?" Castelli echoed.

The Negro boy said, "What have I got to do with those people over there?" He put his hand on Castelli's shoulder. "This boy is my friend. That's all I know."

The reporter went away without his story. I did not bother to read the paper the next day to see if he had made one up.

The problem of intercultural relations was naturally one of the very first that we concerned ourselves about at Franklin. Some years before I had spoken at an education conference in Philadelphia, where I met Dr. Rachel Davis-Dubois who had been pioneering in this field. She asked me to become a member of the Board of the Institute for Intercultural Education. I now spoke to her about doing a study at Franklin. The services and staff of this organization were placed at our disposal to conduct a human-relations project among our boys. While this was to be primarily a study of racial attitudes, it was also designed as a means of developing sympathetic attitudes between the different races and nationalities.

This is not to deny that there were racial incidents at Franklin, even hostility in certain cases. Individual fights did occur, usually stemming from some insignificant argument that built up to the name-calling stage and when they did, we had to make sure that the trouble was straightened out immediately to prevent it from spreading and becoming a group clash. Then, most difficult of all to combat, were the prejudices, originating with the ignorance of the parents and carried into the school by the pupils—the insidious, stupid kind of racial prejudice that makes a white boy label every Negro a "no account nigger" and every Puerto Rican a "dirty spick," without having any conception of what he is saying except that in some way it salves a feeling of inferiority within himself. One boy actually said to me, "I hate Negroes and Puerto Ricans and I'm going to do everything I can to stop them from coming to East Harlem."

A questionnaire was worked out involving four racial and nationality groups: Japanese, Latin American, Slavic, and Italian. There were thirty-five questions about each group. The test gave students a chance to answer questions in one of three ways. 1) A mistake showing an *unfavorable attitude;* 2) a mistake showing a *favorable attitude;* 3) an answer based on *facts.*

The questions themselves followed this pattern:

JAPANESE: Japan does not get along well with China because

———1) The Japanese are deceitful, sly, and crafty.
———2) The Japanese people need raw materials and mar-

kets outside Japan in order to make manufacturing
in Japan profitable.
——3) The Japanese are too trusting and kind.

The tests were given, one at the beginning of the term and
another one at the end, after an intensified campaign had been
carried out to acquaint students with facts concerning each
culture group. The last test showed a marked improvement
in the attitudes of the boys toward other peoples.

Between the two tests we conducted assembly programs in
which lectures were given by prominent people from each culture group, as well as entertainment and exhibitions of art and
music. Dr. Scott Mijakawa spoke on Japan's contribution to
civilization. I introduced the Puerto Rican assemblies where
there were music and dancing by Puerto Rican artists, singing
and dancing by Puerto Rican high-school girls, and education
talks by Dr. Abraham Kroll, who had taught for several years
in Puerto Rico.

Dr. Rachel Davis-Dubois instructed the teachers in classroom work on intercultural relations. I remember her saying,
"Much can be done in the classroom to foster changes in attitudes while enriching the day-by-day routine."

Facts omitted in ordinary textbooks and reading materials
were woven into the regular work. For instance, if a class in
American history was studying the American Revolution, it
seemed appropriate without changing the curriculum for the
teacher to mention that the first person to lose his life in the
struggle for American Independence, Crispus Attucks, was a
Negro; that the man who did most to finance the war, giving
his whole fortune and consequently dying a poor man, was
Haym Solomon—a Jew; that of the important military leaders, Baron Von Steuben was a German, Pulaski and Kosciusz-
cko were Polish, Lafayette, French, and Filippo Mazzei, whose
writings profoundly influenced Jefferson, was an Italian.

We tackled the problem of improving intercultural rela-

tions at Franklin in many ways. Often after assembly, a few
selected students came to my office and had the opportunity
over a cup of tea, of talking to a Japanese actor, or a Jewish
rabbi, or a Negro poet. One Irish lad after shaking hands and
saying a few words to Dr. Mijakawa whispered to me, "Gee,
Pop, he's just like anybody else!"

Just how valuable all this activity was could be argued interminably. It has been said that it sometimes takes fifty years for
an educational idea to take hold and become accepted as an
integral part of school work. I believe that the very essence of
education is a child's knowledge that his neighbor or school-
mate or another child half way around the globe is as good as
he is and has both many similarities and fascinating differences. Though the situation between Italians, Negroes, Puerto
Ricans, and others in East Harlem is far from solved even
today, there was a better understanding among our boys.
When a white boy at Benjamin Franklin heard a recitation of
Countee Cullen's poem in Lee Lombard's English class, he
thought twice before using the word that once came so readily to his lips.

> Once riding in old Baltimore
> Heart-filled, head-filled with glee
> I saw a Baltimorean
> Keep looking straight at me.
>
> Now I was eight and very small
> And he was no whit bigger
> And so I smiled, but he poked out
> His tongue, and called me 'Nigger.'
>
> I saw the whole of Baltimore
> From May until December.
> Of all things that happened there
> That's all that I remember.

A few years ago I was invited to attend a Fourth of July gathering to commemorate the Puerto Rican dead of the Korean

War. The meeting was held at the Eternal Light on 26th Street. There was a huge crowd. When the ceremony was over and I was leaving, I heard someone call, "Pop!" and turned to see a grinning policeman.

It was one of my early Benjamin Franklin students by the name of Charley Matushek, son of Polish immigrants. We talked for a little while. He told me about his family. It was hot and he took off his cap and mopped his forehead. "Boy, these Puerto Ricans get all steamed up! But you know, Pop, I don't feel about them the way some of the other cops do. I remember those lessons at Franklin. I remember myself and my own people. They may look and act and talk differently, but underneath they just got to be the same as anybody else."

24/O

ccasionally, on a Sunday, Rose and I
would take a drive up to Monroe to spend a little time with
my father and Mamma-Nonna. For the rest, I slept six hours
and the remainder of the time I spent at the school.

During the first year of its existence we were mainly concerned with the internal organization. We established an adult
program, an evening school, and an afternoon and evening
recreational program for children and young adults at the
main building. I was kept busy between our main building
and the annex at 79th Street.

The plan for the community program had been worked out
during the summer of 1935 with Harold Fields, who transferred to Franklin and assumed the chairmanship of our Social
Studies Department, and Fred Kuper, who was then law secretary of the Board of Education. Not only in the creation of
the council but in the various educational and community
projects undertaken by our school, Fred Kuper has always
made himself available. I could always count on his advice,
help, and active participation in all our undertakings. He was
born in Russia of Jewish parents and came to America as a
child. He grew up on the lower east side of Manhattan, where
so many outstanding civic, educational, and political leaders
got their start.

The result of our summer conferences was the creation of
the Community Advisory Council of Benjamin Franklin High
School, whose membership consisted of representatives from
civic and social agencies and community leaders from East
Harlem and Yorkville, with Fred Kuper as chairman and
Harold Fields as our Community Coordinator.

In a community such as East Harlem of the thirties, composed primarily of foreign-born parents and American-born
children, the most critical period in the life of the family was,
we felt, that in which the children reach and live through
adolescence. It is the age when the so-called American idea
of "living one's own life" begins to clash with the European
idea of family solidarity, of obedience and respect for elders,
and of subservience to family needs and requirements.

The real educational problem among the Italians and Jews
of yesterday and the Puerto Ricans of today lies in the emo-
tional conflicts that are particularly tormenting to the boy
whose parents are deeply oriented by centuries of foreign
tradition and custom. The feeling of scorn and shame that
builds in these children because of the pressure of adverse
opinion from outside often produces antisocial attitudes dangerous to the boy and to the community—in short, the delinquent.

There was no denying the fact that outside the school there
were vital, powerful, and compelling forces constantly edu-
cating the boys and girls of the community in spite of, or contrary to, the school ideal. On one side the community's motion-
picture houses, its dance halls, its streets, its gangs, and on the
other its churches, its community houses, its welfare agencies,
its law-enforcement agencies—these could either promote or
destroy the work of the school. And the school itself had to
be both leader and coordinating agency, to a certain extent
the pivot upon which much even of the social and civic life
would turn.

Almost immediately the council in cooperation with the

Works Progress Administration set up an afternoon community playground from three-thirty until six P.M. for the children of the neighborhood. Next, an evening community center for adults, open from seven-thirty to ten P.M., was established, in an effort to place all the facilities of the school at the service of its neighbors. We also had an evening center for teenagers. All this was in addition to our regular evening elementary-school classes.

Every Wednesday night I was available in my office in the main building to anyone who wanted to see me for any purpose whatever. We called this Wednesday Night Principal's Conference, but almost always there were other teachers present besides me. When we were not discussing school problems among ourselves, we interviewed parents and people of the community who sought our advice on everything from citizenship to childbirth.

It might be an Irish mother whose son had a fine voice, trying to find a way to further his musical education. Or an Italian woman with a black shawl tied over her head looking for her son who had not been home for a week. Or a father wanting his son to quit school, to go to work in his grocery store or shoe shop, and questioning our moral right to hold him there. Or a Puerto Rican couple with three children having difficulty with their landlord. Or a Jewish storekeeper complaining about the pranks played upon him by some of our boys.

We heard them all, talked to them in the language they understood, helped them when we could, referred them to the proper social agency, or just listened with an ache inside when we could do nothing at all.

Lunch period at the school also became a work period while I munched a sandwich and discussed with colleagues the problems of individual boys.

"You will get ulcers," Rose admonished. "No man can eat the way you do and stay healthy."

I laughed at her fears. When a man is happy in his work, a chunk of bread, an olive, and a piece of cheese sustain him.

Always we were interested in the individual boy—the non-conformist who would vent his resentment by refusing to follow school regulations—repeated absence, cutting classes, tardiness, disrupting school work, and generally driving the teacher to distraction. In the majority of these cases the primitive measures of correction only increased resentment and rebellion. The boy was made to feel an outcast. He was upbraided before his fellow students, suspended from school for a few weeks, even expelled. The problem student more than ever felt himself apart from the rest of society, thrust out, vilified, condemned. Even worse, he felt that "they" had given up on him.

Nothing that lives and breathes can be successfully handled in this way. The adolescent who has difficulties and in whom rebellion stirs must be drawn closer to those who would help him. He needs and wants understanding. The teacher must learn how to listen with his heart.

The Wednesday night "open house" sessions in my office at the old building at Franklin came closest to fulfilling my dream of the school as an integral part of the community. Throughout the building, classes were in progress. I could sit in my office and listen happily to the hum of knowledge. Young men and adults who for one reason or another had been unable to graduate from day school were now completing their high-school education at night. In other rooms immigrants of varying ages and nationalities struggled with the complexities of the English language, sometimes taught by their own sons, while still others prepared for citizenship tests. In the gymnasium a basketball game was in progress, as often as not involving two Jews, two Italians, three Negroes, two Puerto Ricans, and a fellow named O'Reilly. In the library, the Parent–Teachers Association was holding a meeting, while from the auditorium might come the shrill sounds of an argument that meant that the Community Advisory Council was in session.

One night I invited an older student and his girl to have coffee with me after the usual conferences were over. On such occasions I was host, serving coffee and the cookies Rose always baked for me. This particular boy was a barrel-chested Italian by the name of Lupino, who in his early school career had caused the dean and teachers a great deal of trouble by fighting in the corridors and disrupting his classes. When he felt like it, he would get up and walk out of the classroom and return at his convenience. He was so rugged and powerfully built that few dared provoke him. Finally, after repeated trips to the dean's office, the dean brought him to me with a note from his teacher. "This trouble-maker is more than I can stand. I do not want him in my class."

I had talked with Lupino before. Underneath the characteristic sulking and resentful attitude of a boy in trouble, something else struggled for release. There was a feeling of life that was irrepressible and would not be chained. After letting him sit in a corner of the office for a while, I finally looked up from my desk and said, "All right. What is it this time?"

"You know. You got the report."

"I want you to tell me."

"That English teacher! She hates my guts. It seems everybody in this place hates my guts!"

"Just a minute," I said. "Come over here next to the desk. Don't shout. When you shout I can't hear anything. Now then, in a low voice, what were you saying?"

Lupino shrugged. "What's the use? When something goes wrong I'm right there to get the blame. Know what I mean?"

"You mean you were born unlucky?"

"That's me all right. You can say that again."

"And you can say that this time your bad luck carried you

right out of school because that is what the dean wants and
that is what your teacher wants. And, unless I'm very much
mistaken, that's what you want."

Lupino shook his head vigorously. This was not what he
wanted at all. He wanted to finish high school. Even if it
killed him there had to be one member of his family who
graduated. It was just that he was unlucky.

I had often come upon this particular contradiction. I
turned in my swivel chair. "I know how it is," I said to him.
"You know what you want inside, only somehow you act
just the opposite. Your mind gets away from you. Before you
know it you've forgotten what the teacher is talking about.
And when she catches you, you get mad. But you're not really
mad at the teacher, you're mad at yourself."

Lupino considered a moment. "It certainly looks like I'm
in a mess," he said.

"You certainly are. And at your age it's the kind of mess
that will wind you up in jail. But why should you worry? It's
what everyone expects. Your teachers. The dean. You yourself, for that matter. It would not surprise anybody, probably
not even your mother and father. Another East Harlem kid
going wrong."

Lupino dug his hands into his pockets. He tried to say something and then his lips clamped together.

"This time I haven't any choice, I've got to expel you. How
can I run a school like this? How can anyone who wants to
learn make any headway with you in the class?"

With almost superhuman effort to put down his pride,
Lupino said, "Please, Pop, I've got to finish high school."

I was in a spot. I would have to appease the dean and the
teacher. If he made more trouble it would be on my neck and
I told him so. Besides his mother and father were Italian, and
it would look as though I were making an exception.

"I promise," Lupino begged. "This time I give you my

word of honor I won't let you down, Pop. I promise on the
soul of my dead grandmother!"

I thought awhile. Then I said, "I don't know. Let me think
about it. Go home and come back tomorrow morning."

The dean proved to be no particular problem. Though
often severe in his punishment, he had a basic instinct for handling boys and knew his job. The teacher, however, was another matter. She was young, new to East Harlem, and could
not wait to be reassigned to a school in a better neighborhood.
I knew it without her telling me. She had been raised in Pel-
ham, a peaceful suburb of New York, and this was her first
regular job. While by sheer strength of character she could
hold a class of my East Harlem boys together, Lupino was
too much for her. After a few moments in my office, she broke
down and started to cry. "It's as if he ridicules me. He's utterly
contemptuous of everything I say. There in class I'm always
conscious of his presence, like some animal ready to pounce on
me. I've never handled such a student. Tell me, Mr. Covello,
how do you do it?"

Her appeal was almost pathetic, as if I had some magic
formula I could give her. "I don't know," I said. "It's easier
for me, I guess, because I was raised the same way and have
lived all my life in the same neighborhood. But then there are
other women teachers who come from other parts of the city
who understand the boys too. I don't know what it is, exactly.
I do know, however, that if you convince yourself deep down
that these boys, Lupino included, are basically not much different from others you have known, and that they would
like to be liked by you, then most of your troubles will be
over."

As for Lupino, I told her not to concern herself about him.
"If he disturbs you or the class in the least way, just let me
know. He'll be out of here that very day. But let's give him
another chance. I know we can straighten him out." After she

had gone, I sent for Lupino and made him write out a statement to the effect that at the very first adverse report he would voluntarily expel himself from school.

Lupino kept his word. He graduated a few years later. I never had cause to regret what I had done for him. Nor had his teachers, for that matter.

One night Lupino came to present me to his girl, Dolly, who lived on the same block and whom he had known most of his life. He told me he was working in a garage. "I like fooling around cars. In a couple of years when I've got some money saved, we'll get married, Dolly and me. Then I'll save some more and pick up a gas station and repair service someplace. That's what we got figured out." He patted the girl's hand and smiled. "How's that strike you, Pop? How's that for old Lupino who you thought was headed for the clink?"

Lupino's conversation touched on the neighborhood problems. "Boy, these kids today. I'm telling you, Pop. I saw a bunch of them just yesterday, breaking bottles and emptying garbage cans on the street. I said, 'Hey, whatsamatter with you guys? You got sawdust for brains or something? Even a bird don't foul its own nest.' "

After we had finished the coffee, Dolly rose to gather the cups and saucers and bring them to the washstand in a corner behind a screen. I made her sit down. "Oh, no," I said. "You are a guest here. He'll wash the dishes," pointing to Lupino.

Lupino bellowed like a bull.

"What's the matter with you, Pop? You wanna spoil my wife before I even get married?"

"Wash the dishes. It'll do you good. At home I help my wife. It's about time you started to learn."

I will always remember that hulk of a boy named Lupino— Lupino, the terror of 108th Street, who could probably lick any two boys in the school put together. He was not a student every teacher would be proud of. He would never set the world on fire and the school would never inscribe his name on its honor roll. At best he would own a garage and raise a family, that's all. But when he picked up those dishes and said to his girl, "This Pop Covello, he sure is one for the book!" I knew all over again why it was that I was a school teacher.

25/At Franklin we had constantly to be on
the alert against those who wanted to lower academic standards.
It was amazing how many people clung to the notion that because a school was located in an economically and socially depressed area, its academic standards should be practically
ignored, if not eliminated.

We were determined to use all our resources to meet city
and state requirements for graduation, including state Regents'
Examinations for the academic diploma. In fact, a survey based
on a questionnaire done by the mathematics department
showed that many of our students wanted to feel they could
continue on to college and would not have voluntarily accepted
a modified course. The idea of a "watered-down" curriculum,
insisted upon for this type of community in so many quarters,
was rejected by the pupils themselves.

Countless personal interviews proved to me that the desire
to achieve had nothing to do with where a person was born
or how he lived. Our job and our responsibility was to help
our boys to the achievements they themselves desired. If there
was a retardation in reading, the answer was simple. Provide
remedial teachers. If students were deficient in mathematics
and still wanted a college education or an academic diploma,

it was up to us to furnish the remedial instruction to overcome this handicap.

Never in all my years of teaching have I said to a boy, "You can't do it." Who is there who can pretend to know the hidden capacities of another human being? I believe that more than often it is lack of faith on the part of adults which mars and even destroys the hopes of young people. Some of the boys, it is true, are not cut out for academic work. But the best thing for them is if they find it out themselves, in sympathetic surroundings.

Joey Waldman was by no means a physically attractive boy. Along with a slight limp he had a speech defect, which made him shy away from other boys. Nor did he even draw the attention of sympathy of his fellow students. They simply were polite to him and left him alone. Puzzled by the fact that he was always by himself, I engaged him one day in conversation. He seemed perfectly contented in his loneliness and had no desire to join activities of others. He was an ordinary student, in fact, a little backward. But he had one overwhelming ambition—to become a pharmacist.

I was surprised. "But your marks are too low. You'll never be accepted," I said. "What's the trouble?"

"I don't know," Joey said. "I study hard. The teachers go too fast for me. I go home and I struggle with the books until it almost drives me crazy. But somehow or other, I've got to make it."

I could not abandon Joey, erase him from my mind, even though it seemed impossible that he could meet the necessary requirements to be accepted in the school of pharmacy. I spoke to his teachers. They agreed to give him extra help. I also had him assigned to the WPA remedial-reading class. We helped him in every way possible until he eventually achieved his goal. Some would say, "He just wasn't cut out for it." I would answer, "But he wanted it enough."

At Franklin, in addition to meeting the academic requirements, we believed we had to prepare our students for the very serious business of living and sharing in the responsibilities of society.

In the English Department, Austin Works channeled literature in the direction of books that gave the pupil a realistic picture of the world he lived in, as well as what was expected of him in return. Along with Shakespeare and Milton and Scott, the student was given writers such as Upton Sinclair, Lincoln Steffens, and Ida Tarbell, who dealt with contemporary social problems.

Social-study classes stressed the theme "Know Your Community!"

The Art Department worked out a huge map of East Harlem, carefully outlining individual blocks. From this original which hung in my office duplicates of a smaller size were printed and distributed to the various departments of the school and civic organizations of the neighborhood, to be used for their own purposes.

Slowly, on the master map, we began to accumulate information which, in turn, was fed out to the smaller maps. Before anything else, we wanted to know where our students lived. In varying colors to indicate nationality, we spotted them on the map and were astonished to find distributions and concentrations of population never before realized. As part of their social-studies experience, the boys took to the streets after hours with pencil and paper to gather statistical information about their neighborhood which the Art Department, in terms of symbols, transferred to the master map.

The map showed that in East Harlem there were forty-one churches and missions, twenty-two political clubs, nine labor organizations, five hundred and six candy stores, two hundred sixty-two barber shops. There were twenty-eight liquor stores, one hundred fifty-six bars, twenty-six junk shops, six hundred eighty-five grocers, three hundred seventy-eight restaurants, two hundred thirty-two tailors, and sixty-three radio repair shops, as well as two hundred ninety-seven doctors, seventy-four dentists, one hundred and two furniture stores, and fourteen loan offices. Hungrily our map devoured these statistics. With all the different markers in it, it began to look like a pin cushion.

While many of the things we discovered we already knew, it was both significant and depressing, both to the students and to us as teachers, to realize that a community which could support forty-one religious institutions and twenty-two political clubs and one hundred fifty-six bars could boast only a few open playgrounds for its children, three public halls, and no neighborhood newspaper at all. The analysis of all this research was directed by Alexander Stevens, a sociologist and former captain in the Russian Army during the First World War. He and several WPA workers were assigned to the job.

At this time we had already started our campaign for a housing project in East Harlem and a new building for our school. But the leg work of our students showed that it was one thing to talk about modern housing projects such as those being launched in other parts of the city but another to overcome the many problems involved. The idea of compact units with thousands of families living in comfortable apartments, each with independent toilet and bath, was wonderful to contemplate and fight for. But what happened to the dozens of little merchants in each block who would be dispossessed? Was no one to consider the five hundred and six candy-store owners, the six hundred eighty-five grocers, the two hundred sixty-two barbers, most of whom had never known a home outside of East Harlem? Where would they go and what would they do when the wrecking crews came in to wipe out six square blocks to make way for the new housing projects? Where would the students wander off to when the candy store on the corner gave way to the red brick of an apartment house?

We had a lot to learn before we achieved the millennium.

Meanwhile the need for more room outside of the school building which we could use particularly over weekends for meetings and special classes became pressing. After a meeting of the Community Advisory Council one night, one of the PTA members, Mrs. Anna Russo, who lived next door to the school, came to my office. "We have a wonderful idea, Mr. Covello. All the empty stores in the block! Why couldn't we get some of these old stores, clean them up and fix them over, and use them like classrooms?"

"That's an extraordinary idea," I exclaimed, "if it's possible."

"You just leave everything to us," Mrs. Russo said. "We'll find out how it can be done."

This was the beginning of our unique "store fronts" or "street units" as we called them.

The owner of the building next to the school was willing to give us the use of a store, rent free for the first year. I inspected the store with Mrs. Russo. It was dirty beyond imagining and hopelessly in need of repair. My natural inclination was to turn aside from the unpleasant task of making it serviceable—postpone action. A few days later, Mrs. Russo returned, saying that the landlord now was willing to give us the use of the adjoining stores and that he would also permit the removal of the partition between the two.

These stores were even dirtier than the first. Though the space was now adequate, I still avoided making a commitment. I continued to inspect the premises with Mrs. Russo and some other PTA mothers. A crowd began to join us from the street. "Hey, Pop, what goes on?" one of the men from a plumbing shop asked.

"We're trying to figure out if we could clean up this mess and make a neighborhood meeting place," I said. "It looks hopeless."

"Ain't nuthing hopeless, Pop. You know that better'n any of us."

Several men offered to tear down the partition and do the plastering. The janitor of the building said he'd keep the place clean when the work was done. The women promised to take care of the furnishings and decoration. Everyone seemed anxious to have the club and eager to get started. "All right," I said. "Today is Tuesday. Saturday morning we will begin."

I returned to my office at the school, lingering doubts still in my mind. At lunch time I told my colleagues, Dr. Guerra and Mike Decessare about the arrangements. Both were as skeptical as I with regard to the work getting done.

It was May. Saturday was hot and humid. Of the men who had offered their services, only one showed up, and he did not have any tools. I managed to borrow a hammer and a piece of pipe that could be used for a crowbar and we started to hack away at the partition. As we sweated, the usual crowd began to gather in the doorway. Mrs. Russo and the women appeared. They began to upbraid the idlers.

"Aren't you ashamed, just standing there?"

"You'll be the first to use this club after everybody else has done the work."

Sheepishly the men began to grin. A few of them moved inside. One of them took the piece of pipe from my hands. "This ain't work for you, Professor. You got brains to operate with. Here, let me have that thing."

The spirit caught on. Work gathered momentum. People mysteriously appeared from all over the neighborhood. When some of the students offered to lend a hand they were shooed away to their Saturday games and activities. I was thrust aside, given the dubious, strictly honorary title of "supervisor," while the artisans of the neighborhood took over.

The assistant to the janitor scraped away all the dirty wallpaper and washed the walls clean. The Jefferson Post of the American Legion sent men to replace the broken sink and patch up plaster. Women of the PTA donated the money with which to buy paint. Though the work was well in progress, there were those who doubted that the club would ever amount to anything. Even when the Works Progress Administration furnished us a social director in the person of a stately, blue-eyed woman from Georgia by the name of Mary Carter Winter, some still argued that she would be sitting inside the store all day long, reading a newspaper and watching the crowds go by.

The painting was not quite finished. There were loose boards in the floor to be repaired, furniture to be acquired, curtains to be hung, a hundred-and-one details before an official opening. Yet, whenever Mrs. Winter entered the store for one reason or another, children trooped in at her heels and stood around waiting for something to happen. Mrs. Winter began to talk to them of books and tell them stories while she sat on a wooden box and they gathered around her on the floor. Before anyone realized it she was running an open house for the children of the block.

Women donated odds and ends of furniture. Mrs. Redmond, chairman of our Music Department, contributed a piano, a large mirror, and some chairs and tables. Some of this furniture needed paint to freshen it up, and a group of the high-school boys insisted that this would be their contribution. They were working at this task one evening when I happened by. All the boys were fond of Mrs. Winter, but a few of them thought her a trifle simple-minded with respect to the ways of a city jungle like East Harlem. Unobserved for the moment, I listened to a lad of seventeen give her advice as he put a few finishing strokes of paint to a chair. "You don't know it, ma'am, but you got guys in here who don't belong in here."

"I don't understand what you mean," Mrs. Winter answered. "This is going to be a club for friends and neighbors. You must not talk about friends and neighbors in this manner."

"That's right," a younger boy said indignantly, "who don't belong in here!"

The boy who was painting smiled cynically. "I know what

I'm talking about and you don't. Right here you've got guys who will steal things—grab stuff that don't belong to them. I know, because I'm one of them. And there's that one. And that. And that," singling out three others standing around.

Mrs. Winter was silent. The boys now all looked at her, intent, an interesting study, ready to deny direct accusation, waiting to be attacked individually and, at the same time, trying to appear indifferent about the club. Mrs. Winter turned once more to the youth with the paint brush. "Now we know how things stand. All you have to do is watch each other. You will have to watch each other because I won't have the time. Nor will anyone else, for that matter."

Such was the beginning of the Friends and Neighbors Club.

In the seven years of its existence, of the countless articles contributed to the club, rarely was anything damaged or stolen.

We soon discovered that people who would never dream of going near the school, feeling self-conscious, would make use of the facilities of the store fronts—making us further realize the need for small social and educational centers scattered around a neighborhood to supplement the work of the main building in community education. There were several workmen in the neighborhood who liked to sing. They would not think of setting foot in the school building, but Mrs. Redmond got them to organize a singing group and twice a week they never failed to be with us.

Soon after, out of another vacant store we made a library. One of the retired old men of the neighborhood took over the job of librarian. There were books for young and old in three languages, Italian, Spanish, and English, donated by our many friends. The library was followed by another unit for the Franklin Alumni Association, another for the Italian Educational Bureau which I had transferred from Columbia, and still another for the beginning of our work among Puerto Ricans.

During the period from 1936 to 1942, before the school moved to its new location on the East River Drive, we had five separate street units in operation, all maintained—with the exception of a very few salaried personnel—by independent funds raised through special drives and campaigns, dances, dinners, and social functions.

The New York Times sent Benjamin Fine, its education writer, to do a story on our plan of carrying education and the school into the empty stores of the neighborhood. The article showed pictures of some of the last units in the process of renovation. "Actually, a true 'school and community' project has been developed," the text read. "Educational theories have been put into practice. Each afternoon from five to six o'clock is set aside for the 'children's hour.' A dozen or more youngsters, up to eight years of age, come in regularly and listen as Mrs. Mary Carter Winter of the club relates the adventures of Cinderella or the tales of the early Dutch settlers. Then a rhythm band enters the room; boys and girls in their early teens receive instruction in Mozart or Shubert. Instruments are lent by the school. A fife and drum corps is a regular visitor. The Ladies International Garment Workers Union made uniforms for the youngsters.

" 'Instead of hanging around the street corners with nothing to do, these little fellows come in and play in the band,' Mrs. Winter related. 'You can see a spiritual quality in some of the thin, ragamuffin boys—their eyes get so big and shine so bright!' "

Very early in the history of Franklin, I tried to carry out a policy that under no circumstances was a boy to be expelled or drop out of school for any reason without an interview with me. Wherever possible, no student was to look back upon this period of his life with resentment toward the school or any of his teachers. The last impression was important—a moment of kindness, a few well chosen words, a bit of laughter, an arm about a shoulder, the bitterness and disillusionment melted at least in part.

But what became of the students who for one reason or another had been forced to leave school? Except in rare instances, nobody knew and nobody seemed to care. We had to make some attempt to keep them close to us and the school, to guide and encourage them, for these more than the others were the boys who were apt to get lost in life's struggle.

There was Tulio Cellano, a handsome lad possessed of an even more attractive mother, who concerned herself in every way with his future and well being. Unfortunately, Tulio had what almost amounted to a genius for misconduct. He could not stay an hour in a classroom without picking a fight with some companion, annoying the teacher, or generally misbehaving in a dozen different ways. Having talked repeatedly to his mother and threatened him with expulsion several times, I finally had to lay down the law. "You're through, Tulio," I said. "Get out of here and don't ever let me see you in this school again."

I had had all I could stand of Tulio Cellano. I had never been so abrupt with a boy before. And yet, next morning, as I came out of the door of my home at 116th Street and Third Avenue, a few blocks from the school, there he was standing across the street waiting for me. Without saying a word he took my heavy briefcase from my hand and walked along at my side. He walked with me right into the school and into my office, set the briefcase down and went off. Never once did he open his mouth. This little act repeated itself every morning for nearly a week. Tulio would take my briefcase, walk with me into the school and then leave. It began to get on my nerves. "What am I going to do with him?" I said to Rose.

"Give him another chance."

"I can't. I can't afford to take the risk. He's too unreliable."

I tried to be firm. I wanted to tell Tulio not to wait for me every morning, that I was perfectly capable of carrying my own briefcase. I couldn't do it. It was no use. Finally I called in his mother again and the three of us sat down and talked out the problem. Tulio returned to school, settled down, and was able to graduate with his class.

But there were the others who never came back. . . .

We worked out a plan, together with Mary Giacobbe, Annita's younger sister. A list of all the boys who had dropped out of Franklin during the three years of its existence was compiled, and a letter signed by me was sent to each one of them at the last address in our records. In the letter we explained that although they had dropped out of school, we were still interested in what they were doing. We invited them to join us, their teachers, at a meeting to form a club which we would call the "Old Friendship Club."

Many of the teachers felt that these boys would not wish to return to the school. I did not believe it. From my own experience and knowledge of boys I felt certain that many of them would be happy to come. Mary Giacobbe felt the same way. The students were to reply by return post card. I told my secretary to be sure to pull out these cards from the mail pile the moment it came in. Never in our most optimistic moments did we expect the enthusiastic response we received.

The answers were many and varied. One boy who signed himself "Your old friend," wrote, "A million thanks for your kind invitation. It will be an honor to attend." Another by the name of George Leblanc wrote that he would very much like to attend but unfortunately was recovering from a serious illness at Fordham Hospital. I called the hospital, hoping that it would be possible for us to drive him to the reunion and then bring him back again. I discovered that it was a bad case of tuberculosis. George Leblanc would never attend a school reunion of any kind. There were dozens of similar letters, as well as letters from parents thanking us for our interest in their sons. And the replies reflected a cross section of all the nationalities represented at Franklin.

The reunion was a success, made so by the gratefulness of the boys. Not only had a special entertainment program been prepared for them, but a great many teachers and heads of departments were there to talk and spend an evening with them. It was curious to see how eager they were to discuss their work and their experiences and their hopes for the future. At the end we sang the school song.

26/Often

people ask me if I ever got bored
with teaching, or tired of the boys in my school. In return I
ask them if they get bored with their own children or tired of
the people they love. I am reminded of the story Dr. Albert
Schweitzer tells of the old Moslem who was forever reading
the Koran. Taunted by some young men who asked, "Don't
you get sick of always reading the same thing?" he replied,
"For me it is by no means the same Koran. When I was a boy,
I understood it as a boy. When I was a man in my prime, I
understood it as a man, and now that I am old, I understand it
as an old man. I read it again and again because for me it always
contains something new."

My pupils have always been a source of wonder and delight
to me. At the varying stages of my life, I have loved and
sought to understand them, finding in each face the suggestion
and spark of something different and new. But, above all,
what has never failed to amaze me is the tremendous latent
talents and capabilities of adolescents, which very few people
will accept or recognize but which readily come to the surface
when given only half a chance.

Take the world of art, for instance. In too many city schools
in those days, the art work produced by students used to
depict a woodland scene, a landscape, or a seascape. Art, like

poetry, was treated as something apart from the reality of daily living. We tried to get away from this at Franklin. There, art study tied in closely with our concern with the community. What many of the boys produced, as an expression of themselves, reflected their thoughts and ideas about the daily business of living in East Harlem.

Instead of a waterfall with a mill, a painting would show a mud-colored brick tenement with ugly fire escapes and laundry hanging on the roof; but on the front stoop, men in shirtsleeves caught a moment of sunlight. Instead of the surf and rockbound coast of Maine, a charcoal sketch showed a dock on the East River and tugboats and kids swimming. It was vital art, and alive. In the midst of squalor it spoke the yearning for a better life.

The walls of our old building were not decorated with reproductions of old masterpieces. We hung the best work of our students. It made them proud and gave them an incentive to do better.

Twenty years later I received a telephone call from Morris Schwartz, one of the boys who had worked on a series of murals for the school depicting the growth of American democracy. He had become a competent lithographer. As a present, he brought me an example of his work, a moving drawing of a fine old synagogue amid the tumble-down tenements of East Harlem. "One of my early things," he said. "I think you'll like it because it shows the Franklin influence. It shows that I learned that in art you must always keep your eyes open. You must try to see the world around you as it really is and not just put down the sugar and honey."

Participation of students in committee conferences about important civic, social, and education problems was encouraged. They took their places along with parents, teachers, and representatives of city-government and social-welfare agencies as part of the Franklin Community Advisory Council.

In connection with student activities, Austin Works organized a special class for English seniors who had passed their four years' Regents in English and showed unusual qualities for leadership. The title of this special course was "American Social Problems in the Light of American Literature." Its aim was to acquaint students with the thoughts and attitudes of outstanding American authors on the current problems of American democracy. Class work, individual and group work, was based on reading from specific lists of books written by American novelists who dealt with problems of social justice, the slums, the melting pot, war and peace, religion, and individualism versus social control.

Each student was required to select a problem and follow it through. The group studying the problems of the slums was expected to make a personal investigation of actual slum conditions. The group studying problems of the "melting pot" had to ascertain through actual observation and personal investigation the difficulties presented in the adjustment of racial differences and animosities.

Each student had to turn in a midterm theme and a final term theme showing his personal reaction to the problem studied. These individual themes were something personal—essays, possibly stories, even verse, showing by the student's reactions to external stimuli what went on deep inside of him.

I have still in my possession one such theme given to me as a gift. It is a story in photographs done by a student named Hans Geissler. I remember him as a shy, blond lad always coming to class with a camera dangling from his shoulder. The photographs, bound into a book, show on the cover a Negro and a white man seated together in front of a fire made out of a few pieces of cardboard, trying to warm themselves, while the wretchedness of the slums spreads all around them. Inside the cover, Hans wrote "In view of the fact that unemployment and slums seem to be the greatest problems of the common people, I have selected these topics for my report. In preparation I did a great deal of field work, but instead of relying on my memory to describe what I saw, I took pictures, which are far more convincing than anything I can say."

About the cover illustration itself he reported, "These two men earn their bare living by selling paper cartons which they pick up from refuse thrown out by grocery stores. It was a cold Sunday morning when this photograph was taken. The dying fire may well illustrate their dying souls, but do not let it be thought that they have given up all hope or ambition. What little work they have to do they do well. They can be found at this spot every afternoon sorting their cardboard to take to the paper mill."

The last photograph is a closeup—a portrait of a man's head. The mouth is firm, hard. The eyes sullen. The brow furrowed, as if the brain reaches for a balance between fury and despair. "The forgotten man—the refuse of the depression," wrote Hans. "His problems are our problems, because if we do not help him solve his, ours will never be solved."

I do not know what became of you, Hans Geissler, whether or not you fulfilled your ambition as a photographer or whatever else you may have decided to become. No matter. Even as a boy you fulfilled yourself as a human being. Life could not harm you.

This social awareness and vitality of students at Franklin, working in conjunction with the adults of the Community Advisory Council, culminated in two important community projects which were carried on simultaneously. They were new housing for the people of East Harlem and a new school building for our students. We coined the slogan "A New School in a New Community."

Low-cost housing projects financed by Federal funds were beginning to appear in the city; but pressure for such projects was great and in order to obtain them it was necessary to secure coordinated community action.

We started with showing our students housing exhibits—

old and new concepts of housing reproduced with the aid of models, graphs, charts, and photographs. One of the models on display depicted a building common in the neighborhood and had a removable roof, making possible interior as well as exterior views. The largest model, weighing nearly a ton, represented a ten-block area. Several of the models showed what housing could be like in areas where it was feasible to have garden apartments, something most of the boys had never even seen.

An original panel of photographs was worked out by students in the Art Department who were allowed to develop their own ideas about living quarters. Other panels depicting interiors were loaned by the Museum of the City of New York and were electrically lighted to produce realistic effects.

The exhibition was open to everyone. Parents mingled with teachers, social workers, civic leaders. It resulted in the heightening of the interest of our boys in a very specific and practical community project—housing. And it showed them that they need not be helpless spectators but could become active participants.

But the East Harlem housing project faced another problem. That was the movement of speculators to grab up the river frontage for the purpose of erecting expensive apartment dwellings like Tudor City and others to the south. Our committees had to act fast. Delay might mean loss of the beautiful East River Drive which was in the process of construction. To permit this would have been an injustice to the people of the community. It would have meant the creation of a "Gold Coast" along the river and a further deterioration in "backyard tenement areas" between the East River and Fifth Avenue. This danger quickened everyone's interest in housing matters.

We organized mass meetings, held parades through the streets of East Harlem, distributed leaflets calling for the help of every man, woman, and child in our efforts to obtain better housing for our people. We circulated hundreds of petitions addressed to the Mayor and the New York City Housing Authority.

> We, the undersigned tenants of East Harlem, living in one of the worst slum areas in the city, urge you to allocate funds for a low-cost housing project.

Thousands of signatures were affixed to these petitions.

The Harlem Legislative Council, with Congressman Marcantonio as chairman, appointed an East Harlem Housing Committee, which joined forces with the Community Advisory Council of Franklin. Meetings were held every Monday night at the Friends and Neighbors Club in the store unit adjacent to the school, under the direction of two of our teachers, Clarice Smith and Sadie Jacobi. By the time the housing project was completed, Sadie Jacobi had in her possession a record of seventy-three such meetings.

Federal aid on the housing project was approved, and in 1939 we held a victory parade and mass meeting in East Harlem. A news account read:

> Residents of East Harlem celebrated the allocation of funds for a new $7,390,000 low-rent housing project which is being planned between 102d and 105th Street, east of First Avenue to the East River Drive. Under the auspices of the East Harlem Housing Committee, hundreds paraded from the Benjamin Franklin High School last Sunday afternoon. . . .

It is all very fine to preach sermons and make speeches about the brotherhood of man, but more important and effective is the work that different peoples actually do together, regardless of color or national origin, to achieve a common purpose.

The campaign for new housing in East Harlem had been realized. Now we would work together for our other objective—the new school for the new community.

27 / About this time, 1938 to be exact, an incident occurred at Park Avenue and 107th Street which the newspapers transformed into the kind of sensationalism which has always been the curse of underprivileged communities. A group of Italian and Puerto Rican boys got mixed up in a block fight. A few heads were cut by flying tin cans, some eyes were blackened, and then the patrol cars, sirens screaming, pulled up. Next morning a New York daily found an amazing parallel between this street battle and old murderous gangs known as the Hudson Dusters, the Whyos, and the Dead Rabbits. This particular newspaper, after heading its piece "New York's Sorest Spot," commented, "The section for the most part is sunk deep in squalor. It is not safe for a well-dressed man to walk at night. It leads the rest of the city in dope addiction, sluggings, stabbings, holdups, and prostitution. Thousands of persons, most of them unfortunate but many of them vicious, live in the rows of dilapidated houses which are unfit for human habitation. . . ."

In the days which followed, other minor street incidents occurred, probably triggered by the publicity given to the first episode. However, it was an exaggeration to attribute them to pathological and criminal aspects of the neighborhood. They represented, rather, "frontier clashes" in a community where a new incoming group met the opposition of an older and more established group. Such conflicts were far from new in the history of New York City, or in the history of the nation, for that matter.

The question of harmonious living between diverse groups was, and still is, one of the major problems with which the city of New York is confronted. The terrible truth is that the press adds to this problem by a tendency to magnify the unsavory side of slum areas, at the same time doing positive injury to the morale of the community.

As guardian of community prestige, the school had to take a stand. I wrote a long letter to the paper that had editorialized on East Harlem, trying to present an accurate picture of conditions there, making a plea for understanding of our problems and the work we were trying to do to improve conditions.

> As you may know, we have about thirty-four different racial and nationality strains in this single community. There are many problems connected with the life of the community that require sympathetic and intelligent handling. . . . I am firmly convinced that the solution does not lie in blanket condemnations of foreign-born communities or in the application of police force to periodic outbreaks of violence caused by conditions that are not understood by the general public. . . .

To get a more accurate picture of the situation and fearing that all the publicity might give rise to greater violence, I spent several evenings driving around East Harlem with two of my students, talking to groups on street corners. One of the boys with me was Joe Monserrat, a slender, fine-featured Puerto Rican with curly black hair, now director of the New York Office of the Migration Division of the Department of Labor for the Commonwealth of Puerto Rico. My American representative was Texas-born Bob Streeter, whose parents somehow came to live in East Harlem. He was a big, good-natured youth who loved to talk and got along with everyone. The boys called him "the Senator."

We would just stop and talk to people, regardless of color or nationality, telling them that we were from Benjamin Franklin High School and interested to know why people in the same neighborhood couldn't live peacefully together. I would talk in Italian, Joe Monserrat in Spanish, and "the Senator" in English. Mostly, people shrugged their shoulders. "Do you believe everything you read?" they said, looking at us as though we were a little simple-minded.

Occasionally we did encounter resentment. Usually it was from the Italians, and I would take over. One group of younger Italian workmen argued against the Puerto Ricans coming into the neighborhood and working for less wages. "They're not like us. We're American. We eat meat at least three times a week. What do they eat? Beans! So they work for beans. That's why we have trouble here."

I asked them, "What do you think your parents ate when they came to America? You don't want to remember. I was there. *Pasta e fasul*," I said. "Beans and macaroni—and don't forget it. Don't forget that other people used to say the same things about your mothers and fathers that you now say about the Puerto Ricans."

When you can strike home with the truth, it does not take much to make men stop and think again. I argued for solidarity, for the necessity of all people sticking together in the fight for a better life. At the end of what had started as a hot discussion, they smiled and shook hands with us all. "Anyway," one of them said, ending it on a macabre note, "when we get stuck with a knife, we all bleed in the same way."

We organized a "good will" demonstration which was held at the Odd Fellows Temple on 106th Street and Park Avenue. Better than two thousand persons attended. Both Italian and Puerto Rican leaders spoke in English and Italian and Spanish, urging cooperation and understanding and friendship for the sake of the community as a whole. The school was represented by Joe Monserrat, Elmer Glaser, and "the Senator," all of whom gave the viewpoint of the student on racial equality.

Speakers were cheered until the crowd went hoarse. When the meeting broke up, people went off with changing attitudes, arguing the points in question, drawn closer to each other.

There is an incident I must tell, however, in connection with the racial unrest of this period. It happened only a few days after the mass meeting. While walking to school I was stopped by a student, Jesus Morales, who had graduated just the term before. He was Puerto Rican, but he could have been Italian or Jewish or almost anything at all. "I was at that meeting, Pop," Morales explained. "I believe everything those guys said there. A man should never be ashamed of his nationality, but I can't help it. I gotta change my name."

Here was the name-changing routine all over again. How many times had I heard it during the course of my life! Each succeeding wave of immigrants seeking to lose their identity, seeking to lose themselves in a nothingness, a characterless void in which one human being was exactly like the other. I sometimes wonder why a law was not passed for such people so they could all legally assume the name of John Smith the moment they entered the country.

Morales told me about the jobs he thought he had lost because of his Puerto Rican origin. But he was never really quite sure until he applied for work in an office. It was a good job and the office manager was about to hire him until he heard the name. "Morales! That's Puerto Rican. I can't hire Puerto Ricans here."

It was useless for Morales to explain that while his mother and father were Puerto Ricans, he was born in East Harlem. The office manager was firm. "Change your name, that's all I can say."

"So you see," Morales added, "that's how it is. I've got to change my name if I wanna get a job."

We walked along the street together, not speaking. I could understand everything going on in the boy's mind. He was right, in a way. Just the simple business of dropping a few letters from a name and the world might become another place. But would it, really? "You could get away with it, Morales," I said. "No question. You don't have the trace of a Spanish accent. You could change your name to Jerry Morrel and say your father was Scotch-Irish and your mother was a Pole. Who'd know the difference?"

The youth nodded.

"The only trouble is *you* would know the difference. Your mother and father would know, as well as all of your friends and the people who have been around you since you were born. That's the trouble. But if you believe that you can deny the mother and father who gave you birth, if you believe that you can deny your friends and at the same time live with yourself, then go right ahead and do anything you want."

I left Morales standing there outside the school building. I never saw him again, and I never found out if he did anything about his name. But I like to believe that he did not.

The following summer, Rose and I spent in Italy. Rose insisted that I needed a vacation. I did not think so, and I hated to leave the school even for this long; but something had been preying on my mind for a long time. It was my doctorate on the social background of the Italian immigrant. I had to gather the last of my material together, and this could only be done in the libraries in Reggio, Calabria, and Rome, where they had special collections on southern Italy.

It was a beautiful summer, and in a way, a sad summer, apart from the many hours I spent with Rose searching out and transcribing information for my thesis. I was in the Italy of my childhood again, but the people who had given my life shape and meaning were gone now. My father had died just a short while back; and as I walked the streets of Avigliano my footsteps echoed dully and I longed for the sound of his voice and for the sight of my uncles whom I would never see again—who were buried in the *camposanto* among their own people.

Far away from the activity of the school—away from the hectic adolescent life, I had time to think and really feel the loss of others who had meant so much to me. John Shedd was gone. He had died, bequeathing his Lincoln collection to Berea College in Kentucky, leaving to me his writing desk and favorite Italian books and memories of laughter and generosity and the desire to help others. It was John Shedd who had written in his little volume of aphorisms, "In education there is no danger of forgetting that men have heads, but we must remember that they should have hearts and souls also."

And there was Leone Piatelli—dead of a heart attack—gone the poet, the old friend who had given meaning to Dante, who had truly introduced me to the life and culture of the land where I was born.

28 / From the very first, the 1,800 boys who had been transferred from De Witt Clinton to form the student body of Benjamin Franklin could not reconcile themselves to the idea of continuing their high-school days in the two old elementary-school buildings that were originally annexes of Clinton. They had envisioned that when they became "upper termers" they would enjoy the beautiful new Clinton building and athletic grounds at Mosholu Parkway at the northern end of the Bronx. "We must be step-children here in East Harlem," they commented among themselves.

The boys deplored this state of affairs in the school newspaper, *The Franklin Almanac*. They even published an angry open letter to Mayor La Guardia.

> The City of New York promised its citizens a new high school to relieve the sorely overcrowded classes which were in existence at the time. Until this late date the city has not made good this promise. . . . We appeal to you as the Mayor to remember the forgotten promise which the people have not overlooked and as a citizen of the district in which Franklin is situated, we call upon you to support the movement to wipe out this disgrace to a community's dignity. . . .

The many efforts expended toward obtaining a new building finally proved successful. At about the time the housing project was terminated, the Board of Education made the necessary appropriation for the new school. There was great excitement, particularly when the building division submitted five possible locations. Four of these locations were in the tumble-down tenement section of East Harlem, and the fifth, the most desirable one, on 116th Street on the East River Drive. On this site the boys set their hearts.

"Why shouldn't we have the most beautiful location for our school?" everyone asked.

The answer was that this site would probably cost more than any of the others. The students took matters into their own hands. Shortly after this at a radio panel discussion, they had a chance to discuss this same question of site with Mayor La Guardia. "The East River location is much more expensive," he said. "I'm afraid we'll have to settle for one of the others."

The spokesman for the student committee got up. "Mr. Mayor," he said, "our social-studies teachers arranged for us to make a study of land values. We checked the record and we found that according to the assessed valuation, the East River Drive site would actually cost less than any of the others."

Mayor La Guardia seemed flustered for a moment. Then with the humor and poise characteristic of him, he said, "We'll discuss it after the program, boys."

In fact, after the radio program, the Mayor had quite a talk with the students. He was both impressed and delighted by their initiative in seeking to determine the land values. "If you're right," he said, wagging a pudgy finger, "and I believe you are, I will do everything possible to make this the site for the new school."

At the ground-breaking ceremonies for the new building, two young girls representing the school children of the city

took part. One, Christina Claxton, was a descendant of Benjamin Franklin and the other, Rita Aluto, was the daughter of
immigrant parents. Along with the Mayor, the Superintendent
of Schools, and the Borough President of Manhattan, the girls
each made a brief statement. Christina Claxton said, "I wish
my great ancestor could be here today. He would be glad to
see gathered together, as members of one group, young men
whose fathers came from so many countries." Rita Aluto
added, "The good things of life that you and I enjoy we owe
to all God's children of every color, and nation, and creed."

After his own address, Mayor La Guardia took off his coat
and turned the first shovel of earth on the school site. The
eighteen hundred members of the student body and the hundreds of gathered spectators started to cheer, while the Father
Duffy Cadets struck up a march. It was a moment I shall
never forget.

It took two years to complete the new building. During
this time we were living in a brownstone house just a few
blocks away. On my way home from the old school at 108th
Street, I would stop to watch the work which progressed with
exasperating slowness. "I can't understand it," I would say to
Rose. "At the rate they're going I'll be ready to retire before
they finish."

I was not alone in my concern. The boys from the camera
club who used to take photographs at various stages of the
job would complain to me, "What goes on, Mr. Covello? They
building Rome all over again?"

Slowly but surely the building took shape, and its beauty
began to lift the spirits of all of us, not only those of us who
were to occupy its halls but also the people who lived within
the boundaries of its influence. We could begin to realize the
words of Franklin when he wrote, "If a man empties his purse
into his head, no man can take it away from him. An investment
in knowledge always pays the best interest."

Dedication of our new high-school building was held in

April of 1942, the week of the one-hundredth anniversary of
the Board of Education. Classical in design, reminiscent of the
architecture of the later colonial period, the school was built
at a cost of three and one-half million dollars and was considered one of the most beautiful in the city. Thousands attended the ceremony, but it was not the happy occasion we had
hoped for. Between the breaking of ground and the completion
of the building, war had been declared.

War colored the entire ceremony that day. Mayor La
Guardia reminded the boys that whether or not the war ended
before they could serve in it, they would face another war
against dislocated conditions and that they had to bring themselves to realize the enormity of their responsibilities and prepare for them.

As I stood up on the platform of our magnificent auditorium,
capable of seating thirteen hundred people, facing my students, my friends and neighbors of East Harlem, I could hardly
speak. "To those of us who have lived and worked in this
community for many years," I said, "this occasion marks the
fulfillment of a long cherished dream—the dream of transform-
ing dirt and ugliness into spaciousness and beauty, of bringing
light into darkness. . . ."

In speaking about the program of the school, I added, "Fulfilling the ideal of Community Service to which it has been
dedicated, the Benjamin Franklin High School will now
operate on a round-the-clock program of use by all community
organizations. Believing that a school building should be available to all the members of the community, all the time, the
Board of Education has conferred a signal honor on Benjamin
Franklin High School.

"By a special vote it has decreed that our building is to be
open every hour of every day of the year. This means that we
who live and work in East Harlem are free to use its magnificent resources at all times."

A congratulatory telegram sent to me by Harold G. Campbell, Superintendent of Schools, launched the community-centered school as an established fact.

WE ACCEPT THE CHALLENGE TO MAINTAIN IN THIS CITY THE COMMUNITY HIGH SCHOOL WITH CONFIDENCE THAT OUR SUCCESSFUL EXPERIMENT AT FRANKLIN WILL DEVELOP A TYPE TO USE THROUGHOUT THE GREAT SCHOOL SYSTEM OF THE CITY OF NEW YORK.

During the construction of the new building, we started a project which had been on my mind for a long time. East Harlem needed a newspaper. I decided to put the matter up to my students and called a meeting of the editorial board of our school paper, *The Almanac,* and the faculty advisor, Joe Gallant, who was chairman of our English Department. "Boys," I urged, "here we are a population of 200,000 in East Harlem and the people have no way of knowing what is going on. Through the regular news sources they can find out more about what is going on in Afghanistan than they can about their own neighborhood. We've got to do something."

The boys showed interest. I informed them that before taking the matter up with the Community Advisory Council, I had to know whether they were willing to give the project their full cooperation. This meant gathering news, getting advertising, writing the paper, distributing it—a tough job. Once we made the pledge to produce the paper we had to stick by it.

"They'll do it," Joe Gallant assured me. "If they give their word, they will turn out the paper. The teachers will work with them."

Tall, well built, Joe Gallant was an inspirational teacher. He came to Franklin as chairman of the English Department, succeeding Austin Works, who had retired. Gallant contributed much to the success of the *East Harlem News,* spending many hours after the school day and its full teaching load, editing the contributions of our young journalists. In addition he directed a course for teachers on intercultural education. He wrote and spoke extremely well. The six years he devoted to Franklin will not be forgotten by those of us who had daily contact with him. When recently, at the age of fifty-three, Joe Gallant died of a heart attack, I felt a deep regret, knowing that the young people in our high schools had lost a real teacher and a good friend.

At a public meeting which represented a cross section of people and interests of East Harlem, we laid down the broad policies of this newspaper that should be run on a strictly non-profit basis and was not to be associated with any political or partisan group. Also the paper was to have an Italian and a Spanish section in its format in order to reach those of our people who could not read English.

Its fundamental object was to call attention to special problems, such as the war effort, health, recreation, housing, racial cooperation, and better schooling as they affected the community of East Harlem. We intended to concentrate on one problem at a time. Subscription rates were practically nothing and advertising so reasonable that almost every type of business, no matter how small, could afford to advertise in our pages.

The staff of the *East Harlem News* was recruited from teachers, students, and interested outsiders, all of whom plunged into the venture with enthusiasm. Often they would be working in the school until late in the evening. To finance our introductory issue, we held a folk festival in the grand ballroom of the Yorkville Casino. The *Coro d'Italia* I had organized at Columbia was there under the direction of Maestro Benelli. We had Negro dances and folk songs and spirituals, Irish jigs and ballads, Czechoslovak polkas, a German chorus, and the Pan-American singers of Benjamin Franklin. This festival netted us several hundred dollars and set the presses running for the *East Harlem News*. Immediately the paper inaugurated a campaign for a badly needed East Harlem hospital. For, as our editorial said, "This is not a dream. This is something that we, the people, can secure. Weren't we interested in getting a housing project here? Don't we have a new school? Yes, because we got together and fought. We can do it again."

All during the war we sent copies of the *East Harlem News* to Benjamin Franklin boys overseas. Of the many letters we received, Ben Rienzi's is typical. "The nights are cold here in Africa. You're miserable and you freeze. And you're lonely. You don't know what it meant to read about Ben J. and names of people you remember. I am looking forward to the next issue. Say hello to the boys on the block on 115th Street. . . ."

Word filtered through to me that because of certain "left-wingers" on the staff, a prominent local organization would not support the *East Harlem News*. As with the usual rumors of this sort, no names were actually mentioned. All was hush-hush. Mike Decessare, one of my indefatigable teachers who seemed to know everybody in the community, came to me about it. "You've got to do something about this," he said to me.

Mike Decessare was right. The only way to go about a thing like this was to stand up before the membership of this particular organization at one of their monthly meetings. I knew that they could not deny me the right to speak. Mike went along with me. There were about fifty members present when I got up to speak. I drove straight to the point.

"Let me make my position clear," I said. "I am the principal of an American public school. We accept everyone without inquiry into their political affiliations. Now if there is anyone who wants to make a direct accusation against anybody in my school, let him stand right up and make it now."

There was muttering and general uneasiness. They looked at one another, but nobody stood up.

"Unless a person actually preaches politics in a public schoolroom," I resumed, "there is nothing you or I or anybody else can do to curb his free speech. Just remember that. But if you're all so concerned about the problem of left-wingers, why don't you do something about it? Instead of talking about boycotting the *East Harlem News*, why don't you cooperate with us in trying to build up the paper and make sure for yourselves that nothing subversive gets into its pages?"

The upshot of it all was that the organization voted unanimously to lend support to the *East Harlem News*. On the way back from the meeting, Mike and I discussed the complete turnabout accomplished by our simple statement. We had done no more than squash a few rumors. How quick people are to believe anything they hear! Had we not spoken out, these rumors might have swollen into monstrous tales of subversion.

The *East Harlem News* became another part of the legend of Benjamin Franklin High School and its community activities. We published for several years until the ever-present financial bugaboo made it impossible to go on.

Rose said to me finally, "Leonard, just how long are you going to dig into your own pocket for these projects—the Educational Bureau, this newspaper, and I don't know what else? Pretty soon we won't have enough money to buy even dog biscuits for Benjay." (Even our beagle hound was named after the Benjamin Franklin basketball team, the "Benjays." Poor Rose!)

The Second World War brought additional responsibilities to our regular school program, particularly our community program. Franklin became the center in East Harlem for war activities. We created the East Harlem Defense Council. The Red Cross Disaster Unit, the Civil Defense Volunteer Association, and the 23d Police Precinct Coordinating Council merged with our Defense Council and worked intensively with us during the war years. At night, in order to save fuel oil, we used electric and kerosene heaters, because it was at night that most of these activities were held. The East Harlem Defense

Council also functioned during the day, planning various campaigns, giving information on war measures such as rationing, and acting as liaison between our unit and the New York City Central office for the war effort. All materials we prepared were done in several languages so that the people in the community would know what was going on.

What caused us a great deal of concern was the long summer vacation, when thousands of children and young people would be on their own most of the time, on the streets of East Harlem, while their mothers and fathers were working in war plants.

At Franklin we had been working closely for some years with Teachers College of Columbia University and the School of Education of New York University, in a teacher-training program during the school year. Both institutions had been sending us students on a term basis to get their teaching experience on the job—combining theory with practice. These two institutions have a summer program to which thousands of teachers from all over the United States come to receive more training and get higher degrees. Dr. Rita Morgan, coordinator of the Franklin Community Program, suggested that we arrange with the two institutions for teachers to work with us on a summer program which would give the teachers a valuable experience and give us an opportunity to be of some limited service to the children, youth, and adults in our community. The deans of both institutions were more than willing to share in the venture. Some of the Franklin teachers volunteered their services. Dr. Morgan coordinated our summer plan for the summers of 1942 and 1943, and Bessie Redmond, chairman of our Music Department, directed the summer program of 1944.

It was a broad program. There was the formal academic program—coeducational—for high-school boys and girls who needed remedial work or wanted to advance in some of their high-school subjects; a Childhood Center to attract children who had no place to go during the summer—"latch-key children"—children whose mothers were working and could not give them any attention; and activities for adults, including a course in food canning for which the school borrowed pressure cookers and utilized our school kitchen to can much-needed food; a canteen for teenagers; and weekly dances.

In addition to the day-by-day activities on these various levels, the summer school held a series of conferences on such topics as delinquency, racial problems, and the role of the community school in American education.

In short, an attempt was made to utilize the resources of a new building as an educational civic and social center all year round, on the premise that the investment the public makes in its school buildings should be fully realized.

29 / On Saturday, September 29, 1945, news٬ papers all over the city of New York blared the following headlines:

2000 STUDENTS STAGE RACE RIOTS

500 BOYS BATTLE IN EAST HARLEM

STUDENT STRIKES FLARE INTO RIOTS IN HARLEM SCHOOLS

USE SCHOOLS TO PROMOTE RIOTS

ADULT WHITES PUSH CHILDREN TO REVOLT

During the eleven years of its existence, except for the Puerto Rican incident, which was a community problem and did not actually involve any of our students, there never had been a fight involving one group against another at Benjamin Franklin. Now practically overnight a scuffle between a white student and a Negro student over a basketball became a subject for screaming headlines.

For some time now, students in the city high schools had been aroused over the refusal of the Board of Education to pay physical culture instructors for their additional time and services given to sports. It even looked as if there might be an end to baseball and basketball and track events. In some schools the students had walked out in protest, while in the newspapers

talk of student strikes began to appear. The police were
alerted to watch out for such disturbances.

The two boys who had fought over the basketball clashed
again in the locker room and threatened to have it out after
school. Word reached me in my office. Ordinarily a fist fight
in a boys' school is nothing much to get excited about. However, because of the general uneasiness among the students and
the attitude of the press, I sent Sal Pergola, a man equal to
any situation where boys were concerned, to post himself outside the school when school was dismissed. With him was Bill
Spiegel, the brawny basketball coach who was turning out
some of the best teams in the city; physically and tempera-
mentally they were capable of breaking into any squabble and
handling the most difficult student.

The fight never took place. Sal Pergola gave me the story.
"We didn't see the kids who were supposed to fight. We hung
around watching some of the Negro students who were waiting for the bus. All of a sudden a gang of about six hoodlums
came charging from around the corner with sticks. There was
yelling and cursing—then the siren of a police car, and everybody scattered. A couple of Negro boys got some head gashes.
The whites were all older kids I never saw before. It was all
over before Spiegel and I realized what was going on."

That night I went to see the Italian boy who had been involved in the fight over the basketball. He lived near the school.
All I could get out of him was that the two boys had simply
swung a few times at each other and that, as far as he was concerned, the incident was closed. Under the circumstances I
certainly could visualize no great problem.

Next day, Friday, was when things started to happen. A
prominent newspaper reported the events in its Saturday morning issue in the following words:

> Twice during the day street fighting broke out in which
> knives flashed and bottles were flung from rooftops, and

> five hundred white and Negro students and their elders
> battled eighty uniformed and plain-clothes policemen.

Both in terms of the general picture presented and in its details, this report was utter nonsense.

On the morning of the day when all this was supposed to have happened, I was standing on the school steps as I often did at this time, watching the boys arrive. One of my teachers came running up to me in a state of excitement. "Dr. Covello! Dr. Covello! There's a whole gang marching on the school. I just saw them coming, getting off the bus at 116th Street and Lexington Avenue."

Without thinking, I rushed down the steps and started along 116th Street. Not more than a block from the school I came upon a white boy running in my direction and not far behind him a band of Negro students, hooting and hollering, a couple of them waving broomsticks. There were about twenty-five Negroes in this group. At sight of me, they stopped shouting, while the white student ducked into an alley. Before I could get close enough to talk to them, however, police cars, in answer to frantic telephone calls, began to appear. Six of the Negro students were caught by the police before they could run off, and were brought into my office. When their cases came up in the Magistrate's Court, Walter O'Leary, then Chief Attendance Officer for the Board of Education, and I took up the matter with the Chief Magistrate. The boys, since their scholastic and behavior records were good, were released.

While it is true that three of them carried knives and appeared ready for battle, it was a fantastic exaggeration to claim that knives flashed and that five hundred white and Negro students and their elders battled the police. The arrival of police cars naturally brought out large numbers of curious people in the neighborhood, who massed themselves across the street from the school—many of them parents of the boys. But there was never any attempt at violence by the crowd or the students. The police were able to keep everything under control.

On the spot, we invited several hundred parents of the boys into the school auditorium where we could talk to them. I assured them that there was nothing to worry about and that their boys were perfectly safe in the classrooms with the Negro pupils. "Come on," I said, "you've all been in America long enough to know what it is. People who struggle for bread can't hate each other." Pretty soon a few were nodding their heads, one or two even managed a smile. Sal Pergola spoke to the Italian parents, using the Neapolitan dialect. "Go home. Make the spaghetti sauce. Take care of the washing before your husbands come home. You've got more important things to do than worry about the street fights of boys. Let us handle things." Another teacher spoke in Spanish, and pretty soon the parents began to rise and file out of the assembly, feeling a little foolish.

For a short time that day, Negro and white boys in the school kept to their own groups, somewhat fearful of each other. Finally, at ten o'clock, after sending the parents home, we got the two groups in the auditorium and proceeded to carry out the program for the day. The scheduled assembly —an amateur hour in which Negro and white students participated together—went along splendidly and helped break down the tension. From then on we continued with our usual daily schedule. The only precaution we took was to dismiss fifteen minutes earlier in the afternoon and have the buses stop a little closer to the school, so that the boys going west could board more quickly. A group of Negro students chose to walk home as usual and did so. Threats and angry words were spoken, but no one molested the students.

> Divided into morning and afternoon engagements, the battle was not terminated until the Negro students had been put aboard buses by high police officials to take the

pupils out of the area. The buses were pelted with stones,
sticks, bottles, and other missiles.

This battle occurred only in the imagination of the reporter.
In fact, several students reported to me later that one press
photographer tried to get them to fake a fight just so he could
carry away some pictures. It was discouraging to realize how
the work of years in our intercultural relationships was being
put into jeopardy by newspapermen so eager for a story they
would make one up.

> The police found other alleged causes of the strife . . .
> in friction over dominance of the school's activities be-
> tween the student bodies of each race, and in reports
> which had a Negro teacher striking a white pupil.

In all the eleven years of existence of our school, no attempt
by either group to dominate school activities ever occurred.
On the contrary, at that very time the leader of Arista, a city-
wide scholastic honor society, was a Negro elected by the
students themselves. The salutatorian at the previous June
graduation was a Puerto Rican, and the basketball team which
in ten years had won four New York City championships was
always a mixed group. In fact, the student body was so upset
and indignant over these malicious newspaper accounts that
they held an all-day student conference in the auditorium of
the school, at which they decided to march in the forthcoming
Columbus Day Parade as a sign of unity and solidarity among
the student body, and as a protest against the press. The significance of a student of Italian origin bearing the Benjamin
Franklin High School flag surrounded by a guard of Negro
students and members of the other ethnic minorities was well
understood by the people of East Harlem.

The stories of "race riots" were investigated by the National Association for the Advancement of Colored People,
by the District Attorney's office, the Police Department, the
Department of Investigation, the Mayor's Committee on

Unity. For weeks my calendar was filled with meetings and interviews on the subject. All of these organizations declared the news accounts to be unfair. One statement that a group of mothers had gone to the Mayor's office and demanded segregation I investigated myself. I telephoned the Mayor and found that no mothers from East Harlem had called there and that there had been no letter.

Just the same, damage was done to the prestige of the school, making it less effective as an educational institution and stigmatizing the community and the students. Some of my boys complained, "When we go for a job or even want to go to college and they hear we come from East Harlem, it's going to make it much harder for us to get by." A former student wrote to me from the army, "I spent three years at Franklin which were very enjoyable. To me Franklin stood as a symbol of tolerance, and then this shameful event had to occur."

But the most touching letter came from a graduate by the name of Harry Olsen. "Dear Dr. Covello," he wrote. "I'm very depressed by what I have read the past few days in the newspapers. Things sure must have changed at Franklin. Maybe it's the war which changes people. For my own part, when I read of race riots at Franklin, I can only think of Le Count Russell, the Negro boy who was killed in a car accident—the boy who was photographer for the school paper and went everywhere with his camera. You remember how we went to his funeral at the Methodist Church with some of the other boys in his class? Also the special memorial assembly we had for him, and the poem written by Louis Relin which said something about, 'What matter if a man be white or black, gentile or Jew?' It's hard to forget Le Count Russell and my other friends at Benjamin Franklin. How could things have changed so?"

For days I carried with me a feeling of great discouragement, even bitterness, which I could not shake—frustration when I thought of all the work we had done at Franklin in an effort to lessen racial friction and hatred. What was wrong, I kept asking myself. Where had we failed? What forces were coming into play which we had not considered, or which up until now had not existed? During these days I discussed the problem with Sal Pergola, my Dean of Boys. We had been working closely together now for some years.

"Sal," I said, "I just can't reconcile this incident. Here we were with the feeling that such a thing could not happen at Franklin and then suddenly a group of Negro boys are set upon by whites. We were lucky to escape a serious race riot. But just the same, how did it happen? Why should it happen?"

"I don't know, I really don't," Sal answered thoughtfully. "Maybe it's related to the forces that the war unleashed. We can't even begin to appraise the effect of world violence on our kids. Violence always begets violence. People are no longer the way they were when you were young—or even I, for that matter. Their children are not the same."

I could begin to grasp what Sal Pergola was searching to describe—the pattern of violence repeated endlessly through war and hatred—but I did not want to believe it. I wanted to live with the firm conviction that through the school and education the problems of each generation could seek and find a solution.

30/T̲he racial incident receded into the limbo of a half-forgotten nightmare. In a few weeks there was hardly anything to indicate that it had ever happened, as far as the school was concerned. I moved about the building, watching the boys in class, in the lunchrooms, talking together in the corridors, Negro and white, and it was heartening to see how every trace of animosity had been cast aside. We were back once more in the normal healthy routine of Franklin. The only difference was that now we knew better than ever that the story of the community school in East Harlem had to be told beyond its own boundaries. If we were misrepresented again, great harm would come of it. For no man can revile his less fortunate neighbor without weakening the entire fabric of a democratic society. And no man is safe unless all men are safe.

By complaining about the sensational treatment newspapers too often give various school situations, I do not mean to suggest that we had no delinquency at Benjamin Franklin. In the same measure that we had crime in East Harlem, an admittedly and understandably "tough" section of New York, we had delinquency at Franklin. But we never let it get out of control. We treated the rough boys in the only way they could understand—firmly—and they respected us for it. We never considered a boy hopeless unless he was implicated in a serious crime, in which case it was no longer the school's business but the law's. Quite frankly, we kept the police out of our school problems with so-called delinquents until we had absolutely no other choice. Always we followed two cardinal principles: get to the boy, make him feel that we represented hope; and go to the family to dig for the root of the problem.

I remember literally hundreds of boys sitting tongue-tied, frustrated, doubled up inside with shame and confusion in my office. For many of them we went to court, to police stations, to hospitals, interceding for another chance. But to intercede is to assume responsibility. We got jobs, "big brothers," psychological and welfare help. We tried to give them a mixture of discipline and affection. How well I recall our successes and our failures. As I look back today, these are my joys and my sadnesses.

One of the most obstinate cases of juvenile delinquency I ever came up against was that of Jack Varga O'Neill. This difficult student was sentenced to the State Training School for Boys for breaking into and robbing a hardware store. I went to some trouble to have him released, writing letters to the judge who had committed him, to the superintendent at the training school, and even having Marcantonio intervene from his seat in Congress. At that, I was only able to succeed because his Irish stepfather had a job all lined up for him as a plumber's helper in the Bronx.

My first actual contact with Jack came one afternoon at Franklin when I heard a terrific commotion outside my office and went out to find one of the gym teachers and several students grappling with him in the hall. Jack had gone suddenly berserk, and they were trying to bring him to my office. Once we managed to get him inside the office, he calmed somewhat and I sent everyone away. I let him sit for a while, watching out of the corner of my eye. I had learned that in handling an excited boy a cooling-off period was necessary and important.

You just left him alone with his own thoughts and, above all, talked to him with no one else present.

"What is it, Jack?" I finally asked casually. "Why did you fly off the handle?"

"I don't know. I don't know what's the matter with me. I'm confused. Everything is all mixed up."

"There must be some reason."

He rocked his head. "All of a sudden I want to smash things or belt somebody. I guess I must be off my rocker."

That was about all I could get out of Jack Varga O'Neill. In a little while he seemed perfectly normal and extremely sorry for all the commotion he had caused, and promised never to let it happen again. "I don't want to cause you any trouble," he said. "I don't want to cause anybody any trouble." There was a kind of melancholy sincerity about this boy which made me particularly anxious to try to help him. And yet I was always conscious of barriers beyond which I could not penetrate.

It was not long after this that East Harlem detectives picked Jack up for breaking into the hardware store and he was sent to the State Training School at Warwick. His Italian mother with her Irish second husband, Tom O'Neill, came to see me at the school. "He is not bad," the mother pleaded, giving me the eternal story of all mothers of boys in trouble. "It was the bad company, the older boys. If you could only get him out, I am sure that he will never do anything wrong again."

The stepfather promised to assume full responsibility. He had a genuine affection for the boy. "I will see to it myself that he behaves. I have a job ready for him in the place where I work." In fact, he even showed me a letter from a plumbing-contracting firm offering employment to Jack immediately upon his release.

I discussed the matter with the judge at the Children's Court. He had no objection to the boy's release into the custody of his stepfather, providing the superintendent at the

State School approved. Then I had Marcantonio write to the superintendent from Washington. Marc forwarded me the reply which I still have in my files and which reads in part, "It is our feeling that Jack needs to acquire real self-assurance through achievement, to relate to adults in a more constructive manner, particularly to adults in authority. This will require a somewhat longer period of treatment, and we expect to re-view Jack's case again in November. In the meantime he is receiving training in our shop to prepare him in an adequate manner for the job which his stepfather is apparently trying to provide him with."

This was in May—six more months before Jack's case would come up again for review. I wrote another letter to the super-intendent, sending more information about the boy and affi-davits from the parents promising supervision of all of Jack's activities. On the basis of this urging, the superintendent agreed to release Jack in August.

I was watching some activity at the Franklin outdoor Sum-mer School one afternoon when I saw Jack Varga O'Neill again. The State Training School at Warwick hadn't changed him much. He looked a little older, more mature, perhaps, but his manner was still shy, as though he hesitated to thrust himself forward. "I would like to wash your car, Mr. Covello," he said. "I would like to do something for you."

"You don't have to do anything for me, Jack."

"But I want to wash your car."

"Then I'll pay you for the job."

"I don't want any pay."

"Then I can't let you do it."

He walked away shaking his head. I had definite views about accepting service from my boys. But in Jack's case I had an uneasy feeling that somehow I was making a mistake.

Jack lasted about eight months at the job with his step-father. The lure of the streets of East Harlem was too strong—

the attraction of older companions—the easy thrills, the money from the narcotics racket. Next thing I knew he was picked up as a "pusher" and sentenced to the reformatory. The case was out of my hands. I would not think of interfering when the charge is of such a serious nature. However, one day I ran into his mother on the street. What she said to me was curious. "I received a letter from Jack. You know, he never could understand why you would not let him wash your car."

Some people believe that reformatories do endless damage to juvenile delinquents—giving them the contacts and schooling to become seasoned criminals. I agree with them in many instances. But in Jack's case, the reverse was true. The rugged reformatory experience seemed to straighten him out. Afterward he became an honest, law-abiding citizen. The straightening process came from somewhere within himself while he was behind bars. Though I had been unable to help him, I can feel some satisfaction in the fact that the last time I saw him, when he told me about being married and the plumbing shop and his child, he said to me, "Pop, I certainly gave you a hard time. I'll never forget how much you did for me."

Today's teenage gang members seem to carry a frightening arsenal of guns and knives, if newspaper reports are accurate. In my time at Franklin, the majority of boys carried the ordinary pocket knife, and, on more than one occasion, teachers and I were able to confiscate the villainous looking "switchblades" from boys who were seen displaying them. But I can honestly say that in all my experience as a high-school principal in East Harlem, I do not recall that a knifing took place in the school.

In the collection of knives and assorted weapons, which were confiscated, was a murderous pair of brass knuckles fitted with sharp spikes taken from a boy caught clowning with them in the hall with some of his companions. I'll never forget Tony Zucco. Stubborn as a mule. When I got him in my office he refused to tell me where he had obtained the brass knuckles.

"I just can't tell you, Pop. I just can't."

It was exasperating. I couldn't pry the story out of him. I finally had to let him go. After he finished school he became a cab driver, and I used to see him every now and then in the neighborhood. When I mentioned the brass knuckles he always became vague and avoided the subject. Not very long ago I asked him point blank. "Come on, Tony. It's years now. Tell me the truth about the knuckles."

He grinned, scratched his head, and told me the truth. "I found them in a garbage can. I never used them, but I couldn't tell you that, Pop. It was too tame. A tough kid like me, naw!"

It was Tony Zucco who told me how his father handled matters of discipline at home. "Some kids when they did something would get one whale of a shellacking. Not in my house. When my old man wanted to scare us, all he had to say was, 'I'll turn you over to the cop on the corner.'" Actually this was a common, though rarely carried out, threat in our neighborhood.

In a boys' high school like Franklin, one develops an instinct for ferreting out misbehavior. A teacher "gets wind of things." He catches a word in a conversation, he sees a group of boys in a huddle, or a boy jingling some change, or another making a gesture with his fist—and he can almost be certain that a dice game is about to take place. Usually it is outside the school, in an alley or an empty lot, and there is nothing much that can be done about it. But sometimes the dice games take place right in the school.

One afternoon I was standing at the window of my office looking out across the East River Drive when I happened to look straight down and see a student sneaking into the basement. Immediately I knew that something was going on. I went downstairs to the basement and made my way along a corridor which led to a secluded little vestibule behind some swinging doors. I remember that it was unusually quiet, and somehow I was reminded of the time when I was a little boy that Mingo and I stole into my uncle's church to wash our hands in the Holy Water. Near the swinging doors I could hear the hushed voices, "Fade you, Nick! Acey ducey! Mamma's little baby! Got you covered, boy!" followed by dice rolling and striking against the baseboard.

Through a crack in the swinging door I could see six students gathered around a pile of nickels and dimes. I waited just long enough to make sure that I had recognized them all and then I thrust the door open.

Before any of the boys could try a dash for the exit I said quietly, "Hold it! I know every one of you."

Those who were kneeling rose to their feet. One boy started to gather up the money. I held out my hand. "Let me have it."

The boy hesitated a moment, looked at the others, and then dumped the pile of change into my hand. There must have been a couple of dollars in all. "All right," I said, "this will be your contribution to the Student Aid Fund. Any objections?"

There were no objections. I took the names of all the boys. None of them had ever been caught before and I let them off. The offense would be marked in pencil on their permanent record cards. If repeated, it would then be inscribed in ink—if not, it would be erased at graduation.

In offenses like gambling and stealing, repetitions were not so common as people might suppose. The temperament of the chronic offender did not permit him to remain long in high school. Usually he quit of his own volition after the first or second term. Rarely did we have to refer a case to the police. We had a working arrangement with the patrolmen on the beat and particularly with the Youth Squad in case a serious situation might arise. As a matter of fact, the police would bring in boys they picked up hanging around in candy stores, in Jefferson Park, or just roaming the streets, feeling that the school was better able to deal with them.

Our continuing community concerns at Franklin were with health and housing, and we worked with other community agencies to realize such projects as a new hospital and low-rent housing units. Also we instituted a playground program for the children of the immediate vicinity of the school.

Over the years I had received many complaints from mothers about crowded streets which made it dangerous for children to play. Typical of these was a letter addressed to me at the school from a group of worried mothers.

Dear Dr. Covello:

Knowing the fine work you are doing for our community through your school newspaper, we thought we would appeal to you for a good cause. We are the mothers of East 114th Street between First and Second Avenues.

It seems that lately there is a child run down by a motor vehicle nearly every day. We find that this is due to the fact that the sidewalks are cluttered with pushcarts, and the children have no place to play but in the streets. In most cases the drivers could avoid hitting anyone by swerving to the other side of the street, but this is impossible because they are blocked by pushcarts. Not only are these pushcarts causing accidents, they are also very unsanitary. The streets are full of flies and at night when they leave, there are about thirty ashcans on the sidewalks full of garbage. Now that school is over, we dread having the children around in such a filthy street and most of us cannot afford sending them away.

We have signed several petitions to have them eliminated but up to the present time nothing has been done. We therefore ask you to try to do something to have these pushcarts taken away from our streets and make it a better and safer place to live in. Also there are quite a few empty lots in our street that could easily be converted into playgrounds for the children.

We leave it up to you, Dr. Covello, to see what you
can do in this matter.

Thank you.

> Yours truly,
> Mothers of 114th Street
> (Between 1st and 2d Avenues)

Although some recreational facilities were available in afternoon play centers in a few of the schools and in several community houses, these were hardly enough to take care of thousands of children of elementary-school age. Moreover, the
distances children had to go to reach these centers and the
hazard of crossing heavily congested city streets often proved
to be a deterrent to the children as well as the mothers. The
teenager and the young adult found haven in the numerous
candy stores spotted around the neighborhood—about five
hundred of them in one hundred sixty city blocks. But where
were the younger children to play?

Though the era of the pushcarts was dying, they lingered
on. Already a law had been passed prohibiting the renewal of
pushcart licenses once the original owner had retired or passed
away. Empty lots were another matter. Created by the demolition of unsanitary and unsafe tenement houses, filled with
debris and refuse, an eyesore in the neighborhood, they still
had owners and value as property. How to acquire one of
these empty lots for a period of at least five years, how to
clean it up and transform it into a playground was a challenge
given to the students of the Civic Club.

They concentrated on the renovation of one particular lot,
but soon discovered that even this was not a simple matter.
While the owner, Carmine Luongo, agreed to their use of his
property, the students had no facilities for carting away the
debris. Also the lot had to be fenced and paved. Equipment
had to be procured and recreational leaders had to be found
who would direct the play activities of the children. The students finally reached the conclusion that the total job could

only be done in cooperation with interested citizens, community leaders, and city departments—Sanitation, Police, and the Borough President's office.

The outgrowth of these student deliberations was the Playlot Committee, which held its first meeting in my office. This project was under the leadership of Simon Beagle, our Community Coordinator. Si Beagle not only had ideas but also found the time to carry them out, even if it meant working after school hours, in the evening, and over weekends. Adults together with student representatives discussed the matter fully. It was agreed that the students were to carry the major burden of the work. The adult members were to act mainly in an advisory capacity, to make the necessary contacts, and to lead the way.

The Department of Sanitation, with whom we had established friendly relations, agreed to remove the debris with their trucks, the students aiding them wherever possible. The Deputy Commissioner of Public Works, an East Harlem leader, agreed to have the lot paved. The personnel director of the Police Athletic League who assigned recreation workers to man the playlot—among them Bob DeLellis, one of our Franklin graduates.

The Police Department also donated an outdoor shower. The only problem left was the money needed for athletic and play equipment. Someone suggested capitalizing on the human-interest aspects of Mr. Luongo, the man who had donated the use of his property for the playlot in the first place, and this idea was immediately grabbed up by the television program *We the People*. Mr. Luongo, owner of a florist shop over on First Avenue, had sixteen children in his family, whom he housed on two floors of a brownstone in East Harlem. Who would possibly have greater interest in a playlot? As payment for the personal appearance of Mr. and Mrs. Luongo and the sixteen children, the program agreed to furnish us with all the equipment we needed. In this way, also, the story of the Benjamin Franklin playlot was told over the air. The only trouble was that when it came Mrs. Luongo's turn to identify her children she became so confused she could no longer remember their names.

The Franklin playlot was dedicated in mid-July. The success of this project led to our turning another rubble-filled lot in the neighborhood into a play area. In order to alert the community and to get its cooperation in expanding the work, we borrowed a sound truck from radio station WNYC. Students, teachers, and parents spoke in three languages from the sound truck in the Italian and Spanish neighborhoods and brought the message to their East Harlem neighbors.

We were excited with the results. We had achieved what we felt should be one of the basic aims of education—improvement of community life, not merely through discussion but through a demonstration of school-community action. It is true that recreational problems are city problems and the responsibility for their solution rests to a great extent with city agencies. But the citizens must assume the final responsibility, and the ability to assume this responsibility must be inculcated in the growing child.

We pay heavily for apathy, indifference, and shortsightedness. We pay heavily for erecting and maintaining jails and other custodial institutions. What is more tragic, we pay in the broken lives of thousands of our children, the great majority of whom have potentialities for becoming fine citizens instead of the delinquents from whom the future criminals of America are recruited. Land is valuable in our big cities, there is no doubt about that. But children are more valuable.

One day in 1948 there appeared a newspaper story, illustrated with photographs, showing the dirty streets and lots of East Harlem. Si Beagle, community coordinator and faculty advisor to the Civic Club, and the student leaders came to my office. One of the boys, Louis Pasquale, said, "You see, Doc, they're picking on us again."

"It seems," Si Beagle commented, "that whenever the newspapers have nothing to write about, they focus their attention on East Harlem."

Another student broke in, "The truth is the truth. You can't fake pictures like this. Why kid ourselves?"

"Well, my block isn't like that," someone else said.

"Maybe so," I interrupted the beginning of an argument. "We can get the facts. But once we have them, what are you going to do about them?"

This simple discussion was the beginning of our sanitation campaign.

Reports of the students showed the newspaper story was by no means an exaggeration. In fact, the total neighborhood picture showed distressing conditions which had grown bad during the war and in no way improved with the succeeding years. We studied the responsibility for these poor sanitary conditions. It was found that landlords were unwilling to spend money on buildings which ultimately might be torn down in the movement toward "housing projects," while superintendents and janitors were overworked and felt that the task of keeping things clean was hopeless. It looked as if the major responsibility must devolve upon tenants themselves.

To obtain information from the Department of Sanitation and to get the benefit of school-wide opinion, a forum was planned for the weekly assembly, the topic for discussion, "How Can We Keep East Harlem Clean?" The Educational Director of the Department of Sanitation and the Secretary of the East Harlem Health Committee were invited to act as forum consultants.

This assembly and subsequent meetings resulted in the students evolving a sanitation campaign which was to include the use of a sound truck to tour the neighborhood with live speakers and printed materials, a movie short on sanitation to be shown in local theaters, leaflets to be distributed from door to door, an original play to be presented by the Civic Club to parents, a parade through the neighborhood, and a mass meeting at the school.

As the movement for a cleaner East Harlem began to gather momentum, the *New York Daily News* came forward with an offer to award several thousand dollars in prizes to the winners of a cleanup contest in a six-block area. The prizes were to be given to the people living in the "Blue-Ribbon Block" and the judges to be the Outdoor Cleanliness Association of the city and Sanitary Engineers from Columbia and New York University. The boys agreed to sponsor this contest. They met with the above representatives and a staff writer from the *Daily News*, Joe Martin, who wrote a series of articles during the course of the campaign and showed a great interest in the work at Franklin. One of his stories was illustrated by the photograph of a street cleaner leaning on his broom, scratching his head, and wondering if he was going to be out of a job.

An "average area" of six blocks was selected in which to experiment with tenants in street cleanliness. According to the Commissioner of Sanitation, these blocks were what one would expect to find in a highly congested neighborhood. In preparation for the parade and mass meeting to launch the contest, announcements were made over the public-address system to all classes each morning for a week. Excitement over the project began to mount. At a Civic Club meeting, Louis Pasquale got up and said, "I thought everybody was picking on us. Here it looks as if everyone wants to give us a hand."

Mayor O'Dwyer and other dignitaries came to inspect the results of our Sanitation Campaign. "No one knows better than I," the Mayor said, "how hard it is for people who live in great congestion to keep their neighborhoods clean. . . . To do a good job we must have the cooperation of every citizen. I am deeply interested in this experiment, and I hope that the lessons learned this week in encouraging neighborhood cooperation will spread to other districts in all boroughs."

Every family in the winning block was to receive one of the prizes which were on display in an electrical store in the neighborhood—radios, electric grills, toasters, sun lamps, electric razors, fans, and the like. The test started with the committee of judges inspecting each block and repeating its inspection every day until the end of the week, when the street which had shown the greatest improvement was announced. The head of each winning family, along with the choice of gift, was awarded a certificate for community achievement.

Several years later I happened to visit the home of one of my boys who lived on this "Blue-Ribbon block." There on the wall of the living room, I was startled to see one of these certificates in an ornate frame, sharing a place of honor among other family mementos.

How much was accomplished by all this is difficult to say. The problem of sanitation in a depressed area of a great city has challenged the wisest of city administrators. In no way did we solve the sanitation problem of East Harlem. But a step was taken in the right direction. The Commissioner of Health made a change in the City Sanitary Code, making it mandatory upon landlords to provide a specific number of garbage cans, depending upon the number of families living in a tenement. The Sanitation Commissioner arranged for a definite time for garbage collection by the department trucks. As a result of our experience, other communities attempted to grapple with the same problem.

In my own opinion as a teacher, the most important result was the experience gained by our students in the planning and execution of a community project which daily affected their lives and the lives of their families and neighbors. They learned that changes in laws cannot be accomplished overnight, that the heads of city departments are strictly limited by the amount of money available. They learned that teachers, parents, and religious leaders, together with community agencies, are anxious to work with them in and out of school—are willing and ready to have them assume responsibility. Thus, they discovered that they too have a job in making democracy work.

My many years at Franklin made me believe more firmly than ever in another aspect of democracy—the opportunity for boys to pursue their education far beyond the limitations sometimes imposed upon them because of the character of the neighborhood in which they happen to be born.

In the creation of Franklin, we argued for a cosmopolitan or comprehensive high school; and when plans for the new Franklin building were under way, we again urged a broad, all-inclusive educational program that would meet the needs and interests of all types of students. In addition to the academic course, we argued for a general course, a commercial course enriched by the industrial arts, and also a vocational or trade course for those students who wanted it. We definitely did not want just a trade school. We wanted to eliminate the sharp distinctions between the different types of high schools which, in my opinion, create social cleavages and develop a type of class consciousness that is the very antithesis of democracy.

It is interesting to note that 40 to 50 per cent of Franklin graduates now make applications to enter colleges or universities. A vocational or trade school would have restricted many of these boys in their preparation for higher education.

The high school has now become the common school of America and it is here where all American youth should mingle and rub elbows, get to understand and appreciate each other—the academic student who plans for college, the student who plans for a business career, and the student whose inclinations and abilities direct him to the skilled trades. This to me represents one of the basic functions of our American high school.

31/ I had always wanted to visit Puerto Rico, but neither the time nor the occasion presented itself until the summer of 1947 when, accompanied by Rose, I went there as a guest of the Department of Education of the University of Puerto Rico. This invitation came about through the efforts of Professor Robert K. Speer of New York University, who was going there to set up a summer workshop for New York teachers in cooperation with the University of Puerto Rico. This workshop has been functioning successfully for the last ten years.

Rose and I spent about six weeks in a delightful suburb known as Rio Piedras. We resided at the University Guest House, and I spent part of my time lecturing to students of the summer session on such subjects as the Community School and the Puerto Rican migrant in New York City.

During my spare time I wandered about the island, getting to know its people and its customs, fascinated, as always, by the sun and the sea, the majestic and rugged beauty of its countryside, which in flashes reminded me of my childhood in southern Italy. In fact, Puerto Rico is no more than a mountainous crest with precipitous gorges and ravines extending into the Atlantic, where the record depth of 27,922 feet has been registered. Discovered by Columbus on his second voyage to the New World, Puerto Rico was colonized in 1508 by Ponce de Leon with a contingent of fifty soldiers, who found the Borinquen Indians a peaceful, friendly, and agricultural people. Early in the island's history the Indians began to disappear as a distinct racial group, as Negro slaves were brought in by the Spanish.

This visit was a rare opportunity for me. By 1947 we already had about three hundred students of Puerto Rican origin at Benjamin Franklin—the largest group in any high school in New York City. The mass air migration which followed the war was in full swing, with travel rates as low as thirty-five dollars in converted army-transport planes—more than one of which, overloaded with Puerto Ricans like herds of human cattle, crashed with terrible loss of life. Just as New York had been able to boast that it had more Irish than Dublin, more Jews than Tel Aviv, more Italians than Rome, it could soon say that it had more Puerto Ricans than San Juan.

New York City, the city of migrations, was once more the goal of a new people. The very problems which had confronted my own family were now faced by these newcomers —a foreign language, a different culture, and the complexities of living in a strange and gigantic city. Except for the fact that these newcomers were American citizens by right of birth, there was no difference at all between them and early immigrants. And often this very right of citizenship increased the resentment against them, rather than contributing to their welfare. "Where do these spicks come off, calling themselves Americans?" I heard again and again, and very often voiced by people who were no more than a few decades removed from the immigrant themselves. As someone aptly stated, the anti-foreign American is the man who believes that it is all right to be descended from immigrants but all wrong to be one.

Compulsory retirement meant that in the not-too-distant future my work as a high-school principal would be over. No matter how I tried I could not visualize myself separated from the neighborhood and the work which had been my life. All that I had learned about the immigrant and his child in the struggle to become part of American society I could not shelve or lock up in a desk drawer simply because a prescribed number of years had marched by. What happens to the mind which remains alert after the law dictates that its owner can no longer work? What happens to the heart that continues to reach out to those who are still groping in a new land? In time, the Lord gave me His answer.

"*Buenos días*, Señora," I said one morning to a wrinkled but vigorous old lady I encountered in the corridor of Franklin during the summer classes. "Are you looking for someone? May I help you?"

"Señor," she answered proudly, "I am going to my class. I am over seventy but I never learned to read or write. Now I am learning."

Shortly afterwards I read a newspaper account of the little Puerto Rican girl who tried to commit suicide by swallowing poison because her school companions laughed at the way she spoke English. The story had echoes for me. I could not get it out of my mind.

Then there was the story Miguel Fernandez told of his first days at Franklin. It was before he was fluent in English and the scene took place in the office of Sal Pergola. "Miguel," Sal Pergola said to him, "two days ago you took an intelligence test. According to the results, you have no intelligence at all. And there are people who believe in the results of these tests. They think you are stupid. We know that isn't true. Today you are going to take an intelligence test in Spanish and the results will show that you are as intelligent as anyone else."

"But even more important than the tests," Miguel told me, "was what the people at Franklin did for my family. We were poor, you remember. Now that I was in high school, my father could not afford to send me to school every day. I needed twenty cents for bus fare and fifty cents for lunch. My family could not even buy decent shoes for me. The school took care of all this. They gave me a transportation ticket and a free pass for the lunchroom, and out of a special fund I was provided with shoes." This special fund was raised by the Puerto Ricans themselves through Latin American festivals held in Franklin, through the efforts of Bobby Quintero.

On my visit to Puerto Rico I knew that I would make the acquaintance of educators and leaders in other fields and meet the circle known as the cultured of Puerto Rico. While this was of considerable interest to me, I was even more eager to meet the families of my boys—the families from which stemmed the great migration that was beginning to cause concern and even consternation in the New York City schools and social agencies.

I asked some of my Puerto Rican students at Franklin to give me letters of introduction to friends and relatives on the island. They gladly complied. In all, I delivered almost fifty letters, covering the one-hundred-mile-long island from one end to the other. It turned out to be a wonderful way of projecting myself into the lives and backgrounds of these people.

Most of the addresses were in and around the principal cities like San Juan, Ponce, and Mayaguez. With the possible exception of two or three families, all the letters I delivered were in the poorer sections of these cities.

No sooner did it become known that I was the schoolmaster of, for instance, Gerardo Vega, who was the son of Anna and Salvador Vega, who had left for New York several years before, than people would come pouring out of the houses on the street where the Vegas once lived to greet me and vie with each other for the privilege of having me honor their makeshift dwellings for a drop of coffee and a taste of rum, while questions were fired at me from all sides concerning all the Puerto Ricans in New York. Usually I had all I could do to tear myself away, and as my car went off with children grabbing at the fenders and trailing after, the elders would wave their hands and cry, "*Adiós*, Señor Professor! *Adiós. Vaya con Dios!*"

However, while slums must remain slums no matter where encountered in the world, there is something about the bright sky and atmosphere of Puerto Rico, the outdoor living, the friendly attitude of its people which greatly lessens the impact of poverty. Away from New York, the city of steel and stone, one is apt to view with indulgent eyes the hastily constructed shacks of wood and tarpaper, destroyed so many times by the hurricanes and rebuilt again, the narrow streets which are more like alleys, and the complete lack of sanitation or even the most primitive facilities.

In Puerto Rico there is a new spirit abroad in the land. In the short space of ten years, Muñoz Marín and his people have begun to take steps to transform an undeveloped area typical of so many others throughout the world into a modern, progressive community. Ultimately it may prove a dramatic example of what can be accomplished when the will to achieve and intelligent planning are added to the will to work hard.

From that first visit to Puerto Rico I carried back with me the ineradicable conviction that nothing could stop these people from bettering the circumstances of their lives. If it was humanly possible, they had to venture where there were greater opportunities—but particularly, as I heard them express over and over again, where their children could have a chance to get an education. It was the now-familiar pattern of the immigrant repeated all over again—the sacrifice of the parents for the children.

In 1948 I went to the island again, this time with a group working with the Puerto Rican people in New York City, to attend the inauguration of Luis Muñoz Marín, the first elected Governor of Puerto Rico. The island had begun to feel the impact of his creative and dynamic leadership when he first

led the new Popular Democratic Party to victory in Puerto
Rico in 1940. These two visits showed me clearly the need
for the Puerto Rican people to know more about their new
home. It was just as necessary for leaders in the city and state
agencies to know more about the problems of these new migrants and how their particular department or organization
could be of assistance.

With this in mind, I arranged a series of press conferences
at Franklin. There were eighteen in all, covering a period of
almost two years. To these were invited such prominent
Puerto Ricans as Dr. Francisco Collazo, Acting Secretary of
the Department of Education, Dr. José Osuna, former Dean
of the School of Education, University of Puerto Rico, and
Hon. Fernando Sierra Berdecía, Secretary of Labor for the
Commonwealth of Puerto Rico. Representing the city were
the Health Department, the Department of Welfare, a Police
Commissioner, a Chief Magistrate of the City Courts, the Civil
Service Commissioner, and educational leaders. The state sent
its Commissioner on Discrimination, and a New York State
Senator on Educational and Social Welfare legislation.

These conferences proved extremely beneficial because they
established contacts not only between the departments of the
city and state with the Puerto Rican community in New York
City but, beyond that, with the island, through the representatives of the Puerto Rican press. Of great importance to me
was the fact that our Puerto Rican boys took part in them. In
some excitement they would arrive at school in the evening
before the guests and learn who they were and how to greet
them.

Now that I have retired as principal of Benjamin Franklin
and am working as Educational Consultant of the Migration
Division of the Department of Labor of the Commonwealth
of Puerto Rico, I take great pride in the fact that in this New
York City office, the director, Joseph Monserrat, my assistant, Carlos Dominicci, and two other workers, Paul Cabal-

lero and Ervin Villannueva, are all graduates of Franklin. They are deeply involved in the task of helping the Puerto Rican adapt himself to his new life on the continent.

One of the significant developments has been the creation of this Migration Division of the Department of Labor of the Commonwealth of Puerto Rico, headed by Clarence Senior. Never before has a government from which migrants have come to us assumed the responsibility of doing something for its people while they were adjusting to their new home. It was an idea conceived by Puerto Ricans, carried out in a large measure by them, and paid for with their own money. From a small staff in 1948 with a budget of $80,000 it has developed into an organization which now employs one hundred twenty-six people with an appropriation for 1958 of almost $900,000, and with centers not only in New York and Chicago but branches in New Jersey, Connecticut, Massachusetts, and Pennsylvania, where there are emerging Puerto Rican communities.

This program has the understanding and backing of Governor Luis Muñoz Marín, no stranger to New York City himself. During his early manhood he lived and worked in New York City as a journalist, and he is equally fluent in English and Spanish and very well acquainted with living conditions in New York City.

In addition to the actual service the Migration Division renders in education, social work, community organization, public relations, and employment, it is a stimulus to the many programs which have been developed in New York and in other cities where Puerto Ricans are making their home. Partly because of this organization, the Puerto Rican is making a far more rapid adjustment to his new life than was possible for the immigrant who came before him. The Puerto Ricans are quick to seize upon any opportunity to improve themselves. The moment they are able they move to better neighborhoods, try in every way to consolidate their position as useful and public-minded citizens, and are quick to support any organization concerned with their welfare. Every day at the employment bureau of the Puerto Rican Migration Division, hundreds of people are processed and aided in the finding of jobs. Some of them are sent to work outside New York and remain there to make their permanent homes. Puerto Rican lawyers give of their time and services for legal aid to those who need it. It is the same with Puerto Rican doctors and welfare and educational workers.

One thing the New York City schools need is more teachers who speak the immigrant's language. My years of struggle for the recognition of the Italian language in the New York City schools and my experience as a teacher in East Harlem indicate definitely to me the importance of the bilingual teacher in the orientation of non-English-speaking pupils. The impact of new surroundings, a strange tongue, the many and difficult adjustments overwhelm the pupil in his first contacts in school. He needs someone who can talk to him, who understands his problems and to whom he can confide the difficulties he is facing. Yet, there are schools where they not only do not use the bilingual teacher but make it a policy to use classroom teachers who do not know Spanish, feeling that the foreign language would be used as a crutch by teacher and pupil. The Puerto Rican child in our schools will learn English in the same way that thousands of non-English-speaking children learned English during the great immigration periods before 1920. It is as inevitable as it is important. But equally important to the non-English-speaking child is the need to communicate in his own language—particularly to his teacher. The bilingual teacher is a necessity in our schools.

I myself speak English, French, Spanish, and several Italian dialects, and have a working knowledge of German. Sal Pergola is fluent in as many. We had a dozen other teachers equally at ease with the different languages of our students. The importance of this cannot be overstressed. It helped gain us the confidence of the boys. It set us on an equal footing with the mothers and fathers. We were not separate, off somewhere in a world of our own, unapproachable to the man, woman, or child who could not speak English. How often have I seen the lightning joy on the face of a dubious immigrant parent when he hears the sound of a familiar tongue! How many barriers crumble before the shared language! I am there, once again at my office at Franklin. I see the careworn face of a little Puerto Rican woman, aged beyond her years from the poverty and hard work in the fields of her native island. She has come to see me on some matter relating to her son.

"Señora," I say to her in Spanish, "sit down. Make yourself comfortable and we will talk about Miguel and his future." And to the boy, also in Spanish, "You sit down over there, and do not interrupt us while I talk to your mother."

The only language of education is the language which people can understand—no matter where it originates. To this simple Puerto Rican woman I have suddenly become more than the principal of an English-speaking high school. I am a human being who understands and is trying to help her. In the eyes of the boy I have given respect and status to his parent. The process of education has been translated into human terms.

There is one important difference between the educational programs worked out for previous migrants and the present program for the Puerto Rican. This difference is a Planning Committee at the Board of Education in New York City, composed of top officials who discuss the various aspects of the educational program. And the policies they outline are carried out in the schools. The *Puerto Rican Study*, a four-year project undertaken by the Board of Education and the Ford Foundation, has resulted in something more than graded teaching materials for the more rapid acquisition of English by non-English-speaking Puerto Rican pupils. It has acted, in addition, as a stimulus to more effective over-all school programs to meet their particular needs. Moreover as part of the educational plan, the schools undertake many direct experiences, such as trips to neighborhood places of interest.

The Board of Education has at the present time assigned to the elementary schools where there are large concentrations of Puerto Rican children over seventy Puerto Rican bilingual teachers who, instead of regular classroom teaching, are given the job of doing community work and helping parents and teachers in overcoming difficult situations. Moreover, hundreds of New York supervisors and teachers have gone to Puerto Rico through the New York University summer workshops at the University at Rio Piedras.

The question frequently arises: Why do the Puerto Ricans come here, anyway? Things are tough enough as it is. Not very long ago in a discussion of the Puerto Rican situation, a businessman said to me, "These Puerto Ricans you are talking so fondly about—by these do you mean the people I see every day on my way to the office? In the summer the women sitting on the stoops nursing their babies? The kids running around without any shoes and urinating in the gutter? The men sullen, evil-tempered, looking as though they'd like a chance to stick a knife in you? Are these your wonderful Puerto Ricans?"

Nodding, I asked him where he was born. "Hell's Kitchen," he answered without hesitation. "Toughest spot in all New York."

The old story. This son of immigrant parents could no longer remember women nursing their babies on doorsteps in his youth, or the drunks staggering along Tenth Avenue, or the prostitutes, or the bucket of beer with the head of foam he used to pick up at the saloon for his father! The memory of man is short. He no longer remembers the conditions of his youth, and if he does—well, it is another time and another period. Times have changed. Things are no longer the same.

While he lives in the latter half of the twentieth century, he still talks like the Mayor of New York who in 1837 declared

that the streets were "filled with wandering crowds of immigrants—clustering in our city, unacquainted with our climate,
without employment, without friends, not speaking our
language, and without food . . . certain of nothing but hardship and a grave." Or, turning the pages back further, he still
mouths the warning of a Representative from Massachusetts
who told Congress in 1797, "When the country was new, it
might have been a good policy to admit all. But it is no
longer."

Since that time, close to forty million immigrants have
entered and become an integral part of the American way of
life. One would be justified in saying that they *are* the American way of life.

My days as a high-school teacher and principal are over.
My mind and my heart, however, are with the boys I taught
for close to half a century. In these pages I have sought to give
a picture of these years. I have tried to show how, though at
first I was only concerned with books and the imparting of
information, ultimately I came to realize how the heart and
mind not only of the individual boy but of his whole community are involved in the education process.

There are those, I am sure, who will argue that I have painted
too glowing a picture of the boys whose lives began in the
slums of Manhattan, that I should have made more of violence,
of juvenile delinquency, and of social chaos. It is so easy to
concentrate on the sensational event in the life of a community
and to ignore the everyday pattern of living of the thousands
of families that struggle to raise their children decently against
tremendous odds. I could have recalled some of the criminal
types I have known, the drug addicts, the boys who contrary
to expectations suddenly went wrong. I could have recorded
many unpleasant things, but I did not. I did not because I felt
it was necessary to emphasize the positive and not dwell on the
ugly; for the ugly in our day and age receives all too much

emphasis. This is not and never was the way I looked upon my job as a teacher. My approach was determined by the fact that in the most difficult boy I always saw another side. I sensed beneath the rough, defiant, and cynical attitude the yearning for appreciation, understanding, and the willingness to struggle to become an accepted member of society. I felt that the difficult boy—yes, even the young criminal, was more sinned against than sinning. We, as adults, do not come to him with clean hands and clear consciences because too often we have failed to help him live by the moral code that we write and preach. I know too that of the almost one million school children in New York City, regardless of national origin, race, or creed, only a small per cent constitute a social and community problem—a menace to themselves and to society.

As a teacher I have witnessed the antisocial behavior that has led to delinquency and worse, and have had the frustrating experience of lacking the resources to arrest or divert it. And so have hundreds of my fellow teachers.

What I did want to stress is that an overwhelming number of boys, in spite of living in difficult communities, with many demoralizing influences, have made fine lives for themselves and are among our civic leaders today.

Not long ago I attended the annual conference of the Council of Spanish-American Organizations which was held at the Benjamin Franklin High School. Fifty-eight separate organizations met and spent the day discussing the problems of their people and what they were doing about them. The theme was "We Help Ourselves." The idea for this council was originated and worked out by Joe Monserrat, its first president, who claims that it was his early experiences at Franklin that gave him the training and desire to work for the good of his fellow American citizens from Puerto Rico.

There are so many heartening examples among the young men who graduated from Franklin which prove that in order to develop civic-mindedness and a willingness to serve, the process must begin as the boys grow up in the school. No better example can I give you of the importance of high-school boys sharing in the responsibility of improving community living than to quote several passages from a letter which I received during the Second World War from Elmer Glaser, a Jewish boy of an immigrant family who graduated from Franklin in 1937 not only with high honors but with the affection of the whole school.

> If the only function of school in these times were to teach the "three R's" I would say better to close them, saving time, money, and effort. . . . But the place of school in society is far greater, and I can hardly believe that this would have to be demonstrated again. . . .
>
> I don't have to tell you about how the inspiration of us Franklin students was fired by the thought that we would be able to participate in something bigger than ourselves that would allow us to translate into action some of the things we had been hearing about and seeing in books. "Democracy" was a little abstract and far away in meaning to most of us. It had begun in 1776, it had an annual ritual each November, and there were guardians of it in Washington.
>
> Almost overnight, it meant something concrete and very close. Part of it meant that I, born of a people that has been discriminated against and persecuted for many years, could meet with other common everyday people from all walks of life and discuss ideas for solving problems we all shared. . . .
>
> I helped older people organize meetings, learned how to write letters, how to make contacts.
>
> We met in the auditorium, heard our committee progress reports, sang together (I'm chromatic monotone), listened to speakers, and in general enjoyed those bonds of fellowship and good will that are rare and when they are found one long remembers. Sometimes I had the privilege to address these gatherings.

Here I met and spoke with neighborhood doctors, trade-union members, priests, teachers, housewives, storekeepers, and others, and education suddenly became meaningful to me, drawing out any talents I had along the lines of writing, speaking, organizing, and so on. This was a change from the routine classroom lecture-and-regurgitation method of education. . . .

My work on community affairs was done mostly after "school hours" but instead of losing out in my studies, I came to class next day with renewed interest in matters under study and a burning desire to learn. A lesson in immigration policy was no longer a matter of arbitrary arithmetic formulae, but a flesh and blood policy that dealt with matters of life and death and freedom and tyranny for the people I had mingled with at Community Night, or last night. The discussion of housing problems really amounted to if and when and how were the people of East Harlem going to have decent homes instead of the dark, dank tenements I had seen last week when I made the rounds with a petition for a housing project for the neighborhood. . . .

I merely wanted to tell you of my belief that I and many others profited individually from participation in the community program and that as a result of our collective efforts the community, and through it, the city and nation, have profited.

If I had nothing else besides this letter from Elmer Glaser to show the value of our experiment at Franklin in school–community education, I would feel well rewarded for the many years that I devoted to this cause.

A teacher is fortunate in that he is left with so many wonderful—if intangible—mementos. A young man named Joe Roberto is now supervising architect of the new Rockefeller Dorado Hotel project in Puerto Rico. He was a Clinton graduate of around the year 1927. I had heard of his work as an architect long before he became associated with Rockefeller. A surprise telephone call at Benjamin Franklin brought us together two or three years ago for an hour or so as he was passing through on his way to California. As I showed him around our beautiful building he confided to me something I had never known. "Pop," he said, "have you any idea how I happened to become an architect?"

He told me that it all started in that tiny office of mine at De Witt Clinton while he was operating the mimeograph machine and I was talking to one of the other boys who wanted to become a draughtsman.

"I never forgot what you said to this kid. You said, 'Why do you want to settle for draughtsman? That's more or less mechanical. Anybody can become a draughtsman. Set your goal high. Become an architect. Try for the top.'"

Joe Roberto smiled. "You weren't talking to me at all, but I'm the one who was affected. From that day on I began to dream of one day becoming an architect."

Just the other day I received a postal card from Joe from Puerto Rico. He finds himself perfectly at home down there. "Doctor, you recognized the fine qualities of these people long before I did. They are best in the knowledge of their craft—masonry, tile work, plaster, and concrete. I thought only the Italians had mastered this art."

The fundamental objectives and the moral ideal are constant. It is the human patterns of behavior which are changeable and must be adjusted to achieve these objectives, for the most stupendous fact of human existence is that man *can* change, for good or for ill. Man has over the centuries made many attempts to achieve the objectives of a higher moral code. At times he failed. At other times he seemed almost to succeed. When some degree of success was achieved, it always appeared to be based on one of the most fundamental bases of human behavior—faith. Faith in the world; faith in man. For the struggle of man to achieve the ideals of a moral world will never suffer permanent discouragement.

What was applicable to me as a child in the little Italian mountain town of Avigliano holds just as firm today; the child must be inculcated with a responsibility toward his family, his elders, and the community in which he lives. In turn, every member of the community has a responsibility toward that child. Only thus can there be progress in the development of the useful citizen.

"The student must suffer," my uncle, the priest, used to say to me over sixty years ago. That also has truth today, despite educators who have advocated the "no-failing theory" and the concept of uninhibited self-expression. For, how is it possible to inculcate discipline—self-discipline—and develop the desire to improve in a child if he is not taught a sense of duty and responsibility along with his rights and privileges.

Yet I do not believe in beating lessons into boys. Far from it. "Foolishness is tied up in the heart of a boy," the proverb says, "the rod is what will remove it from him." This "get-tough" idea which seems to be gathering momentum in some quarters today proves only that man has a short memory. The severity of punishment practiced in days gone by neither corrected, nor reformed, nor lessened delinquency and crime. I never found it necessary to lay hands on a boy. I know that corporal punishment is not the answer. However, I am convinced that a firm hand when the child is young is the best method for instilling in him a normal and healthy attitude toward life and living in the society of his fellow human beings.

The increasingly serious problem of juvenile crime that exists today cannot be shrugged off. Yet we must not use the schools and the teachers as scapegoats. We must search within ourselves for the fault and the solution. Adolescents are hardly responsible for the world they grow up in, or for the influences which shape their lives. One need not seek far to find an environment which successfully controls the adolescent: in Chinese communities in this country, where respect for family and tradition amounts almost to religion, there is no such thing as juvenile delinquency. And these are usually low-income, often tenement, communities.

It is ironical but true that the years of the great depression and immediately following were the most productive in our Benjamin Franklin experiment. Because of the unemployment situation, many capable WPA workers worked without cost to us on our numerous community programs. Bitter irony indeed! Workers in a depression made possible what today is practically out of the question. With a national budget in the billions, we still sorely neglect the education of our young people. The great majority of people refuse to face reality. Education costs money. While they may pay the idea lip service, their minds refuse to grasp the fact that there are just not enough teachers and that they are not paid enough for the significant work they do. At least a part of the answer is as simple as that. The Russians accepted this fact when they decided to give their teachers the same status and pay that they give their doctors.

I believe and will always believe in the potential in every boy to lead a good and useful life—if we as adults will only care enough, take the time and the trouble and the expense to develop this potential. The great boys I have known—Benny Segreto, Le Count Russel, Hans Geissler, Elmer Glaser, Joe Monserrat, Vito Marcantonio, and hundreds more—exist in all boys.

The teacher is the heart of the educational process and he must be given the opportunity to teach—to devote himself whole-heartedly to his job under the best circumstances. Half a century as a teacher leads me to the conclusion that the battle for a better world will be won or lost in our schools.

ABOUT THE AUTHORS

Fiction writing, journalism, advertising, farming, hunting and fishing, and psychological warfare have been some of the varied occupations and avocations of Guido D'Agostino, collaborator with Leonard Covello on *The Heart Is the Teacher*. He is author of four novels, *The Barking of a Lonely Fox*, published by McGraw-Hill in 1952, *Olives on the Apple Tree, Hills beyond Manhattan*, and *My Enemy the World*. His short stories have been published in such magazines as *Esquire* and *Story*, and he has been a successful writer of magazine articles. Mr. D'Agostino began selling his writings while he worked with a Manhattan advertising agency after college. During World War II he served with the United States Psychological Warfare Division in Sardinia and Italy. Born in Greenwich Village, New York City, of Sicilian parents, D'Agostino attended the city's public schools and Columbia University. He and his wife now live on a 250-acre farm in Honesdale, Pennsylvania, which they run themselves. When away from farming and writing, Mr. D'Agostino loves to hunt and fish.

Leonard Covello needs little discussion here, for *The Heart Is the Teacher* is his story—the story of his life and his work as a teacher and later principal in New York's East Harlem.